Project: Strategy

Strategic planning is the starting point for projects and often the primary reason for a project's success or failure. It has the potential to enable every organisation to realise its ideals and actualise its values, whether it be a small start-up business, a large international company, or even an entire society. Project leaders and project-orientated organisations need to understand strategic planning to recognise their position and environment, and make rational decisions when selecting and defining their projects and programs. But, those same principles can have broader, more profound, and more ambitious applications too.

Project: Strategy is a practical handbook that enables organisations of any size, and employees at all levels within them, to form strategic plans and actively contribute to them throughout a project's development. Rather than focus on superficial exercises, this book draws from knowledge outside of business and management – humanities, philosophy, psychology, technology, and engineering – to create a holistic view and a depth of understanding you would never achieve with SWOT analysis alone. Taking the reader on a pragmatic journey, it teaches self-reflexion, social responsibility and creative thinking with application to their projects and plans, but also to their working relationships and to their organisations.

This book is also an ideal introductory book to progressive programs on strategic planning, with a focus on collaborative work, open strategy, and open strategic planning on a social level. It provides a wealth of learning tools and case studies to demonstrate best practice. This is the ideal guide to project planning for anyone that wants their planning decisions to be as wise as they are savvy.

Helgi Thor Ingason is a professor at Reykjavik University, a consultant, and Certified Senior Project Manager. He is the author of several books on management and his work has been published in the *Project Management Journal*, *International Journal of Project Management* and *Journal of Metals*.

Haukur Ingi Jonasson is a professor at Reykjavik University, a consultant, and Certified Stanford Project Manager. His background is in theology, philosophy, and psychology, which he applies to engineering and management. He is the author of several books on leadership and management.

Project: Strategy

Helgi Thor Ingason and
Haukur Ingi Jonasson

Routledge
Taylor & Francis Group

LONDON AND NEW YORK

First published 2019
by Routledge
2 Park Square, Milton Park, Abingdon, Oxon OX14 4RN

and by Routledge
52 Vanderbilt Avenue, New York, NY 10017

Routledge is an imprint of the Taylor & Francis Group, an informa business

British Library Cataloguing-in-Publication Data
A catalogue record for this book is available from the British Library

Library of Congress Cataloging-in-Publication Data
A catalog record has been requested for this book

ISBN: 978-1-138-33872-2 (hbk)
ISBN: 978-0-429-44150-9 (ebk)

Typeset in Goudy
by Deanta Global Publishing Services, Chennai, India

Printed and bound in Great Britain by
TJ International Ltd, Padstow, Cornwall

This book is dedicated to
our families

Contents

•••

Figures

Tables

Acknowledgements

Special thanks to our families for their encouragement, patience, and contributions. Very special thanks to Jonathan Norman at the Major Projects Association Knowledge Hub for his unceasing support, guidance, dedication, and friendship. Thanks to Tim Morissey, who read through the text and gave us some great suggestions for the content. Our thanks also go to Lara Jonasdottir, Jon Asgeir Sigurvinsson, and Jane Appleton for their help with translations and to Olof Embla Eyjolfsdottir for her help in initiating the project with Routledge.

We also want to thank some of our friends and colleagues within the project management community for the many inspiring discussions: Bob Dignen, Beverly Pasian, Darren Dalcher, Mark Morgan, Miles Shepard, Rodney Turner, Steven Eppinger, Sharon De Mascia, Tom Taylor, and Yvonne Schoper. Also, we extend our thanks to our co-workers in the Master of Project Programme (MPM) at Reykjavik University: Asbjorg Kristinsdottir, Benedikt Arnason, Agnes Holm Gunnarsdottir, Gudfinna Bjarnadottir, Ellen Gunnarsdottir, Florence Kennedy, Greta Maria Gretarsdottir, Hannes Petursson, Yr Gunnarsdottir, Pall Kr Palsson, Pall Jensson, Pauline Muchina, Marta Kristin Larusdottir, Morten Fangel, Markus A Zoller, Thordis Wathne, Throstur Gudmundsson, and Thordur Vikingur Friðgeirsson. We want to thank the University of Reykjavik and all our co-workers there and our students for the ongoing invaluable input, support, and encouragement. Special thanks to Aslaug Armannsdottir MPM and Iris Hrund Thorarinsdottir MPM and our co-workers on the Project Leadership and Project Management programme at the University of Iceland, Kristin Jonsdottir Njardvik, Kristin Birna Jonsdottir, Elin Juliana Sveinsdottir; and at the University of Akureyri, Elin Hallgrimsdottir.

We also thank Gudrun Hognadottir, Gunnar Stefansson, Kristjan Kristjansson, Kristinn Orn Vidarsson, Ingolfur A. Johanneson, Margret Bjornsdottir, Petur Maack, Runolfur Smari Steinthorsson, Kristinn Orn Vidarson, and Tryggvi Sigurbjarnarson for their support.

Special thanks to CCP Games in Reykjavik, its CEO, Hilmar Veigar Petursson, and its SVP of Human Resources, Sophie Froment, for their help funding the translations. We want to thank JPV Publishing in Iceland, particularly our editor Oddny S. Jonsdottir and CEO Egill Orn Jonatansson, for their encouragement and cooperation.

Last but not least we want to thank Halldor Baldursson for his wonderful illustrations and friendship and Amy Laurens and Alexandra Atkinson at Routledge for their patience, suggestions, and support.

Helgi and Haukur

Preface to the series

•••

Transparent leadership and sustainable project management

This book is part of a series of four that are written for anyone who needs to be able to lead and participate in various types of projects and in the human, technical and communication aspects of projects, programmes and portfolios using styles and techniques that are adapted to the context and the environment of each project type.

The series is tailored to help you strengthen four key proficiencies in a very creative way; strategy, leadership, implementation, and communication. Use the advice they contain to develop your personal leadership and managerial style and your ability to take ideas and advance them through planning and execution – with the transparency and accountability that successful project management today demands. We put equal emphasis on the technical and human elements of effective management. Success will require you to align the objectives of the project leader, team, and organisation within the project's social and environmental context.

We've written this series primarily for the next generation of project, programme and portfolio managers. The models, techniques, and advice within the books have been taught for many years in the most popular and successful management education and training program in Iceland. They reflect the integrated nature of this successful program which is designed with the needs in mind of those who want to lead well in both their professional and private lives. To do that you will bring a degree of self-awareness and self-realisation of the leadership of businesses, public bodies, NGOs and society in general.

We have aligned the books to the most recent version of IPMA Competence Baseline ICB4. The idea is to provide something that is as practical as handbooks and supporting documentation for anyone aiming to become certified ICB 4.0.

We wanted to make sure the series would be of interest to an international readership since projects today are typically planned and operated across international boundaries and involve teams from different disciplines and cultures.

Our aim is to transform you into an international and transparent leader. Someone who is intellectually and emotionally ready to manage others in a spirit of self-reflection; has the values and ethics to guide them in often complex and difficult environments; and has the flexibility and confidence to listen to and make use of criticism and communication, in all its forms. Transparency implies leading in a way that shows constant, considered awareness of the project's content, context and consequences for you, your team, and your organisation, as well as the society and environment within which you live and work. The series is based on this vision.

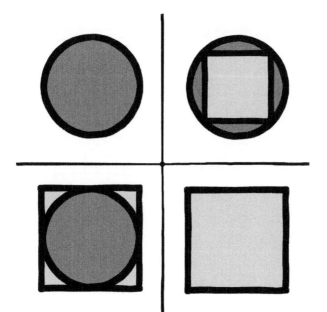

Foreword

●●

This book forms part of a series of four books that each individually focus on one of the following broad topics: *Leadership, Strategy, Communication,* and *Execution.* Although the overall approach taken in this series is strongly influenced by the authors' involvement in the field of project management, we believe that the material presented has wide appeal and is relevant to a broad constituency of readers who wish to become better leaders, managers, planners, and strategists. Our combined background and experience lends itself to a novel cross-disciplinary approach and there is a strong focus on the human element in management and leadership in general. As such, these books are intended to complement the large body of general management and project management literature available that is more technical in nature. With this perspective, our aim is to provide more depth to the above topics by: (a) discussing them within a very broad context; (b) referencing a diverse array of academic sources; (c) including frequent examples to support the various points made; and (d) describing practical tools for real-life applications. The material is written with both the student and experienced practitioner in mind and each book can be read as a whole or used as a handy reference guide to be dipped in and out of as the occasion demands.

In this book, we focus on "strategy" or, more specifically, the process of *strategic planning* to identify a desired *vision* for an enterprise and the formulation of an associated *strategic action plan*, which outlines the actual practical means by which this vision can be realised. The proper implementation of such plans is naturally of vital importance in the overall process and this includes monitoring and controlling activities, closing out and preparing the ground for follow-on work. As the ensuing chapters indicate, there is a lot to consider in carrying out such work and one can benefit greatly by taking a structured approach to decision-making and using an array of analytical tools that are widely recognised for their effectiveness.

Strategy is universally recognised by all leading management associations as being a fundamental aspect of ensuring the long-term health and profitability of a business in an uncertain environment, as well as for the successful management of any type of non-profit organisation. It is also specifically recognised as a key element of competence in project management by the

International Project Management Association in their recently published fourth version of their Individual Competence Baseline for project, programme and portfolio management (IPMA, 2015).

This book is clearly structured and familiarises the reader with the foundations of strategic management theory, together with the leading proponents in the field and their contributions. A number of examples are used to describe the scope and relevance of the topic and to illustrate particular factors of importance. In the practical sense, a concise method for undertaking the *strategic planning process* is outlined that is easy to grasp and that can be applied to any organisation. The different steps in this process are further broken down and a number of analytical tools that can be used as aids are described in detail.

As will be explained, strategic planning can be undertaken at a number of different levels and has the potential to enable every organisation to realise its ideals and actualise its values, whether it be a small start-up business, a large international company, or even an entire society. Yet, strategic planning efforts often fail due to an inability to execute the plan or because of poor decisions resulting in mismanagement of resources, for instance betting on the wrong projects. This book explores the perspective of project, portfolio and programme management, as well as strategic management in general, and it shows how strategy is, in fact, the starting point for many projects. It is therefore imperative for project-orientated organisations and other organisations to understand their position and environment, and to make rational decisions when selecting and defining their projects. Numerous real-life examples are used to illustrate these points that cover a wide range of organisational types operating across many different sectors.

Also included in this book are frequent questions designed to increase your awareness and understanding of the subject matter, with a particular emphasis on the human dimension. By allocating enough time to answer these questions in a proper fashion, it is hoped that your critical thinking skills will improve and that you will see your own environment in a more enlightened way. Through closely studying this book, readers should be able to take on leadership roles in the strategic management of their own organisations or become independent strategy consultants.

Strategic planning in the context of project management

As mentioned, the International Project Management Association recently published the fourth version of their Individual Competence Baseline for project, programme and portfolio management (ICB4). This relates to assessment and certification of professional project managers. In this document, three overall divisions of competences are included – *People, Practice and*

Perspective – and strategy is mentioned as one of five key competences of the *Perspective* division. *Competence* involves individuals having *ability*, *skills* and *knowledge* according to ICB4, where they define ability as applying knowledge and skills in the right manner and at the right time. By way of illustration, ICB4 lists the following as strategic skills for project management:

- *Analysis and synthesis*
- *Entrepreneurship*
- *Reflection of the organisation's goals*
- *Strategic thinking*
- *Sustainable thinking*
- *Contextual awareness*
- *Result orientation*

While ICB4 admirably condenses a lot of material into the one space, the result is that the material covered is only really looked at in broad terms and there is a lot of scope for expanding on these topics and providing greater depth and examples, which are key aims of this book. Other relevant references in ICB4 to the topic under discussion here include *strategic resource planning*, *strategic procurement* and *strategic alliances in stakeholder engagement*. These do not require any special explanation but will be covered at various points in this book where specific approaches are discussed in more detail.

Numerous other sources are also available on good and recognised practices in strategic planning.

We will refer to a report by The Boston Consulting Group (BCG), an American management consulting firm with offices in 50 countries. The clients of BCG are in the private, public, and not-for-profit sectors around the world and BCG is considered one of the most prestigious management consulting firms in the world. In the report "Four Best Practices for Strategic Planning" (Kachaner, King and Stewart, 2016), the authors – BCG consultants – point out that most companies lack an effective strategic planning process. Furthermore, based on their experience, companies that get the most benefit from strategic planning processes have four things in common:

- They explore strategy at distinct time horizons. Long-term vision, medium-term strategy, and short-term plans are revisited. This happens at different intervals, depending on the different business sectors. Typically, the frequency of defining a long-term vision is 5 years or more, the frequency of defining the medium-term strategy is 3–5 years and the short-term plans are revisited annually.
- They constantly reinvent and stimulate the strategic dialogue. Doing the same routines year after year is not creative and does not necessarily lead to new ideas, which is an essential part of the strategic thinking process.

Therefore, they tend to renew the process, e.g. by applying different tools for an analysis and by refreshing discussion questions. Discussion questions should be neither too broad nor too narrow. The report cites Peter Drucker who once said, "Great strategists – and great business leaders – have to learn the art of questioning."

- They engage the broad organisation. In general, experience shows that the strategy development effort will yield better results when a broad group of stakeholders is engaged in the process, as compared to a small and central team. Of course, a central team has a critical role as a facilitator for process.

- They invest in execution and monitoring. It is well-known that translating the strategy into results by actions is usually harder than driving in the strategic planning process. Therefore, companies that get the most benefit from the strategic planning process do what it takes to give the strategy stability and traction, implement clear and engaging communication, and develop quantitative metrics and goals that measure progress.

To conclude, we hope that you will enjoy reading the book and that it will provide you with new insights and further your skills in current or future management. Happy reading.

Helgi Thor Ingason
Haukur Ingi Jonasson

References

IPMA (2015). IPMA Competence Baseline 4.0.

Kachaner, N., King, K. and Stewart, S. (2016). Four Best Practices for Strategic Planning. [online] https://www.bcg.com. Available at: https://www.bcg.com/publications/2016/growth-four-best-practices-strategic-planning.aspx [Accessed 21 May 2018].

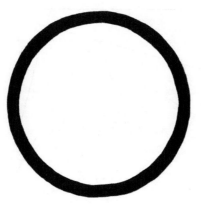

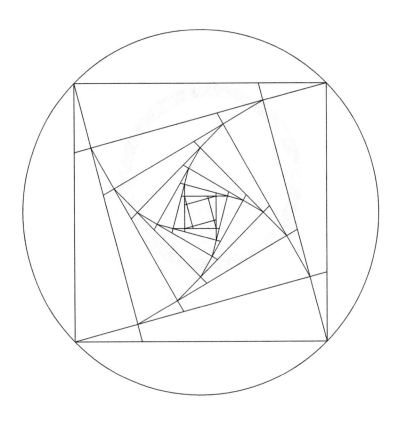

1 The nature and value of strategic planning

Anyone who professionally manages projects inevitably encounters obstacles. The future is difficult to predict – which means you will face situations that you have predicted as well as scenarios that take you by a surprise. This book will provide you with a structured approach to realise your future objectives and deal with future uncertainties – through a process called strategic planning. We use critical, creative and ethical thinking to enable you to use your organisation's strengths to make the most of your projects. This reflective approach allows you to navigate your projects and programmes through uncertainty and changing circumstances and to lead them according to your planning.

Strategic planning is a process that produces a shared plan, informed by the values of the organisation. The plan provides a clear mission to engage everyone both emotionally and intellectually, and a well-defined set of directions explaining how to execute this mission. The discrete vehicles to implement the plan are your projects and your programs – which, collectively are organised into a portfolio. Our approach to project management – the discipline of managing projects, programmes and portfolios – follow the processes and require the competencies as they are described in the Individual Competence Baseline (ICB4) of the International Project Management Association (IPMA, 2015).

A *project* is a non-routine set of tasks with a scope (what you will and won't deliver) and a description of the resources required to *deliver* a particular goal, usually a product or a service or, in this case perhaps, *a strategic plan*. A programme – such as implementing an organisational strategy – is a coherent set of projects to *realise* a set of goals. Thus, a project *makes* (something) whilst a programme *achieves* (something). *Project management* is a discipline within which there are defined principles and one that will greatly vary to reflect the context and needs of a specific endeavour. Strategic objectives such as at getting a candidate elected to parliament; reversing a decline in the number of migrating whales in an area; constructing and relocating to a new headquarters building; and launching a new TV channel are all examples of either – projects, programmes or portfolios. How each is defined will depend on the context and practice of the organisation that owns the strategy and the complexity and scale of the activities involved.

In this opening chapter we begin by defining the term "strategic planning" and discuss why it is crucial for the wellbeing of any organisation; businesses, institutions and non-profit organisations. We then provide some background to the different management theories that relate to strategic planning and give examples of how a strategic plan is then implemented.

What is strategic planning?

Strategic planning is an expression of what we want to achieve and how we intend to do it in order to manage our organisation into the future. Strategic planning is usually seen as a more long-term approach to planning that deals with achieving goals where multiple possible scenarios should be accounted for and/or is of a scale that affects the continuing success of the organisation as a whole. It is similar to more conventional planning. Strategic planning is unlike more conventional budget planning in the sense that it is all about designing a future, rather than planning by looking in the mirror. It may also involve a *business plan* which is something that defines the commercial rationale for a decision to invest time and resources in the form of a project or a programme.

In essence, *strategic planning* is a systematic attempt to determine the future of an organisation by: (1) identifying strengths, weaknesses, opportunities and risks in line with the values of an organisation; (2) creating a clear vision for future direction that entails clear goals and (3) outlining the path to be taken to achieving these goals. For example, a tourist business that starts to suffer frequent late-stage cancellations by customers might have a strategic *goal* to set up a booking and payment system that ensures that non-refundable deposits are paid and losses are hence minimised. The same business may spot an *opportunity* for increasing sales in the form of large group bookings and their strategic *goal* then involves realising this through expanding capacity, networking with the right people, and devising a new marketing approach. For larger organisations, in particular, strategic planning can often mean devising ways to maintain uniqueness, effectiveness, efficiency, dynamism and growth. Figure 1.1 shows three different levels of forward-looking planning.

A business plan is mainly made in relation to new business opportunities, new projects or an innovation of some kind. As part of the process of business planning, the planners will explain the purpose of a new business idea; how it will be implemented and estimate the possible outcome over the life of the idea. Business plans are typically intended to persuade the Board or investors to support a new business idea. The creation of a business plan is a good way to elaborate a business idea in a form that allows investors to understand the risk and the commercial returns.

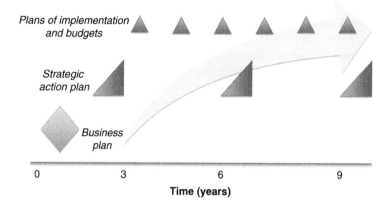

Figure 1.1

Three types of planning and their relation to time.

A strategic plan serves a different purpose for a business plan. It deals with what to do, rather than specifying in detail how to do it. It is a tool used by organisations to express a future purpose and direction; the emphasis lies on improvements, adjustments and long-term growth and development of the organisation. Organisations need to plan strategically on a consistent and regular basis, for instance every three years, or more frequently if the environment – competition, regulation, labour markets and so on – is highly dynamic. Strategic planning involves articulating the strengths and weaknesses of an enterprise; exploiting strategic opportunities and mitigating risks; and developing solidarity, enthusiasm and belief by enabling employees/members to participate in forming the future. A strategic action plan is the output of the strategic planning process and expresses clear and measurable objectives to be reached within a specified time. It should also address the requisite measures to be taken in order to reach the objectives within the time frames and with defined responsibilities for their implementation.

Implementation and budget plans deal with how to implement what needs to be done. Budgets are usually made annually to give an overview of costs and income (sales or some other measure of success) across the whole respective period of the plan. The budget can then be used to compare actual income and cost throughout the year, with what was estimated. Traditionally, budgets are created from the actual results of the previous year, allowing for foreseeable changes and incorporating some of the observable trends of the longer term. These changes may be the result of decisions taken in relation to the company's strategic planning.

A healthy enterprise, whether it be a company, institution or non-profit organisation, must be capable of preserving its identity and growing its assets in the face of the inevitable challenges that arise. Strategic planning is where the most important thinking and planning are carried out in this regard. For example, look at the dynamic field of air travel. The past few decades have seen enormous changes from what was once a very restricted market monopolised by national airlines and travel agents. Whereas before air travel was seen as an exotic luxury for the wealthy businessperson and traveller, it is now generally viewed in far more pragmatic terms as a "no-frills" way of getting from A to B. Deregulation of the skies and the development of airports outside of the major established hubs have played a key role in accelerating these changes. A number of airlines foresaw opportunities in their respective markets and have, through ongoing strategic planning, positioned themselves to avail of these opportunities and increase their leverage and ability to negotiate favourable deals with every step. Strategic actions including: (1) the use of new – and often more remote – airports; (2) online booking and check-in, bulk purchasing (or leasing) of aircraft; (3) increased efficiencies in staffing and scheduling; (4) playing one jurisdiction off another; (5) separating luggage and other charges; (6) fuel hedging and (7) marketing headline low fares; were used to increase competitiveness and market share. In contrast, many former national flag air carriers have lost significant market share and have struggled to adapt to the commercial and practical realities of this new market. Their own strategic planning has focused on downsizing and operational cost reduction as they belatedly adopt some of the methods pioneered by their low-cost competitors but struggle to find competitive innovations of their own.

Elements of your strategic plan may only offer a temporary advantage as competitors or customers adjust to the changes. For example, it is interesting to observe that Ryanair – long associated with low prices but poor service – has recently made a strategic decision to value customer experience more and has been implementing several changes to its policies and mode of operation to bring this about. The overall trajectory seen in the airline industry is reflected in other sectors such as manufacturing and service where many activities have been outsourced to low-cost jurisdictions in order to increase profits. In the "race to the bottom," however, few strategies are without downside risks, not least because customers and clients adapt their habits and so change the commercial context on which the strategy may have been predicated. This theme is explored in more detail in later chapters where specific strategies are discussed and analysed.

It is a fact of life for most private enterprises that they constantly need to look ahead and apply strategic thinking aimed towards attracting new business and consolidating their position in their respective markets. Those who lead engineering consultancies, for example, typically need to devote considerable time and resources to follow commercial leads and submit tenders for projects in order to keep their employees busy and ensure future profits. The tendering process itself can be strategic and enterprises need to be aware of the different markets that exist and the opportunities, risks, and capabilities associated with each. Global connectivity and the breaking down of various barriers to trade have meant that many enterprises of all sizes operate in multiple jurisdictions. In all sectors, intellectual property – perhaps best expressed as commercial insight – and the strategy around knowledge to create and maintain value is a major consideration, both for existing businesses and new investors.

For project managers who work in the field of information technology (e.g. computer hardware, software, internet, telecoms), strategic planning is an essential part of deciding what technology and software platforms to use and the extent to which they are compatible with surrounding systems and of value to users. No other sector struggles as much with the issue of obsolescence, or the challenge of integration. Another key aspect is the overall strategy employed to ensure information is kept secure. For example, high-profile leaks of company emails and personal data leaks have made users very wary of what is communicated and stored online.

Thus, strategic planning is a complex and demanding process of analysis and critical thinking that covers many areas and that needs to be carried out regularly and consistently to find the common area between the needs, ability and identity of an enterprise (see Figure 1.2).

The white area shown in Figure 1.2, where all three elements overlap is drawn deliberately small to reflect the difficulty represented by the search for the common area between these three elements in practice. For an enterprise to prevail in the long term, all the factors shown must be present: a real need for what the enterprise has to offer; the ability to meet this need; and a clear idea about its identity. Imagine, for example, a business that has an established identity and operates in an environment where the need for its services exists. This counts for little if the business lacks the capability to fulfil its role, to live up to what it aspires to be. Alternatively, imagine an enterprise that has a clear idea about its identity, and the ability to fulfil this role, but for whose products or services there is no market. Brand and identity, likewise, are of

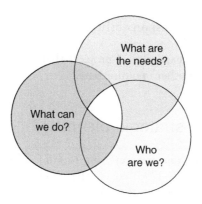

Figure 1.2

Strategic planning as the search for a common area.

importance, as others need to be aware of the existence of an enterprise and its abilities in order to avail of its services or products. Consequently, it is vital for every enterprise to position themselves in the small space in the middle of the picture, common to all three sets. This is the major role of strategic planning and the key aspects of this will be discussed in more detail in the following chapters.

In some cases, strategic action plans can involve small changes in others, radical and controversial transformation. Minor redesigning of a product, rebranding of an enterprise, small organisational changes, exploratory ventures into new markets or limited budget changes are all less likely to provoke strong resistance from those closely involved, whereas decisive change in the form of major restructuring or directional change is very likely to stir up the stakeholders. Fear of losing employment and entitlements or of seeing many years' work go down the drain is very common and those whose role it is to carry out wholesale restructuring, directional change and/or liquidation of assets can be faced with very hard decisions. Strategic planning is therefore as much about emotion and behaviour as about process or technology. This emotion can also apply to the projects which drive these changes that will have a significant impact on external stakeholders.

In summary, strategic planning may be regarded as an element within results-oriented management, encouraging an enterprise and its constituents to succeed in an ever-changing, uncertain environment that is paved with obstructions. The strategic planning process should result in an integral and integrated plan on how an enterprise can form its future, tackle uncertainty and set objectives and attain them.

Reflection points

- What differentiates strategic planning from other forms of planning?
- What aspects of strategic planning are most relevant to the area you work in?
- Who should take responsibility for strategic planning and who should participate?
- Can you think of examples of projects that were not aligned with the strategy of their mother organisations?

Why undertake strategic planning?

"By failing to prepare you are preparing to fail." This famous quote from Benjamin Franklin (1706–1790) covers the two key tenets of strategic planning: anticipation and preparation. When an enterprise fails to anticipate fundamental changes in its environment or is not prepared to deal with them, they can then lack the resources and lose time at the most critical juncture, and find themselves fighting a rearguard action.

Imagine you are devising a strategic action plan to deal with overcrowding in tenement housing and arrest urban decay. Authorities tasked with finding solutions to this common problem face a range of dilemmas and uncertain outcomes, some of which they may be aware of (known unknowns) but others of which they have no awareness at all (unknown unknowns). A good historic example of contrasting approaches is seen in the US city of St. Louis where two social housing projects were undertaken side-by-side in Carr Square Village (completed in 1942) and the Pruitt-Igoe apartment complex (completed in 1954). The former was a large low-rise development (2- and 3-storey) while the latter consisted of 33 individual high-rise towers (11 storeys high). As it turned out, Carr Square Village is now a mature and relatively quiet neighbourhood whereas Pruitt-Igoe was completely demolished in 1976 after it had become virtually derelict and associated with extreme poverty, segregation and crime.

The reasons behind these different outcomes are many and varied. In the case of Pruitt-Igoe, the sources of failure include: (1) the initial high-density design stipulations made by local authorities in conjunction with relentless cost-cutting in the planning and design stages by the relevant federal housing authority; (2) construction budget overruns in certain areas and insufficient resources to maintain the running of the Pruitt-Igoe complex in the face of inadequate income from rents; (3) living spaces that did not promote a sense of self-worth, security and social cohesion; (4) a lack of surrounding amenities and landscaping; (5) increased vacancy rate due to initial overoptimistic projections and shifting economic fortunes in the broader region (also increasing the poverty of residents); and (6) the gradual abandonment of the maintenance of law and order as certain troublesome families and gangs gained more of a grip on their surroundings (Bristol, 1991).

This is an example of a long-term project that is subject to a wide range of external social and economic factors and would therefore be considered very complex. One take-away lesson in this example is the significance of future demand projections and the need to have flexible solutions that can respond to the shifting nature of circumstances. By committing to such a large project as Pruitt-Igoe at the strategic planning stage, and executing it in one go, the relevant authorities were unable to consolidate their position or get things back on track once circumstances went against them.

In the business world, situations frequently arise where a lack of strategic planning, or poor execution, lead to projects burning through resources with little to show for it, and those in charge can be unable to react effectively to changing circumstances. To use a sailing analogy, businesses may have had favourable winds when they start, but later they find that as the weather changes, the first proper headwind can lead to them stalling. Succeeding without a plan is possible in the short to medium term but is not usually a viable approach in the long term. As well as a regular salary, employees need to feel engaged with their work and that what they do is worthwhile. Lack of purpose and direction can lead to morale problems, lower productivity and confusion in scheduling priorities. Warning signs that the organisational culture is not quite right include deeply entrenched views, indifference, short-term and narrow-minded thinking amongst the leadership and confusion and lack of unity amongst employees.

Strategic planning can be directed inwards at keeping people engaged and motivated in their work and broadening horizons. For example, initiatives such as promoting continuing professional development among employees through periodical courses can be a good way for enterprises to broaden their expertise and develop new markets. This is particularly the case in those environments where regulations are frequently updated, and enterprises need to keep on top of these changes. But it can also be a strategic objective to increase the level of loyalty, sense of belonging or contentment among employees and to avoid situations where key people leave for fresh pastures and take their acquired skills with them.

In the world of professional management, strategic planning is widely regarded as a necessary part of best practice. For example, the (European) EFQM Excellence Model identifies strategic management as one of nine core criteria of management. The model requires that companies define a strategy that is in keeping with their role, goal and values, and which is based on the needs and expectations of interested parties. Among other things, the companies pursuing the model must realise their competitive advantage, evaluate how relevant and efficient the strategy is, define key performance indicators and review and update their strategy.

In the US, a comparable model is used to identify winning companies for the renowned Malcolm Baldrige National Quality Award. In that model, strategic planning is one of seven assessment criteria. A company is assessed on the basis of the process they use for strategic planning, who takes part and how efficient the processes are in detecting the company's strengths, weaknesses, challenges and advantages. The assessment process includes how well the companies cope with setting objectives, defining actions to reach them and implementing those actions. Demonstrating efficiency in all aspects is a fundamental requirement (NIST, 2018).

Since 1993, the global management-consulting firm Bain & Company has regularly performed surveys of management tools and trends used in companies all over the world. In May, 2013, a survey was published describing the most popular management tools and trends used in 2012. Information was gathered from 1,268 executives in North and South America, Europe, and Asia and the results are reasonably representative of what management tools are applied globally. In the survey, strategic planning was the top-ranking management tool in 2017. In second, third, and fourth place came "customer relationship management," "benchmarking" and "advanced analytics," respectively. Other high-ranking management tools include "supply chain management," "customer satisfaction," "change management programs" and "total quality management." Strategic planning has consistently been among the top-ranking management tools in the trends survey by the Bain & Company for over 25 years (Bain & Company, 2018).

One of the main reasons why strategic planning has proved so useful and why executives are generally satisfied with its results is that it enables enterprises to plan their future and keep control of their destiny as circumstances change. Failure to anticipate and prepare for upcoming changes means that enterprises can miss the opportunity to react to those changes – to use them to their advantage, or to avoid dangerous threats. Strategic planning is an ideal way to increase solidarity among the staff if they can be encouraged to participate and their creative input is harnessed successfully. In the broader scheme of things, a clear and decisive company strategy is likely to eliminate uncertainty and make it easier for people to focus on urgent tasks and not get distracted. Strategic planning aims to define which projects are promising and which are not, which projects are relevant, and which relevant projects may support each other. It is also aimed at creating and maintaining a spirit of progressive development within the organisation and supporting the setting of ambitious goals.

Reflection points

- In your experience, what are the early signs in an enterprise that indicate that strategic planning is necessary?
- Can you give three examples of known unknowns and how they impact an area you are familiar with?
- With the benefit of hindsight, can you give three examples of unknown unknowns and how they impacted an area you are familiar with?
- In your experience, what are the most important challenges in strategic planning?

The history of strategic planning

The ability to think strategically has been an integral aspect of human success. Our hunter-gatherer ancestral leaders no doubt employed many strategic methods to achieve their goals of supplying food and shelter to their dependents and ensuring their health and safety from the dangers of nature, other tribes, and internal opponents. It was not until much later that more complex societies formed, and the advent of writing ensured that information and knowledge could be recorded accurately and transferred from generation to generation and between civilisations. The superpowers of antiquity such as the Greeks, Romans or Persians all had scholars whose writings covered many different fields from the technical to the philosophical and all areas in between. As trade flourished, these writings were translated into different languages and the ideas within them were also further developed by other cultures. Early developments in management theory may be found in contemporaneous writings on large infrastructure projects such as sanitation works or the organisation of new tax-collection and local administration structures. These types of projects required complex planning and the development of strategic action plans to deal with a range of potential outcomes. There are, of course, also many notable historical figures in the field of military strategic planning such as Alexander the Great or Hannibal whose ideas and experiences have been well documented and widely studied by others. In the political world, strategic thinkers such as the Italian Niccolo Machiavelli (1469–1527) have written about the means to obtain and retain power, albeit, in his particular case, by uncompromising and sometimes amoral means.

With the advent of the industrial revolution, ways of working changed radically as enterprises grew larger and more complex, with machines now performing many tasks. Management theory began to appear as a discipline at this time that traced its roots to the social sciences, political economy and psychology. The rise of computers and the information age was equally disruptive and the foundations of modern management theory (of which strategic planning is one key aspect) began in the 1940s to 1960s. Some of the most influential modern thinkers in the field of strategic management for business include Alfred Chandler, Igor Ansoff, Peter Drucker, Henry Mintzberg, Michael Porter, John P. Kotter and Peter Senge whose works (and also those of others) are discussed in various guises in this book. For a more comprehensive review of the early development of the field of strategic management, read *Historic Evolution of Strategic Management (Volumes I and II)*, edited by Peter McKiernan (2017). While strategic management theory was initially aimed at for-profit enterprises, its scope has broadened in recent years and the tools employed are now to be found in all types of organisations, including those that are non-profit. Below is a brief biographical outline of these pioneering authors:

Alfred Chandler (1918–2007) was a professor of business history at Harvard Business School. He underlined the importance of companies taking a holistic approach to the various elements of management and examining them in the context of an integral strategy. Furthermore, Chandler emphasised the necessity of long-term goals rather than short-term ones. Chandler's fundamental work on this matter, *Strategy and Structure*, was published in 1962.

Igor Ansoff (1918–2002) held a professorship at several American universities, including Carnegie Mellon University and Vanderbilt University. His book, *Corporate Strategy*, published in 1965, was a turning point in strategic management theory. In this book, Ansoff presented various terms related to strategy and strategic planning and defined a few basic types of strategy. Moreover, he elaborated on the important idea of *gap analysis*, which consists of studying a company's present status, its expected status in the future, and the gap between those two points and how it might be bridged. This is returned to in more detail later.

Peter Drucker (1909–2005) acted as a management consultant for companies and organisations all over the world, as well as being a productive writer and columnist. His most famous contribution to strategy theory is reflected in the emphasis he put on objectives, which resulted in a methodology in its own right, "Management by Objectives." In Drucker's view, the fundamental factor in the operation of an organisation should be the definition of objectives and the follow-up of operations aimed at reaching those objectives (Drucker, 1954).

Henry Mintzberg (1939–) is a professor of management studies at McGill University in Montreal. He is the author of *The Rise and Fall of Strategic Planning* (1994), where he criticised known strategic planning methods. Mintzberg is furthermore known for his *Ten Management Roles*.

Michael E. Porter (1947–) is a professor at Harvard University in Boston. He is the most influential contemporary scholar in the field of strategic planning and famous for many theories, e.g. *the five forces competition theory model*, the *generic strategies* model and the *value chain* model. Porter has not solely focused on corporate strategy theory, he has also studied strategic planning at the political level, cf. his book *The Competitive Advantage of Nations* (Porter, 2011). In recent years, he has turned his attention to addressing urgent problems of health care, both in the USA and elsewhere in the world.

John P. Kotter (1947–) is a professor at Harvard University in Boston. His speciality is leadership and change management and studying the best ways of transforming businesses. In 1996 he published the bestseller *Leading change*, where he presented an eight-step transformation process meant to boost the chances of a successful transformation (Kotter, 1996).

Peter Senge (1947–) is a teacher and scientist at MIT Sloan School of Management in Boston and the author of the best-selling *The 5th discipline* (1990). The book's subject is the "learning organisation" and the idea that a necessary prerequisite for a successful business is that companies gain competence in gathering, analysing and utilising information. Senge argued that the learning organisation had to master five basic disciplines, where the fifth discipline consisted in looking at how systems function as a whole, rather than looking at individual parts. "Systems thinking" is the subject of an interesting field of study called "system dynamics," which was originally developed at MIT in Boston.

For a long time, the leading practitioners in the field of strategic planning in management have operated both in the business and academic worlds, bringing their real-world experience into the classroom. Harvard was the first university to offer a course in business policy in 1912. The strategic management discipline evolved from the middle of the 20th century and central strategic planning divisions were built into the organisational structures of many companies with the purpose of developing and executing strategic planning. General Electric, for example, was a pioneer in corporate strategic planning and went as far as developing specific departments with employees working full time as planners. At that time, GE was organised into strategic business units and strategic plans were developed for each unit. During the 1960s, strategic planning became standard practice in most of the companies on the Fortune 500 list. While originally largely limited to the private sector, strategic planning and strategic action plans are now commonplace tools in management for both public and private enterprises.

As in other disciplines, many different methodological schools and movements exist in the field of strategic planning, and scholars often disagree on accents and definitions. While some stress the purpose and role of an organisation, others put emphasis on an organisation's goal(s), or how the strategy is realised. Therefore, more than one method of implementing strategic planning exists and what is applied in any particular situation can depend on the final purpose and intended product of the strategic planning process. What is most likely to work is often a mixture of approaches. In the following section, we give a brief overview of ten different schools of thought that were identified in the book *Strategic Safari* by Ahlstrand, Lempel, and Mintzberg (2001). At the start of that book, the authors stress that, in order to gain a proper understanding of strategic planning, you need to understand that it is a multidisciplinary academic field. They choose to treat each of the different schools of thought as having distinctive features and accents. The reader should be aware that the following section includes only a brief summary and is a simplification of these schools of thought. The intention of this chapter is to only give a glimpse of the theoretical foundations of strategic planning.

i   The **Design School** is associated with Philip Selznick and Alfred Chandler. They introduced the idea of "distinctive competence," and the need to harmonise an organisation's "internal state" and the external expectations towards it. the Design School emphasises the organisation within the competitive environment; one of the school's characteristics is the use of SWOT analysis to evaluate an organisation's strengths, weaknesses, opportunities, and threats. This analysis is, in turn, used to assess the situation and define actions and the Design School has had enormous impact and is one of the most widespread manifestations of strategic planning in organisations worldwide. However, critics of the Design School point out that certain characteristics of it may inhibit and limit creative work. It implies assumptions as part of the process that may not be universally applicable. The approach taken does not reflect the fact that a typical strategy in an organisation is developed step-by-step, over a long period of time. In addition, it disregards the fact that the current structure of an organisation influences the strategy and does not allow for contributions from all of an organisation's employees, focusing instead on the top executives.

ii   The **Planning School** came into being at a similar time as the Design School, tracing its origins to Igor Ansoff's 1965 book *Corporate Strategy*. While there are common traits in the Design School and the Planning

School, the latter puts the main emphasis on the *process* of strategic planning in which the managers of an organisation play a key role. Numerous flowcharts exist that describe the process of strategic planning and many different versions can be seen in books on this topic. The basic idea is usually the same, but may be elaborated in different ways. Normally, the presentation is organised as follows: (1) a SWOT analysis is made; (2) an itemised plan of implementation with checklists and prescriptive approaches is put forward and (3) special emphasis is placed on setting objectives, making budgets and plans of implementation. Early critics of the Planning School maintained that it made planning itself a priority instead of focusing on whether the value and applicability of the results. Other shortcomings of the Planning School have been pointed out, for instance, the assumption that an organisation's environment can be predicted, that it can be controlled and that it is constant. Critics have also pointed out that there is a risk of a rift forming between those who develop the strategy and those who implement it. This is reflective of a broader observation that the strategic planning process can miss its mark if employees are: (a) not involved in it; (b) not aware of it or (c) oppose it. This can happen both at any level in the organisation. They have also highlighted the tendency to define strategic planning as a fixed planning process, which may inhibit the creative thinking that is imperative when setting future goals.

iii The **Positioning School** is normally traced to Michael E. Porter and his book *Competitive Strategy* (Porter, 1980). Both the Design School and the Planning School influence the Positioning School. The distinctive feature of this School lies in its emphasis on positioning organisations within the competitive environment by applying certain analytical methods. By studying the features of different industries, the Positioning School concludes that different generic strategies apply to different organisations, based on the market in which they operate and the nature of their operations. The focus, then, is put on two variables in an organisation's environment: whether the market share is large or small and whether the enterprise is able to grow. Using these variables makes it possible to study the organisation's activities, position them in a simple model and decide in which direction it is sensible to direct the organisation's time, energy and money. Reference is made to a two-by-two matrix of the Boston Consulting Group, which will be discussed later in this book. One of Porter's best-known models is the five forces competition theory model, which describes the decisive forces in an organisation's environment. This model is discussed in more detail later on in this book. The Positioning School has its critics, often expressing comments that common to the Design School and the Planning School too. For example, it has been pointed out that the Positioning School's approach can be rather narrow. Thus the simplification that strategies can be grouped into only a handful of basic types does not always correspond to reality. Since organisations are both big and small, and competing in different market environments, generalisations, and simplifications are rarely appropriate.

iv The **Entrepreneurial School** is associated with Joseph Schumpeter who, in 1950, introduced ideas that well describe the school's basic ideology. The Entrepreneurial School lays all the emphasis on the vision of the entrepreneur who is regarded as the only party within an enterprise to have a clear vision of where to head for new opportunities. The enterprise must follow the entrepreneur, who needs to be sufficiently persuasive to convince people to follow their lead. This is an interesting idea, but the problem is that the whole strategy formation takes place in one person's mind and it is unclear how anyone else can affect that process. Success depends on this one individual whose vision and thinking will, unfortunately, be unique to them. Any enterprise that follows an entrepreneur and experiences difficulties will find it hard to change course in strategy formation process which is never explicit and rarely documented. The only solution will be to replace one entrepreneur with another, which may have unforeseeable circumstances on the culture of the business.

v The **Cognitive School** owes its origins to numerous scholars publishing after 1990. The School's theoretical foundations come mainly from psychology. Strategic planning is regarded as a cognitive process in the strategists' minds. The scholars studied the mental activities associated with how information was processed, arranged and exploited. Even though such reflections remain speculative, they can shed light on what takes place in the minds of individuals. The main shortcoming of this approach, however, is that it is of limited use for understanding or managing a strategic planning process undertaken by a group of people. Therefore, the Cognitive School does not have as practical an application as other schools.

vi The **Learning School** is based on the fundamental principle that organisations learn and develop over time, just as individuals do. The origins of this school can be traced to an article published in 1959 by Charles Lindblom. In the article, he argued that strategic planning in public administration was a complex and chaotic process, which involved an understanding of an environment that was too complicated to be understood. According to the Learning School, the customary approach to strategic planning creates an illusion of understanding, which may accord with the ideas of certain managers but has little to do with what really goes on in organisations. The Learning School emphasises that strategy develops within an organisation in different divisions, and that it is vital to gather the knowledge arising from this process in order to learn, improve and develop the organisation. Critics of the Learning School have commented on its vagueness and limited value if the learning does not lead to added value for an organisation.

vii The **Power School** is based on the idea that strategic planning consists of conversations and negotiations between authoritative parties, both within organisations, e.g. between divisions, and between companies. In such discourse, all viewpoints should be presented, and the conclusion should prove realistic and acceptable to the majority of those involved. A strategy that is formed in this way should, in theory, be easy to implement. The Power School is mainly criticised for the emphasis it puts on negotiations, which may demand much time and effort, possibly with the consequence that issues are not addressed decisively enough. There is also a danger of people losing sight of and missing out on potential collaboration, interplay, and development, which might be more apparent in a consensual rather than oppositional climate.

viii The **Cultural School** is closely related to the Power School. However, it emphasises exactly the opposite phenomena within organisations, i.e. the common interests of all those who belong to the organisation, rather than just the power and influence of those in positions of authority. It regards strategic planning as a social process, which is based on the organisational culture. Culture in organisations has been studied by various disciplines of the social sciences. Initially, this was in a general context, but a number of works have been published since the early 1990s that specifically looked at the connection between strategic planning and organisational culture. Critics of the Cultural School point out that it is poorly defined, hard to grasp and difficult to show direct causality with strategic changes made. Experience has shown that organisational culture is very conservative and the requisite regular changes in organisations are often hard to carry out because of a built-in resistance to change. An undue emphasis on organisational culture is therefore potentially a barrier to progress if it results in a tendency to preserve the status quo at the price of necessary change. On the other hand, forced changes are much less likely to succeed if they do not reckon with the prevalent organisational culture.

ix The **Environmental School** stresses the working environment of the organisation, how this constrains possibilities and builds a requirement for continual change. Even though the other schools address an organisation's environment in various ways, they do not regard the environment as the most important variable. According to the Environment School, an organisation's management must focus on forces in the environment, assess them and respond to them appropriately. This school has mainly been criticised for putting too great an emphasis on external factors, which can be difficult to grasp and predict. The idea of constraint has also been criticised, i.e. the idea that an organisation is, first and foremost, at the mercy of its environment, which controls its destiny. This feels limiting, for it is certainly the case that organisations can influence their environments to varying degrees on the basis of the strategy they choose.

x The **Configuration School** tries to combine various elements present in the nine other schools. Two basic ideas at the heart of the Configuration School are the context of the organisation and its environment, on the one hand, and the processes that lead to a transfer from one state of being into another state of being, on the other. Strategic planning is regarded as a tool to achieve the transition from one state of being to another. The configurations are simple graphic presentations of a number of generic types of organisations, i.e. how the respective organisation would look in a state of equilibrium. The theoretical roots of the Configuration School can be traced back to an article written by Chandler in 1962, which changed people's ideas about strategy and structure of organisations. Critics claim that the theories of the Configuration School consist of great simplifications, which are not actually representative of real life, even though they are easy and manageable in the classroom.

Some key factors of the ten strategic planning schools can be presented in a simple mind map as shown in Figure 1.3.

The figure draws out some of the primary characteristics of each school as well as the main points of criticism.

Strategic planning methods are commonly divided into two broad approaches; *prescriptive* and *emergent*. While recognised as being distinct in the academic sense, real-life strategic planning typically combines these two approaches:

- The prescriptive approach is based on a rigid strategic planning process, broken down into clearly demarcated pieces of work. It presupposes a known and stable environment, making it possible to estimate future conditions and choose a corresponding suitable strategy.
- The emergent approach presumes that a strategy is created and developed in accordance with circumstances that are only partly predictable. Consequently, this approach is experimental and flexible. It places an emphasis on the ideas and creative work of individuals and the strategy is thus largely formed through feelings and insight.

Reflection points

- What lessons from history can you take that relate to strategic planning in your field?
- For each of the ten schools listed write down your own descriptive summary as well as your personalised view of their pros and cons.
- Which three of the ten schools listed best describe your favoured approach to strategic planning? Why?

How is strategic planning carried out?

The process of strategic planning and delivering strategic action plans requires a good deal of initial thought and sufficient support from those whose

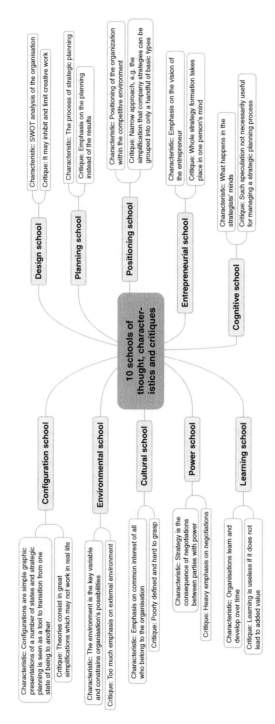

Figure 1.3

Overview of the main characteristics of the ten strategic planning schools.

input is key. Enthusiasm, thoroughness, stamina, creativity, and realism are all required along with the ability to communicate effectively. Keep in mind that defining where an enterprise is now and deciding where it wants to be in the future, in terms of its environment, is the principal reason for carrying out any strategic planning. What follows in this section is an overview of the strategic planning process that will be fleshed out in more detail in later chapters.

In structural terms, there are two approaches to forming a strategy: the top-down approach, in which strategic planning is generated at the executive level and flows down the organisational pyramid; and the bottom-up approach, where the strategic planning process starts at the lower levels of the organisation and grows upwards to the executive levels. The "up" and "down" concepts presuppose the idea of an organisational pyramid, where those with the most authority are positioned at the top, and those with the least authority are positioned at the bottom.

In the first case, top-down, where, when and how to start is the pre-requisite of the organisation's chief executives. They decide among themselves what the purpose of the company is, as well as its values. They define the current situation and decide where the company should be at a given point in time in the future. These decisions are made and elaborated in a work process that is coordinated and guided by the highest-ranking executives. Before the message is sent down through the organisational structure, to all other employees. In this model, the employees themselves have a very limited role in the strategic planning process.

The bottom-up approach starts from the opposite direction. It seeks to exploit the employees' knowledge, creativity and will to act and is predicated on the power inherent in a united group of people to create something unique and special. At the same time, the current status of the company in relation to its internal and external environment is assessed in a realistic manner. When this approach is chosen, united action is necessary in order to encourage as many employees as possible to participate in the strategic planning work process, giving them both a sense of participation and ownership. Proprietors and even customers or other interested parties may also be called upon to participate.

This approach harnesses the forces of creativity, increasing the potential for innovative and exciting ideas to emerge. If this approach to strategic planning is organised wisely and employees are given the chance to express their creativity, you may set aspirational and ambitious goals, confident in the knowledge that those involved will be more united, as well as having increased confidence in, and loyalty to, the enterprise. Typically, employees are given the opportunity to agree on the Human Resources policy, set the procedures and define ethics for the process they want to follow. It works well to allow employees to do this for themselves, as well as contribute to strategic planning in general, since most people naturally resent any forms of compulsion. Setting an HR policy at the employee level is more likely to improve the organisational culture. It can also serve to make employees more conscious of their rights, responsibilities, and obligations, and to strengthen their moral sense and their connection to the objectives of an enterprise.

Both approaches have their pros and cons. The top-down approach has the advantage that strategy can be formed in a relatively efficient manner. At a single meeting, chief executives can reach agreement on key issues and make the decisions they want to make. They are likely to have a good overview of the company and a good sense of the direction in which it should be heading. Consequently, this approach to strategic planning can take a relatively short time. The disadvantage of this approach is that a whole range of viewpoints are never taken into account and opportunities to make use of the employees' impetus are underused. The result may be that employees are unmotivated to put as much effort into achieving objectives they have no part in, and obstacles in the administration of plans are more likely to impede change. All in all, this is a rather old-fashioned approach considering modern knowledge-based companies.

The bottom-up approach should have the advantage of improved buy-in from employees as they have had a hand in the strategic planning process. By having everyone participate and contribute, the resulting strategic action plan should be more realistic, smoother to execute and important aspects are not forgotten or dismissed. A correctly chosen process is of key importance to assure the group becomes tight, united and willing to head in the same direction. Many new ideas may be generated and, in that pool of ideas, many new perspectives may surface, some of which could lead an enterprise in new directions and fortify it in various ways. The advantages of this collaborative approach are that it unites people, generates an extensive view of an enterprise's situation, and it is likely to be successful if it is well managed. However, it is exactly this need for strong management that represents its Achilles' heel. The process needs to be maintained without being so rigid as to hinder creativity. The execution phase is critical as the expectations of employees need to be met and management of these expectations remains very important throughout the whole process. Promising that employee's views will be taken into account but then excluding them from implementation plans without proper explanation can be very demoralising for those who approached the whole process in good spirit.

Any strategic planning needs to be followed by action and employees need to see the process move from plans to realities. The administration, preparation, management of and follow-up to bottom-up strategic planning can be complicated and difficult to execute. Progress needs to be visible throughout the company and based on convincing measurement, such as a balanced scorecard. Failure to do this will undermine the whole process. When employees see progressive plans and promises dissipate because of a failure to take action, it can easily destroy the unity and group harmony that was created during the strategic planning process.

In practice, a mixed-method approach is commonly chosen, i.e. *collaborative strategic planning*, which uses the best elements from each school to run an effective process. For instance, chief executives may define the main policy and on which employees then elaborate to generate the creative work, such as various analyses of the organisation's internal and external environment and the setting of goals. The collaborative approach emphasises strong guidance, with a high level of awareness required from executives of the main elements of the operation, transparency in terms of how objectives will be measured and how things are progressing.

The key questions that lie behind strategic planning are: "where are we now?" and "where do we want to be in the future?" In many cases, carrying out the work and analysis to answer the first question will highlight shortcomings, risks, and opportunities that then strongly influence the answer to the second. A structured way to initiate the process of strategic planning is to first think of it in terms of four basic dimensions. The first three of these are: (1) the relationship between a strategy and the environment of an enterprise; (2) the content of a strategy and (3) methods of setting and executing a strategy (Lynch and Smith, 2006); (4) the fourth basic dimension is simply the *existence* of the organisation in its broadest sense and this can be expressed in terms of however many levels is deemed necessary. Using a simple analytical model that is based on these four elementary dimensions, you can gain an insight into different aspects of strategic planning in all types of organisations. This is shown schematically in Figure 1.4.

The four dimensions may also be expressed as follows:

- Existence – Why does the organisation operate? What is its function? What legislation, regulations, and ordinances demarcate and describe its purpose, role and goal?
- Content – What does the organisation's operation centre around? In which fields does it operate and what is its basis of operations?

Figure 1.4

The four elementary dimensions of strategic planning (Steinthorsson, 1995).

- Process – What processes are employed in the operation and what methods and routines have been developed?
- Context – Where does the operation of the organisation take place; by and for whom? What are, for instance, the outer and the inner contexts of the organisation, its social and economic environment, and premises? Who are its customers and owners? Who else does its activities affect?

In this book, we will be discussing all of the dimensions and analytical models that are of help in answering those questions about the strategic planning process. There are a number of important aspects that should be kept in mind throughout the entire strategic planning process:

- Encourage participation – The process should be motivating for all participants and executed in such a way as to guarantee that as many employees as possible participate directly. In this way, the process should contribute to building up a sense of teamwork and increase the probability of success by extracting as many good ideas as possible.
- Support open discussions – The process should encourage open discussion and constructive critique. It is important to create a joint understanding of the need for change and, at the same time, be careful that no misunderstanding occurs due to poor communication.
- Build on existing work – The process should be focused on developing work that has already been carried out within the organisation, e.g. previous or current strategies, appraisals of the enterprise's status, surveys of customer or employee satisfaction. Former strategies or schedules made in specific areas of the organisation are an important starting point with the provision that they are still relevant to the current circumstances of an enterprise. If a recent move by a competitor has made previous work largely redundant, or some other change of circumstances has had the same effect (such as entirely new regulations), then this should be acknowledged quickly so no time is wasted.
- Adopt appropriate analytical tools – Numerous analytical tools have been developed to study both the internal and external environments of organisations. The process should use any of the main recognised tools such as SWOT analysis, five forces competition theory model as well as other less common analytical tools that are appropriate for the context or industry and useful for making the work more creative and effective.
- Design the process – The process must reflect an enterprise's goal in a clear and understandable manner, and make the participants feel they are a part of it. The process must put the main emphasis on a policy statement, measurable objectives and the methods to achieve them.

These factors that form the basis of the strategic planning process are further elaborated on in the second chapter of this book.

Reflection points

- What lessons from history can you take that relate to strategic planning in your field?
- For each of the ten schools listed write down your own descriptive summary as well as your personalised view of their pros and cons.
- Which three of the ten schools listed best describe your favoured approach to strategic planning? Why?

Skills and methodology of the strategic planning practitioner

Strategic planning skills make it possible for people to prepare, maintain, encourage and deliver an enterprise's strategic planning process in such a way as to bring the enterprise positive results in the long run. These skills can be subdivided into individual strategic skills and group skills. Some people will possess both sets of skills, in other cases, you'll need a team of people whose skills can complement each other. A good facilitator for a strategic planning group may lack the strategic mindset capable of foreseeing all future permutations but nonetheless have good overall experience, critical abilities and people skills, as well as being methodical in their approach, able to bring out the best in other people and convert all of this into a well-crafted implementation plan. Another individual, meanwhile, may be something of a recluse with poor communication skills but have a razor-sharp mind and uniquely focused outlook that can visualise multiple scenarios and make connections that are not obvious but nonetheless very insightful. Yet another may have considerable experience of projects, an in-depth knowledge of planning methodologies as well as plenty of patience and dedication.

All of the skills or attributes will be useful so bear them in mind when building your planning team. Individual strategic planning skills involve being able to think and implement in a creative and thorough manner, both progressively and systematically. They may include explicit, technical skills learned through formal training as well as tacit skills learned from working with others. Whilst explicit skills are often visible, tacit skills may be more hidden but are no less important. For example, a manager may have advanced complex reasoning skills but may overlook some rather obvious common-sense aspects of a particular problem. This is where group skills are also very important. Involving others helps to avoid missing important aspects particularly in situations where "groupthink" and/or an unwillingness to challenge superiors is prevalent.

Having a diversity of opinions is always a key aspect of successful strategic planning; experience and intuition are very important when dealing with future uncertainty. When you form a group to undertake strategic planning make sure you include those whose views are independent and unconventional, as their input can be of great benefit where real insight and change is required and desired. Wherever group work is involved, you will need the ability to build group cohesion and the skills to facilitate getting the best out of others. Many of the skills of successful strategic planning can be developed and cultivated. A number of aspects relating to group skills are covered in the *Leadership* and *Communication* books in this series. An individual with strategic planning skills should be able to define the challenge, recruit people to participate openly sustain the process, encourage the participants, tackle obstacles and turn disagreement into a platform for achieving better results.

Professional strategic management consultants (who may be internal or external to an enterprise), will demonstrate the skill to familiarise themselves with the situation and environment of a client (or employer) and gain an in-depth understanding of these. The consultant must primarily listen and serve; approaching the task with a mix of humility and resolution. We emphasise the role of the strategic planning consultant in this book since it may well be a role to which many of our readers aspire. Typically, the results of a consulting strategic planning activity are delivered in the form of a strategic planning report, for which the consultant is responsible. The report addresses the main topics of the strategic planning process and will discuss the following issues:

- **The values** that characterise the organisation and unite its employees.
- **The mission** that defines the purpose of the organisation.
- **The future vision**, which reflects the situation of the organisation at the end of the strategic planning period.
- **Status assessment** and a summary analysis of the organisation's external and internal environment.
- **A strategic action plan** containing main objectives, project objectives and a list of agreed actions, plus a list of the projects necessary to achieve the objectives set.

A strategic planning report needs to highlight the key findings and be concise and to the point. It is a good rule to summarise the findings in a short and systematic summary chapter at the start of the report and use a layout that is well-structured, uncluttered and does not allow for misinterpretation.

> **The following is an outline of a strategic planning process under-taken by one of the authors acting as an external consultant for a medium-sized European enterprise:**
>
> **We applied a conventional strategic planning method by analys-ing values, roles and goals, making a status assessment, defining main objectives and project objectives, and creating a strategic action plan. The actual work itself started with a meeting between the consultant, the sponsoring director, and the Board, followed**

by a series of meetings attended by the sponsoring director and the consultant and each and every employee. The consultant used an introductory session to present the basic ideas of strategic planning and emphasise the importance of everyone participating in one-way or another. The consultant then conducted an in-depth interview with the director and supervised several full-day workshops, which took place outside the company, first with the company executive board, then with all other employees. Following the workshop, the employees were encouraged to contact the consultant if they had constructive comments about the company, its management, operations and more. A good many employees took the opportunity to participate. The output of the interviews with executives and employees, as well as a study of the operating summary, suggested that this was a good time to look into the operation in order to form a strategy for the future. The deliverable in this case was a comprehensive strategic planning report (earlier drafts of which had been discussed with the board and executives) that reflected, in detail, the process that had taken place and had clearly stated objectives and plans of implementation.

The following example illustrates a possible format that can be used by a consultant to undertake strategic planning. Whilst the approach described above was tailored to the needs of the company in question, Figure 1.5 shows a general presentation of the main actions in a typical consulting strategic planning process.

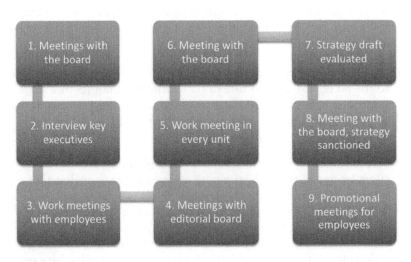

Figure 1.5

An example of the main steps in the consulting strategic planning process.

Guidelines for strategic planning

Stages 1 & 2: Strategic planning requires the close co-operation of the executive management and the Board of Directors. It is normally carried out under the authority of the Board, who will approve the findings and resource its implementation. The process starts with the consultant (internal or external) arranging a meeting with the board and interviewing key executives and selected employees. The ability to understand the governance, structures, and culture of the organisation is a key to success.

3: If the strategy draft is meant to originate at the bottom level of the organisational chart, it may prove useful to hold a large group meeting, to introduce the basic ideas of strategic planning, and encourage those employees present to participate directly in the strategic planning work. The aim is to gather information from the grassroots, build up unity and ambition and encourage the group to advance. This is the time for the consultant to show his/her leadership and ability to facilitate teamwork.

4: Following this large meeting, the board commissions an editorial board, with which the consultant meets.

5: Once everyone is aware of the strategic planning, it can prove effective to initiate a dialogue through which everyone within the organisation can state their thoughts and offer valuable information and intelligence. One way to do this is to call a work meeting in every work unit – department, group, board, and so on – and invite the chosen group to analyse the work unit by way of a SWOT analysis. If you manage and organise this well, it will encourage a constructive dialogue within the work unit about what is currently being done well and what might be improved. Strengths and weaknesses refer to the internal environment of the work unit, while threats and opportunities refer to its external environment. The internal environment of a work unit comprises employee skills, work, communication, and product quality. The external environment may refer to the impact of other work units, of the market and economic conditions. The purpose of the SWOT analysis is, however, both to motivate dialogue and idea generation and help the work unit to face its challenges and opportunities, as well as encouraging the employees to feel empowered and autonomous. A good SWOT analysis should build on the strengths of the work unit and encourage those involved to find ways to compensate for weaknesses and threats by understanding strengths and pursuing opportunities. A SWOT analysis leads to self-examination, brings out useful information and prepares the work unit for participation in the strategic planning. SWOT analysis and other analytic tools will be discussed in more detail later on in this book. You may need to deal with conflict and problems in communication, and it is of the essence to show personal integrity and create a spirit of results orientation in the work.

6: As you start to compose the strategic planning report using the existing data, it is sensible to present this information to those concerned and gather their comments. This early consultation will reassure employees of their role in and relevance to the planning process. Your ability, as the report's author, to interpret all comments as constructive is crucial, and you should either add the feedback you receive to the report or attach it as an appendix. Even though the strategy is by and large set by the report itself, it remains important that the Board and executives make use of all the creative and critical insight the data contains in implementing the strategy. The strategic planning report does not contain the ultimate truth, but is a working document that can prove useful for the development of the organisation. This is when you may need to apply your skills as a negotiator, to reach an outcome that is acceptable and aligned. As the strategic planning report starts taking shape, remember to forward your work in progress a draft regularly to all concerned and request their feedback.

7: A final report draft is submitted to the company Board, which reviews it and makes comments and corrections, particularly in relation to prioritising opportunities financing, resources and more. Thereafter, the strategy draft is sent to all parties concerned (individual employees, divisional managers, directors, councils, departments, work units or committees) who are invited to make comments. It is important to invest enough time in this phase as well as enough effort in encouraging all relevant parties to make their views known.

8: When all comments have been received, the editorial and company boards evaluate them, and the draft text is edited. The final version will involve a compromise that reflects the critical feedback and the work, which has taken place at work meetings and in the work of the editorial and company boards. You may find it hard to agree on a common path on certain aspects, and it is therefore important to guarantee that the process is transparent and to prepare assumptions and arguments to share in the face of challenges.

9: Once you have a final plan, you will need to organise promotional meetings to introduce all parties to the report and its contents. These provide an opportunity for all participants in the process to identify their own contribution. If the report reveals or contains commercially sensitive information, relates to the personal circumstances of specific individuals or trails as yet unannounced product development you may need to anonymise such information in some way. Be careful how you do this is as any compromise in transparency may arouse suspicion and undermine support. In the introduction to your strategic planning report, thank all who have contributed to it in such a way that they can easily identify themselves.

Reflection points

- What are the main desirable skills and attributes for a professional strategic planning consultant in your view?
- In your experience, what factors might lead to encountering resistance and hostility from stakeholders in the course of undertaking the strategic planning process? How should this be dealt with?

References

Ahlstrand, B., Lampel, J., & Mintzberg, H. (2001). *Strategy safari: A guided tour through the wilds of strategic management.* New York: Simon and Schuster.

Ansoff, H. (1965). *Corporate strategy.* New York: McGraw-Hill Inc., US.

Bristol, K. G. (1991). The Pruitt-Igoe myth. *Journal of Architectural Education*, 44(3), 163–171.

Chandler, A. D. (1962). *Strategy and structure: Chapters in the history of the American enterprise.* Cambridge: Massachusetts Institute of Technology Press.

Drucker, P. F. (1954). *Management by objectives and self-control. Practice of Management.* New York: Harper & Row.

IPMA (2015). IPMA Competence Baseline 4.0.

Kotter, J. P. (1996). *Leading change.* Boston: Harvard Business School Press.

Lynch, R. L., & Smith, J. R. (2006). *Corporate strategy.* Harlow, England: FT/Prentice Hall.

McKiernan, P. (Ed.). (2017). *Historical evolution of strategic management*, volumes I and II (Vol. 1). London: Taylor & Francis.

Mintzberg, H. (1994). The fall and rise of strategic planning. *Harvard Business Review*, 72(1), 107–114.

NIST (2018). Baldrige performance excellence program. [online] Available at: https://www.nist.gov/baldrige [Accessed 21 May 2018].

Porter, M. E. (1980). *Competitive strategy: Techniques for analysing industries and competitors* (Vol. 267). New York: The Free Press.

Porter, M. E. (2011). *Competitive advantage of nations: Creating and sustaining superior performance* (Vol. 2). New York: Simon and Schuster.

Senge, P. (1990). *The 5th discipline.* New York: Bantam Doubleday Dell Publishing Group.

Steinthorsson, R.S. (1995). Strategic management of integrated intermediate organisations: An empirical/theoretical analysis of how industrial associations are managed strategically. A Ph.D. Dissertation (5.95). Copenhagen Business School.

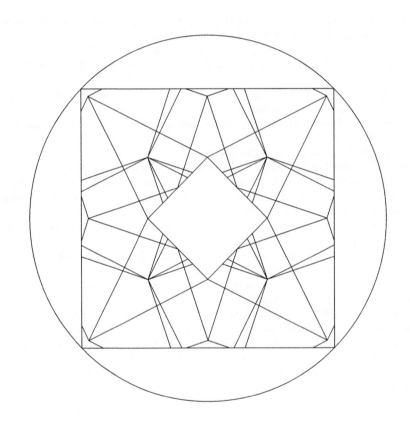

2 The strategic planning process

∙∙∙

Towards the end of Chapter 1 we discussed the strategic planning process in a broad outline. In this chapter, we build on that discussion and provide more detailed insights into different approaches and methods that can be applied. We will define the *strategic process* as a coordinated series of steps or actions taken to achieve a particular end, which, in this case, is a successful strategic plan that can be implemented. The process itself is a reflective undertaking that takes place within the boundaries of an organisation but that may involve external consultants to assist, facilitate or challenge the participants. As the strategic process is such a significant and integrated part of the organisational life it is crucial that the process is well-conducted and transparent to all involved. Typically, the mere act of going through the motions of strategic planning and all that it entails can be both revealing and beneficial, even in cases – which we do not recommend – where a detailed and well-defined strategic plan will not be the outcome.

Strategic planning can take place on several different levels. In Chapter 1, we suggested that formal strategic planning should be carried out routinely, typically every third year, but sometimes more frequently, depending on the environment within which the organisation is expected to thrive. While the main strategic plan will focus on the future of the entire enterprise, there can also be several levels to the strategy, below this; for instance (a) an interim or iterative strategic planning process in response to changing circumstances; (b) separate strategic planning processes for different divisions of the organisation; (c) particular programs may have their own associated strategic planning; (d) as can their constituent projects. Thus, a project to construct a high-voltage electrical transmission line can require specific strategic planning aimed at overcoming objections raised by particular stakeholders.

Without getting too focused on nomenclature, we could refer to various types, or levels, of strategic planning as being related to "projects," "programmes" or "project portfolios." It is easier to simply speak of "projects" as a generic term and emphasise the strategic elements that they all have in common. While planning strategy can be seen as a project, some aspects of strategic planning do refer more specifically to programmes and project portfolios, we will highlight these separately as we go along. In the following sections, we will discuss a generic process that is widely applicable for strategic planning purposes at all levels. In doing so, we will also highlight a number of important considerations and variations that are important when tailoring a solution to a particular situation.

Overall methodology and structure

This book's point of departure is a simple generic model of the strategic planning process that has wide applicability and sees the two elements of strategic design and implementation as both a creative task and a systematic process. This model is based on ideas put forward by Goodstein et al. (1993), combined with our own experience of conducting strategic planning at all levels and for all kinds of organisations. We will also keep in mind some of the implications associated with models from the ten strategic schools mentioned in Chapter 1. We will kick off with a discussion of the preliminary work that can be done in the lead up to, and in the early stages of, strategic planning, including decisions about scope, definitions, and elaboration of the four dimensions mentioned in Chapter 1.

Strategic planning is based on an understanding of the organisation's internal and external environments; this can be acquired by gathering data, analysing it, and interpreting the results. At a basic level, you need to differentiate between *strategic thinking* on the one hand and *strategic planning* on the other. As shown in Figure 2.1, defining an organisation's values, its mission, analysing its current status or competitive position and laying out a vision for the future can be said to be "strategic thinking," while the setting of objectives and making of a strategic action plan come under "strategic planning." The difference is essentially that "thinking" involves where and why, whereas "planning" involves how, with what, and by whom. As already mentioned, either a top-down, bottom-up or collaborative approach can be used although the final version of the strategy; its execution and follow-up will definitely require the knowledge, support, and direction that only top management can provide. It is important to realise that all of the foundational elements in the illustration from values to vision do exist, irrespective of whether you address them consciously or not; indeed, an important aim of systematic strategic thinking involves defining and then realising these essential elements in a deliberate and studied way.

The strategic process may take a long or a short time, depending on the circumstances, available know-how, commitment, scale and complexity required, and level of urgency. Special timelines and processes may apply to strategic planning related to particular projects or sub-elements of projects. Projects may have restrictive deadlines by which objectives need to have been achieved and submitted. A project or programme for a national regulator, for example, may involve inviting interested parties to make a detailed submission by a particular date through a formal consultation process.

To remain credible, we suggest that enterprises should review their strategy at least once a year, even if the enterprise's main role and purpose do not

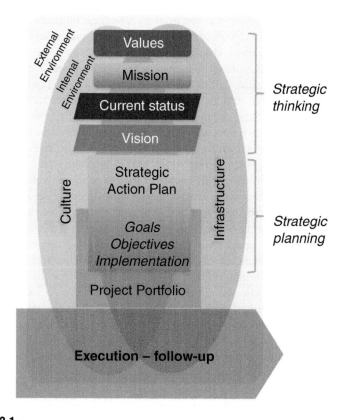

Figure 2.1

The generic strategic planning process followed in this book.

change that frequently. At the end of such a review, you can tweak or adjust the strategic plan as necessary. The environment changes, and new opportunities and risks are constantly emerging. The organisational strategy, including the strategic plan, must therefore be subject to influence, critical review, and improvements. Let's now explore Figure 2.1 in more detail.

Strategic thinking

The first element in our diagram is strategic thinking and within that, our organisational *values*. Values define "who we are" as an organisation. They are the principles or standards that are fundamental to the life of the organisation and they should reflect its core philosophy and approach. The values are the ideals that the organisation, its board, managers, and employees will never compromise. In the case of a public organisation, these may stem from a well-defined constitutional duty. In the case of NGOs, these may reflect the common interests of members. In a private enterprise, they may reflect the beliefs of the founders or owners as to what is essential in how their business is conducted, or express the distinctive DNA of the organization's commercial brand. Values are unlikely to undergo much change over time although some updating may be periodically apt. Take a moment to reflect on these values before embarking on a new project to make sure your new activities align with the corporate values. Values are not just lofty statements, they can be used as key tools to manage motivation, discipline, and commitment. Individuals within the organisation should be encouraged to reflect upon their personal values and mirror them in the values of the organisation to ensure synergy and cohesion. For example, a project manager who has strong environmental views, lives in accordance with them, cycles to work, and separates waste at his home. If he works with a civil contractor and is entrusted with managing a major street construction project in his city, he may be in trouble. That is, if he doesn't believe that such construction solves the problems in the transportation system and, in addition, has a bad environmental impact. Another example could be a city employee who is commissioned to follow up a ban on keeping dogs in the city. If the official has no faith in such commandments, then he may be in trouble.

The next element is the *mission*, which defines what "we do" as an organisation. The mission should derive from and be in line with the values. For any for-profit enterprise, this involves making money for shareholders alongside its ambitions in its designated area of activity, while a not-for-profit enterprise will typically have a central reason for its existence that delineates its actions. In order to provide more clarity, the role of an enterprise can be further elaborated to reflect the particular scope of a strategic planning exercise. Some examples of mission statements can be found on the web site of Unum (Unum.co.uk, 2018).

Current status is an all-encompassing term that covers all critical aspects of both the internal and external environment of an enterprise. "Where are we now?" is the basic question and many different considerations and metrics can feed into this overall aim to describe the present status and "health" of an enterprise.

Elements pertaining to the *internal environment* include the enterprise's various resources, such as employee know-how, the knowledge that has been accumulated in past and present operations and projects, or intellectual property that the organisation has acquired, developed or purchased. The organisation's culture may represent another internal resource if it has been developing over a long time and can play a big part in the formation and implementation of a strategy. Be careful to include both the defining features of the culture as well as their implications to avoid any meandering into vague intangibles. Thus: "the company was founded on the principle of balanced stakeholder needs, which means that we approach the needs of the owner, the employees, our customers, and our suppliers with equal weight when making decisions." There are also concrete elements to the internal environment such as the organisation's infrastructure, instruments and tools, working environment, and facilities, which ensure employees are secure and provide the resources to meet customer needs. Last, but not least, elements such as the organisation's financial status, its assets, liabilities, revenues, and cash flow are all part of its internal environment.

The *external environment of an organisation* includes everything that stands outside the organisation but nevertheless influences it or is influenced by the organisation's operations. The economic situation in the regions or countries where an enterprise operates or wants to operate is one such element. The political environment may be significant too, i.e. whether it is stable or unstable, and the nature of political views and sentiments regarding environmental issues. A further element is the level of market competition, whether it is growing or declining, and how the market will grow in the foreseeable future. Customers (or clients) are, of course, a very important consideration, and knowing about their needs, loyalties, profiles, purchasing power, numbers, and strength is likely to be essential. Various social issues in market areas or in the company's environment may matter, such as the age distribution of the inhabitants and their level of education. Natural conditions must be assessed – for instance geographical circumstances, location or locations, whether the climate of other natural phenomena affects the company's operations, and so on. The culture, religions, customs, and potential social tensions in both the organization's places of operation and its markets should be considered. Legal requirements, regulatory standards, and industry standards are also of great importance, as are the views of various stakeholders and interest groups. If you are looking to develop a new wind farm in an area of outstanding natural beauty, for example, it is inevitable that there will be a number of groups and individuals that will vigorously oppose it. You should anticipate planning battles or make contingency for other, less-sensitive, sites.

The last element of strategic thinking shown is *vision*. Vision describes the desired status of an enterprise at a designated time in the near future and, by extension, outlines the specific goals that you need to achieve in order to make this a reality. The inputs into the Vision include everything that has been described relating to the internal and external environments of an enterprise. Synthesis of all these different elements through vigorous analysis and debate should lead to agreement on a vision that reflects the ambitions, capabilities, and values of an enterprise. If these elements do not accord, the vision may become incongruous either by contravening the role of the enterprise, violating its core values or otherwise going against what is appropriate. We will return to this topic in later chapters when we look in more detail at how to evaluate an organisation's values, role, and vision. Some examples of vision statements of non-profit organisations can be found on the website of Top Nonprofits (2018).

When carrying out strategic thinking, be realistic, base your activities on facts derived from the various analyses undertaken rather than simple wishful thinking. There are many tools to aid the analysis of the internal and external environments of an enterprise and its current status. These are discussed in detail in Chapters 3 through 6. But remember that analyses of different kinds carried out during the strategic planning process itself are important but are still only part of a bigger context (see Figure 2.2).

Figure 2.2

Strategic thinking.

Planning

When the strategic thinking process is complete, and a vision has been set, it is likely that it will differ markedly from the current status assessment. The vision will probably allow for more growth, more markets, more profit, more customer/client satisfaction, for the development of further knowledge, and so on. In order to realise the desired vision, you need to create a strategic action plan where the organisation's mission and vision are translated into projects. This breaks down the strategy into a series of goals, which are further divided into objectives, each with its own implementation plan describing how to achieve the respective objectives. It will usually also describe a management system for measuring performance and assessing whether the desired changes have been met at a point in the future.

In the end, the strategic action plan and its inherent implementation plans must be brought to fruition. During the subsequent execution of the plan, you should be alert to any changes in the enterprises internal and external environments that materially alter the original premise of the plan and the actions that have been derived from it. You may have *put* or *take options* that you can exercise (basically opportunistic or defensive and pre-determined actions) that you identified as a result of your initial scenario planning. For example, legislation requiring congestion charging for traffic in cities might increase the immediate demand for public transport. If you have anticipated this as a scenario, then you may have planned provision to accelerate or extend your program of railway upgrades. If these changes have not been anticipated or have a far greater impact on the project or program, you may need to re-evaluate various parts of the strategic plan; they may impact the status assessment and even the overall vision. This may, in turn, affect the strategic action plan. In order to achieve a strategic action plan's main objectives, you need a disciplined methodology, and success will only be achieved if an enterprise has sufficient knowledge and, preferably, a tradition of project management methodology. Unfortunately, it is common for careful strategic planning to fall far short of its original purpose because project management knowledge, process, and infrastructure are lacking. This applies to projects relating to an enterprise's internal operations, as well as to services granted and production. The connections between strategic planning and project management are explored in Chapter 8.

Reflection points

- How would you explain the terms culture and infrastructure in the internal environment of an enterprise?
- In your experience, what are the key factors that influence the vision of an enterprise?
- In your experience, what elements in both the internal and external environments of an enterprise are likely to prove most problematic in trying to realise a desired vision?
- Would the strategic planning process shown in Figure 2.1 be different or similar for profit and non-profit organisations? Explain.
- What should the follow-up aspect of strategic planning involve?

Participation and analysis

The principle of "garbage in, garbage out" applies to any strategic planning processes that involve gathering and then analysing data. Individuals and teams working on internal and external environmental analysis need to ensure that they are rigorous in their approach and that the information they obtain is accurate and reflective of reality. For example, if your rail upgrade project overlooks particularly interested parties, or their concerns are knowingly or unknowingly misinterpreted, then you may find you need to divert from your original route when the execution of the strategic plan is already in motion and significant resources have been committed. Equally, a poorly performed customer needs analysis that is not reflective of the market as a whole can give misleading signals to management to pursue particular strategies, so, if your forecasts of passenger traffic are wildly optimistic, they may undermine the whole commercial basis of the project.

The processing of information gathered is equally important. If models are used to manipulate data and provide answers to questions posed, then the assumptions that lie behind this modelling and the limitations of it need to be widely understood and acknowledged.

Report presentation

The results of the strategic planning work materialise in the form of a document called a strategic planning report, or a strategy document. The report contains the strategy's key elements and the emphasis for the future, together with a systematic plan of action. It is important to underline that even a well-elaborated strategic planning report should not be thought of as something fixed and definitive. A good strategic planning report is a living document, which serves as a guideline for the board and executives of an enterprise. Those concerned need to be aware that the strategy is a guide into the future, and since the future is uncertain, must be ready to make changes and discontinue projects that are not successful or no longer have relevance. The report is one of the manager's most powerful working tools. Success is best guaranteed by taking the report very seriously while, at the same time, realising that it needs to be constantly re-evaluated, balancing the importance of the actions and direction it dictates with the need to adjust the direction in light of ever-changing circumstances.

A good strategy document is simple and accessible, short and free of jargon. To ensure that the strategy document's main message and intent come through clearly, use a concise summary of no more than 1–3 pages to preface the main strategy document. Following the summary, more detailed discussion on various phases of the strategic planning process may be added, such as clarifications, analyses, and results. The format and layout of a strategy document, as well as its standard of writing, can have considerable impact when it comes to the readability and application. Spelling and grammar are important in the sense that errors can convey the wrong impression of the material contained therein. There is always the danger that the reader overlooks the quality of the contents because of the poor layout and writing of a report make a bad impression. Make sure you reference sources of information, when applicable, with a list of references at the end, as readers may need to consult these in the event of changing conditions or assumptions. Appendices and attachments should be added if relevant. These might consist of further reading material that supports the discussion in the document and which might prove useful for the reader.

A strategy document sums up the results of the strategic planning process and presents a clear picture of an enterprise's role, values, vision, objectives, and action plan. It documents the research done, the analyses of data carried out, the vision that the team envisages, and last, but not least, the action plan best suited to advance the enterprise into the future. The report may include considerable detail but should still emphasise the main actions and the most useful information to make it a living witness to the strategic planning. It is meant to be a practical work document rather than a source of detailed historical data. A strategic planning report is, as a matter of course, written for an enterprise, its employees, managers, and board. It is not written for the external environment, e.g. supervisory bodies, clients or suppliers, nor is it primarily meant for investors. In this regard, it radically differs from a business plan. Nevertheless, a strategic planning report can prove useful in deciding how to communicate with these external parties.

There is no fixed layout for a strategic planning report and there are various ways to structure and write it. Since it is a document that is meant to be a foundation for discussion, and needs to be assimilated by management and workers alike it may prove clever to format the report in such a way as to make it suitable for presentations, e.g. with presentation slides, as well as for reading in print. Another option is to develop a version of the report as a web page, for display on an organisation's intranet.

The outline of a strategic planning report might use the generic strategic planning process presented graphically earlier as a template. Different circumstances will mean that you need to put varying emphasis on the different elements, perhaps for different groups, but we believe all of them should always be referred to, however briefly. We stress again that each enterprise needs to be fully aware of its own external environment and all the different factors that can influence events and impact the achievement of objectives. In terms of the internal environment, we believe this can be viewed from two overall perspectives for simplification: culture and infrastructure. These categories will be discussed in more detail later. It is good practice to state at the beginning, of any presentation, how the final report was constructed including reviewers at various stages, who the interlocutors were and how the strategy contents were acquired.

Professionalism and best practice

Strategic planning in any particular enterprise can be carried out by people with very different backgrounds and with varying levels of experience and knowledge. An entrepreneur, for example, may have little formal training but, nonetheless, have an in-depth knowledge of the relevant internal and external environments, and be highly competent at strategic planning, at least in the formative stages of an enterprise. As the business grows and its markets or services become larger and more complex, strategic planning can quickly become a specialist area where experience and an understanding of networks (of people), management structures, systems, and different environments can be essential and formal training may be a requirement.

Reflection points
- What criteria apply in assessing whether data and modelling used in strategic planning are reflective of reality and appropriate? Explain by showing an example, if you can.
- What approaches can be taken to avoid knowledge gaps in the strategic planning process? Explain with an example.
- What might be clever ways to make sure that a strategy planning report becomes a "living document"?

Considerations and main difficulties

There are a number of mistakes that are made in the strategic planning process. Olsen (2007) and Mezger and Violani (2011) point out the following dangers and potential mishaps (Table 2.1):

It is also useful to keep in mind the warnings of Henry Mintzberg who wrote *The Rise and Fall of Strategic Planning* (1994). Mintzberg emphasised the difference between strategic thinking and strategic planning and defined three basic assumptions as the principal fallacies of strategic planning: (1) that prediction is possible and that the environment of an organisation will stay still while a plan is developed and implemented; (2) that *thinking* strategy

Table 2.1 Dangers and potential mishaps in strategic planning

Potential risk	Impact
The analysis factor of the strategic planning process is underestimated.	The necessary information on the enterprise's status has neither been gathered nor analysed properly before a plan is made.
Information gathered and analysed is then ignored in the planning process. This may be a conscious or unconscious omission.	Results in a false picture of reality, leading to unrealistic plans.
Too much energy is put into the planning process and little energy is left when it comes to the implementation	Little is actually completed. Better not to start in the first place.
The working procedure is careless and previous work is thoughtlessly ignored in order to write the strategic planning report as quickly as possible.	Ignores the fact that one of the most useful things about strategic planning is precisely the process itself. Poor engagement and little chance of success.
The strategy is too general, includes everything plus the kitchen sink and cannot say "no" to anything.	Companies have limited resources and need to make choices and focus on what is most important and most relevant. An unrealistic or over-ambitious plan will either drain common resources from other priorities or undermine the chance of delivery.
The strategy does not take into account competitors and their actions	An enterprise exists in a dynamic and connected environment and should assume that the actions it takes will lead to responses by its competitors. A strategic plan that fails to factor in the potential competitor responses along with their own corresponding counter-responses, is likely to be fragile.
A strategy cannot be implemented if it is not feasible for an enterprise.	An early step in strategy formulation should be a proper capability assessment, otherwise, the defined strategy risks being so ambitious that the enterprise lacks the capabilities to implement it.

can be detached from *doing* strategy, and that strategies should be formed by "thinkers" who are detached from the "doers" in an organisation and (3) the assumption that a strategy-making process can be formalised.

In this book, we present a strategic planning process that has been tested successfully in many organisations. The process itself does not automatically protect you from the perils we have described. Take these warnings seriously and keep them in mind as you read Chapter 4 on internal analyses where we specify the first steps that need to be taken in introducing strategic planning within an organisation. These consist mainly of discovering the true concerns and desires of managers and employees alike.

Reflection points

- One of the dangers in the strategic planning process is that the analysis factor is underestimated. Have you experienced this? Can you imagine the opposite, i.e. too much analysis? What might be the consequences?
- One of the basic strategic planning mishaps is that the strategy is too general, includes everything and does not say "no" to anything. Have you experienced this? What was the consequence?
- Look at the warnings of Henry Mintzberg in his book *The Rise and Fall of Strategic Planning*. How can these be taken into consideration in the strategic planning process? (see Figure 2.2).

References

Goodstein, L. D., Nolan, T. M., & Pfeiffer, J. W. (1993). *Applied strategic planning*. New York: McGraw-Hill.

Mezger, S., & Violani, M. (2011). Seven basic strategic missteps and how to avoid them. *Strategy & Leadership*, 39(6), 19–26.

Mintzberg, H. (1994). The fall and rise of strategic planning. *Harvard Business Review*, 72(1), 107–114.

Olsen, E. (2007). *Strategic planning for dummies*. Hoboken: John Wiley & Sons.

Top Nonprofits. (2018). 30 example vision statements. [online] Available at: https://topnonprofits.com/examples/vision-statements [Accessed 21 May 2018].

Unum.co.uk. (2018). The 24 most inspirational company mission statements. [online] Available at: https://www.unum.co.uk/hr/the-24-most-inspirational-company-mission-statements [Accessed 21 May 2018].

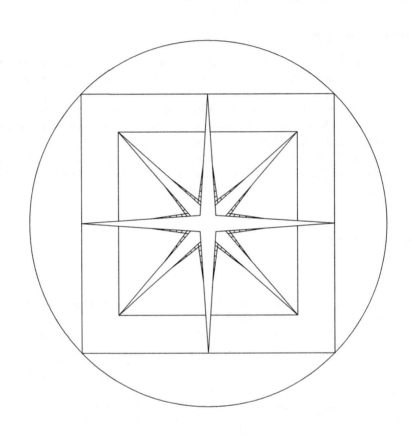

3 Understanding your stakeholders and sources of organisational capital

The next two chapters focus on the analysis of the internal environment of the organisation as an essential aspect of the strategic planning process. In order to manage the future of the organisation, it is necessary to have a good understanding of both the past and present state of affairs. This means studying available information on the organisation: its history, its infrastructure, its culture, its performance, and its current and past triumphs and failings. Various methods and analytical tools may be used to assist in this work, and a number of these will be described in this chapter.

To kick off the strategic planning process you need to take time studying various sources of existing information pertaining to the internal environment of the organisation: annual reports, interim statements, and client and personnel attitude surveys as well as any previous strategy reports, if they exist. While the enterprise may have invested both time and money in previous strategic planning, it is not uncommon for the resulting report to end up unimplemented and on a shelf. Even if this is the case, provided the earlier work was undertaken with integrity, all such previous reports can be used in the current strategic planning process, as they are likely to contain valuable information and insight into the workings of the enterprise. Therefore, all such data should be requested, reviewed, and analysed in a systematic manner.

A number of key points may be extracted from this analysis that can help answer important questions, such as:

- What particular objectives have been achieved?
- What challenges have been experienced?
- Has the customer base been expanded?
- Have new products been developed?
- Have new and competent employees been hired?
- Has the enterprise's knowledge base developed?

- Has the internal environment changed to a significant extent?
- Have previous strategic action plans achieved the desired results?

In terms of this last question, it is important to gain an understanding of why projects succeeded or failed. In this case:

- Where did people make mistakes?
- Why were particular objectives not achieved? In retrospect, which decisions should not have been made?
- Which aspects were not completed or took too long?
- What aspects were of insufficient quality or exceeded the cost estimate?
- What overall conclusions can you draw here for the future?

If all parties have the same understanding of the success criteria of the enterprise, this discussion should be unproblematic. However, in some cases, different people have different ideas about success and it may be that managers have never defined what the desired results are for the enterprise. In which case, it is better not to dwell on the past, but focus on the future and the objectives for the years ahead. We will return to this theme in Chapter 7.

In the following chapters, we outline a number of analytical methods that are important tools for enabling the internal environment analysis stage of professional strategic planning. The coverage here is far from being exhaustive and there are numerous other analytical tools. Whichever tools you adopt, you should understand their pros and cons before you start and make sure each is applied appropriately given the circumstances. Your analysis should be planned in the context of the overall strategic planning process (described in the previous chapter). Analysis of the internal environment of an enterprise is a part of the current status assessment, which takes place after values and roles have been defined. In some situations, it may not necessarily be a good idea to compile too extensive data or discuss the internal environment too thoroughly if this material has little bearing on the defined role and future plans of an enterprise.

Is your enterprise ready?

In the earliest stages of strategic planning, it is important to determine whether an enterprise is, in fact, ready for the process and whether the challenges and cost of undertaking the process outweigh the benefits. Figure 3.1 outlines a number of considerations that you should assess in a systematic manner. Typically, the answers to these questions can be gleaned through your initial interviews with key personnel.

The management's sentiments

The first question to ask is whether the management of the organisation is ready. In your interviews with management and directors, i.e. the top

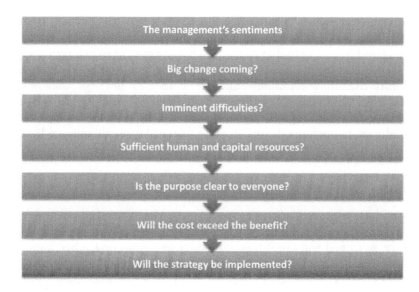

Figure 3.1

First analysis, the organisation's sentiment towards the imminent strategic planning.

executives, you will quickly determine whether there is a real willingness to carry out strategic planning and the consequent operational changes. Do the top executives seem to be genuinely interested and engaged and are they going to participate directly? If the intention is insincere and superficial, it pays to stop and rethink the whole process, because the chances of success are low if management does not believe wholeheartedly in the need for, significance of, and commitment to the strategic planning work.

Big change coming?

Most enterprises operate in a continually shifting business environment, but they may also experience exceptional changes from time to time. The catalyst for these changes could be a merger, large administrative changes, or alterations in the regulatory environment. Both the management team and the person facilitating the strategic planning need to be aware of what lies ahead and prepare accordingly. Any substantial strategic change process will suffer if the organisation's resources are already committed elsewhere. Or it may be that the organisation's ability to respond to this exceptional change is compromised by your self-inflicted change programme.

Imminent difficulties

Is the enterprise facing difficult, imminent problems such as internal rivalry, communication problems, or technical problems, or is it struggling with competitors or facing litigation? Such operational issues call for an enterprise's immediate attention and demand great administrative effort. If you are engaged in an internal fire-fight, you will struggle to switch your focus to the future. Put the fire out and make any immediate changes to strengthen the infrastructure and minimise the risk of another outbreak. Lack of cash flow is an obvious example of an imminent difficulty. Strategic planning may prove very difficult, impractical, or unworkable if it appears foreseeable that wage demands, unplanned costs, or other financial commitments are likely to overstretch the organisation's reserves for working capital.

Sufficient human and capital resources?

Do you have the necessary resources for successful strategic planning? A key resource, for example, is the participants' time, both the individual(s) leading the work and the executives, divisional managers, and other employees directly involved in the planning and likely implementation. The employees' aggregated work contribution may be substantial if the strategic planning is to be based on the widespread participation of all employees. You will need to budget for direct expenditures, for instance in relation to consultancy services, data gathering, and analyses. If capital and human resources are limited and the organisation estimates it cannot afford the time strategic planning inevitably demands, then it pays to think twice, rather than start something that will deliver little or nothing.

Is the purpose clear to everyone?

Are the employees generally conscious of the whole purpose for undertaking the strategic planning process? Ideally, the employees should see this change journey as a real opportunity to plan for the future and achieve better results for the benefit of the enterprise, and consequently for all who work there. However, unless you have prepared them for this, the reality may be somewhat different – employees may regard strategic planning as yet another craze, particularly if they have experienced other apparently fruitless attempts to achieve change. If this is how the process is seen by staff, you will need to find a way to engage all the internal stakeholders and make them susceptible to change. The staff must buy into the idea of strategic planning as a process that implies constructive opportunities for all who are willing to participate.

Will the cost exceed the benefit?

Much thought should go into deciding whether the cost associated with strategic planning will exceed the resulting benefit. You need to consider this in the context of the other points on the list, e.g. whether the management is ready, whether the necessary resources exist, and whether all parties concerned grasp the purpose. It is likely that the benefit will not exceed the costs if the majority of these requirements are unfulfilled. In order to convince all those involved of the importance of the process, you might use a "do-nothing" scenario to illustrate to those affected how things are likely to pan out and how current risks may turn into negative realities.

Will the strategy be implemented?

Last but not least, we should ask the million-dollar question: whether it is likely that the strategy, which the planning will produce, will be implemented, or whether it will suffer the destiny of thousands of impressive strategic planning reports around the globe, and end up simply on a shelf in a director's office, or as a classified document for the company board. If that seems likely, then ask yourselves whether it pays to start the journey in the first place.

Reflection points

- What reasons could managers and directors have for resisting or disregarding the strategic planning process?
- What reasons could employees have for resisting or disregarding the strategic planning process?
- How can engagement from managers and directors be encouraged and their belief in the process secured?
- How can engagement from employees be encouraged and their belief in the process secured?

Internal stakeholders and organisational background

It is prudent to begin by carrying out an analysis of interested parties within the organisation. Strategic planning may be undertaken for an organisation as a whole, but sometimes the work is focused on some specific division or work unit. Your frame of reference should be clear and aligned with the content of the strategic planning process. Identify and allocate the main roles in the strategic planning process: which individuals, groups and departments are involved in, affected by, or just need to be informed of each role? Who is leading the process? Who responsible for the outcomes and on which parties do the results depend? Who are the primary stakeholders within the organisation (top executives, middle management, specialists, employees, project sponsors, and project managers)? Who will provide information and carry out the work involved in the strategic planning process? It is important to understand all of these roles and to identify who will be making the most important contributions to the strategic planning and what their views and expectations towards it will be.

Strategic planning builds inevitably on the organisational foundations of an enterprise, no matter whether it has a long or short history. Everything is contingent on the past, and there is no point in disregarding history, even though some may feel it is of little relevance. How has the organisation been successful and where has it failed? By advocating this approach, we are not saying that it is necessary to dwell in the past – rather you should try to learn from experience and respect the good intentions and endeavours in the history of the organisation.

A good strategic planner takes time to study the beginnings of an organisation, its foundations and keystones in its history up to the present day. It is sensible to take older strategic plans into account as they contain evidence and important information about the development, state, and vision of an organisation and reflect in what ways that vision has been successfully realised. These documents will typically contain a summary of what the organisation represents, how it sees its role, and what its main values are. It is necessary to review this data, examine which objectives have been achieved from earlier strategic plans and which have not and assess the reasons for this. You may then reference this data in the introduction to the new strategic planning report without putting too much emphasis on it.

- We will return later to the topic of organisational values but note briefly here that the prevalent values of an organisation are an important factor in strategic planning and that it pays to define them at the beginning of the strategic planning process. An organisation's values should readily become apparent through your interviews with employees and managers. It is very common for organisations to have their own heroes (and villains), i.e. individuals who have, in one way or another, played a decisive role in an organisation's history. Such persons may, for instance, be the entrepreneurs who founded the enterprise, executives who directed it during a boom period, or the ones who saved it when it was going downhill. These heroes will all have had a decisive impact on the history of the enterprise in question and serve as an inspiration to others. They may be the subject of stories and they are certainly part of an organisation's background and a formative factor in its culture.
- You will also need to summarise the success of an organisation from an historical context. This can be presented as an infographic, or in a table with a brief explanatory discussion. This is where you should summarise the times when the organisation was experiencing its greatest successes and when it experienced its worst difficulties along with the reasons for these. Information on turnover, profit, and expenses through these periods will be useful, as will data on changes to the numbers of people employed, the rate of personnel turnover, and how attitudes towards the company among the staff have varied on the basis of your employee surveys. This kind of data is particularly useful for surfacing correlations between success and the various factors and variables in the organisation's

internal environment, which can then be valuable when making plans for the future.

- It is important to be aware of and examine the customs and traditions that have developed within an organisation. The social life within an organisation may be the best window into its customs and traditions. For example, there may be a tradition of employees communicating and meeting with each other outside of work. These social events may sometimes be planned and even paid for by an organisation. They can have the positive results of increased unity and better working spirit, which, in turn, may result in increased efficiency and lower personnel turnover. Reward and recognition for a job well done is an example of a custom or tradition within an organisation. Other examples might be acknowledgments for a long period of employment, employee summer trips, festival parties, festival gifts or handicrafts, special coffee mornings, or trips involving employees' families.

- In some organisations, particular shared interests can result in formalised extracurricular group activities. For instance, the authors know of a knowledge-based company where employees banded together to form a company choir. They subsequently got permission to practise weekly during lunch breaks and a piano was bought and a conductor hired. The choir then performed both for the company as well as outside it and, at one stage, around one-fifth of the employees were members of the choir. This involved some financial cost for the company, but it was a shrewd investment as it meant there was a much better working atmosphere in the company as a whole and greater productivity.

Reflection points

- What methods might you use to gain a real insight into the internal workings of an organisation independent of the conventional management viewpoint?
- What kinds of sensitive issues might you encounter while in the process of learning about and understanding the internal environment of an organisation?
- Can you give an example of a "hero" in an organisation and how this could be relevant in the context of strategic planning?
- Why can it be important and beneficial for the strategic planner to talk about older strategic planning efforts in context with the present one?

The combined capital of an organisation

In this context, we define capital in the broad sense of all the wealth and resources that an organisation owns or has access to. There are a number of different forms of capital and in the following sections we will discuss the following types: human capital, social capital, structural capital, intellectual capital, and customer capital (see Figure 3.2).

Human capital encompasses all the inventiveness, knowledge, commitment, loyalty, and experience of employees. This is the capital that goes home for the weekend and returns on Monday morning. Human capital is important for all organisations, to a greater or lesser degree. It is less important in organisations where jobs are simple and repetitive, while it can be of vital importance to those organisations with complicated work that calls for a high degree of expertise. Many organisations in the modern world are knowledge-based enterprises relying on their human capital. Their worth is, to a large extent, based on the people who work for them. The mobility of key personnel and retaining talent can be a major consideration for the organisation, not least because people have their own individual interests, ambitions, and goals (see Figures 3.3 and 3.4).

It is useful to look at the human resource processes and functions within the organisation. These processes and functions should support all the organisation's activities, for example, programmes and projects linked to incentivising team members, training, temporary employment, and even ethics. Two specific examples of relevant human resource activity are how recruitment takes place and the formulation of employment contracts. To what extent do the HR team assess the need for a given employee and define the abilities and skills they should possess, prior to recruitment? Are other elements a factor in the candidate selection process? After recruitment, how is an employee trained and how do they then develop and acquire knowledge? Are they just parachuted in and expected to have all the skills and experience from day one? Knowledge can have a short shelf life, particularly so for high-tech industries where skills such as programming in certain computer languages can become redundant in a relatively short time. It is sometimes said that the half-life of

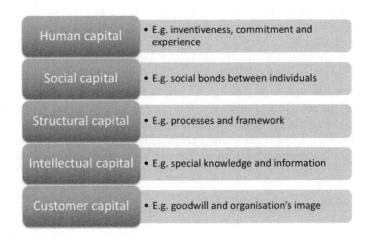

Figure 3.2

A breakdown of an organisation's capital.

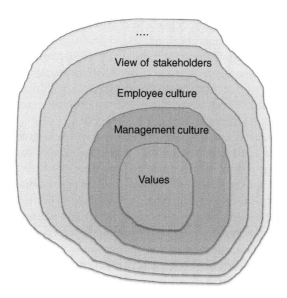

Figure 3.3

Layers of organisational culture.

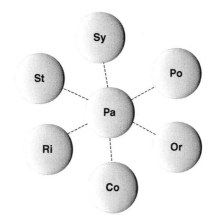

Figure 3.4

The cultural molecule of an organisation.

knowledge is counted in years or even semesters in some cases. It is therefore essential to develop employees' knowledge consciously and systematically in order to avoid stagnation. This can be a considerable challenge, especially if the organisation is a big one. But it remains vital just as knowledge remains the most important resource of a knowledge-based enterprise.

Social capital is a term worthy of mention in the context of organisations. Here, we define social capital as the wealth contained in social bonds created between individuals at the workplace and also in families, groups of friends, communities, voluntary organisations, and so on. Such bonds can have diverse positive effects on the prosperity of individuals, groups, and organisations. We recognise the different dynamics associated with social capital and consider it a separate entity worthy of special consideration. This form of capital is particularly apparent in times of adversity and can provide a means to overcome challenges and sustain organisational resilience.

Structural capital encompasses the supportive infrastructure, processes, frameworks, and administration systems that allow human capital to function within the organisation. These include a broad range of physical assets such as buildings, equipment, and tools, as well as software, databases, patents, and developed processes that enable an organisation to operate. Established routines for making decisions are an important aspect of structural capital where a typical decision-making process involves information preparation, presentation, acceptance, recording, communication, and implementation. Such routines can be either formal or informal. The structure of an organisation is also influenced by other intangible sources of value such as working spirit and organisational culture, which will be discussed further towards the end of this chapter.

The processes and frameworks that are used in the operations of an organisation are an important consideration. Many organisations now operate in accordance with top professional standards; well-defined and standardised work processes, policies, and procedures. If these elements sustain and improve operations and make things more efficient, they are of value to an organisation. Companies that have introduced administrative systems in accordance with international standards, e.g. ISO 9001 or ISO 14001, will have mapped all their work processes in a systematic manner. They will have defined and documented their work methods and adjusted them to international demands where applicable. They offer customers and employees a consistent and predictable working environment in which requirements are clear. ISO 9001 was originally developed with the needs of manufacturing businesses in mind but is now adopted by a very broad range of organisations. Different sectors will place different emphases on various aspects of this overall standard and it is important to note the particular characteristics of the organisation in question when interpreting the standard's requirements.

A large number of organisations worldwide have now developed a quality system based on ISO 9001 to design good work procedures and effective management methods and provide quality assurance. These include police authorities, football clubs, manufacturing companies, and professional service providers amongst others. The standard's requirements are based on the eight principles of quality management put forward in the ISO family of standards, which are as follows:

- Customer focus.
- Leadership.
- Involvement of people.

- Process approach.
- System approach to management.
- Continual improvement.
- Factual approach to decision making.
- Mutually beneficial supplier relationships.

The expression of the quality system (in terms of the organisation's processes) and the experience of it by customers and employees are likely to be part of your initial data gathering.

Intellectual capital implies all the accumulated knowledge of an enterprise which can generate value and sustain continued competitiveness and is closely tied to human capital. Every enterprise should be aware of those areas of knowledge that are most important for its operations. These include the enterprise's key processes, such as communication and customer service and dealings with suppliers and interested parties as well as personnel matters. As an exercise, take a moment to imagine what would happen if a number of key employees in your enterprise were to quit simultaneously? How would that affect its operation? What knowledge do they possess that is necessary to preserve and maintain? Organisations increasingly seek ways to identify, document and share the explicit knowledge of their key employees and to build the kind of social networks and activities that support and share their tacit knowledge. Enterprises where intellectual capital is especially important include knowledge-based companies such as engineering firms and accountancy offices. Within such companies, those who carry out the main work possess specialised knowledge based on experience and education. In recent years, there has been an increased focus on the intellectual capital of such companies and how it is managed and preserved.

The **customer capital** of an enterprise is contained in goodwill, customer loyalty, trademarks, and the enterprise's image. An enterprise will be of little worth and short-lived if it does not have sufficient customers. It is vital, therefore, for every enterprise to define who their customers are and which ones are of most importance and to reach out to them to gain market traction. We will return to this topic later where we discuss external environment analysis. The *reputation* of an enterprise refers to how the external environment, and all the different individuals and groups that this constitutes, regards and assesses an enterprise. An enterprise will typically have a distinct *brand and reputation* that it is broadly identified by and can be the result of actively cultivating that image, e.g. in advertisements and public relations. Their reputation may also be imposed externally through the reported views of professional critics, journalists, or other commentators.

The role of a corporate communications department is to create and maintain a certain image of an enterprise in the external environment. The products or services provided must appeal to customers in order for an enterprise to flourish. Marketing and PR can add great value to a company, but they can also be a very significant draw on resources and need to be reinforced by actual positive customer experience of products and services. Established companies with a long history of successful marketing and communications will have gained considerable capital in this regard. Intangible assets associated with *reputation* such as goodwill and customer loyalty can be extremely valuable and highly regarded by potential investors.

The *reputation* of an enterprise can be somewhat fragile, however, and it is not just the quality and value of the products and services they provide that are important, but also the corporate social responsibility (CSR) and ethics of the enterprise, which are influenced by its strategic choices. Poor customer or employee relations, unfair treatment or use of unethical suppliers, inappropriate or corrupt contracting, or disregard for the organisation's environmental impact will all have significant knock-on effects on the organisation's reputation

Reflection points

- Briefly describe the combined capital of an enterprise with which you are familiar using the headings given above.
- Discuss Apple, based on the model of an organisation's capital – guess if you don't know.

Organisational culture

A large body of research has conclusively shown that the culture that prevails within an organisation, whatever form it takes, shapes how you approach communication, management, and decision-making. The means of cooperation within an organisation, how problems are solved and how various tasks are tackled are key aspects that are all directly linked to organisational culture. Management theory has paid a lot of attention to this area in the last few decades and it has been the focus of numerous studies of organisational success. Strong and weak organisational cultures have been distinguished by strong culture correlating more often with success (Collins & Porras, 2005). The concept of "organisational culture" is somewhat ambiguous, however, and a clear definition remains elusive. The well-known image of the iceberg may be used as a metaphor here. As we know, only the uppermost tenth part of it is visible above the surface of the sea. This visible part reflects the situations, conduct, customers, official data, organisation charts, rules, and generally everything that is easily discernible. The invisible part of the iceberg reflects the intangible parts of an organisational culture – feelings, communication, traditions, expectations, and various other things that are hard to grasp but have nevertheless much to say about what is to be seen on the surface. Strategic planners need to have an insight into both the visible and hidden aspects of organisational culture because any initiatives by an organisation should be aligned with its values and correspond with formal and informal cultural rules within an organisation and its various subsidiary parts. Formal and informal influences can stem from, for example, group ambitions and personal interests, and can urge for self-development or doing something for the greater good; they can be crucial in the context of strategic planning and project management and need to be assessed.

For instance, employee activities are shaped by factors in the organisational culture such as values, ideals, and views that are, in some way, collective and characteristic of an organisation. Discretion among employees working in a respected law firm or bank would be one such example. Self-evidently, organisational leaders are the ones who play the biggest role in shaping organisational culture. Other things can also be very influential such as processes and frameworks, goals, organisational structure, and vision as well as external influences like technology and science, politics, ecology, economy, and even religion. The culture or atmosphere within an organisation is one of the biggest sources of influence, both positive and negative, on the success of strategic planning work. It is therefore important to understand what is meant by organisational culture and how its characteristics may be distinguished. In discussing organisational culture in its entirety, it is good to be aware that it consists of several layers.

The most visible layer is the promoted values of an organisation, but there are other layers such as management culture and employee culture as well as how both management and employees within an organisation view particular types of external stakeholders. If, within an organisation or part of an organisation, there is a pervading culture of bribery or inappropriate influence, for example, then no amount of high-level strategic planning will work unless this behaviour is not understood and tackled at the source.

The recent Volkswagen Group diesel emissions scandal raises questions about organisational culture. The scandal involved senior executives in the company endorsing a programme of deception as part of a routine technology development and marketing strategy. In this case, a computerised system linked with various sensors was developed and installed that could identify when a vehicle was being tested and which then triggered temporary measures to reduce nitrous oxide (a known pollutant) in the exhaust gases. This bore no relation to what the vehicles were producing in reality during normal driving and was simply a means to beat regulatory requirements and enter lucrative markets. It's difficult to know how best to describe this decision – inexplicable, unethical, short-sighted, fraudulent – and the financial and reputational repercussions are sure to go on for a long time to come. But how could this happen, in spite of extensive organisational quality management systems and standardised procedures, strict professional regulations, and ethical codes of conduct?

There are many aspects to organisational culture, e.g. socially driven, highly emotive, historical, symbolic, capricious, unfathomable, and so on. Culture can be recognised in the form of unwritten rules that define "how we do things around here." It is primarily reflected in the things people take for granted, e.g. values, roles, and visions of employees. Stories connected with an organisation, what employees know, symbols of various kinds, power structures, image, internal organisational structure, control and quality systems, traditions, and habits all play their part in defining the overall organisational culture.

A sound organisational culture can be described as one where all employees in each respective field of work have an understanding of the combined financial, social, and environmental responsibility of an enterprise and are willing to do their job according to accepted fair principles. Individuals in a healthy culture will look out for each other and be willing to act for the greater good without focusing solely on personal recognition and reward.

An unsound organisational culture, on the other hand, manifests itself in an overall unwillingness to work together towards achieving the goals of an organisation. The root causes can be a lack of respect between parties and a failure to recognise the importance of leveraging the resources of an enterprise as well as a lack of understanding of the importance of financial, social, and environmental responsibility. Corporate politics, bullying, and manipulation may be part of an unhealthy culture. The cause of this may be localised or widespread. In the former case, an enthusiastic, diligent, and creative part of an organisation may produce great work without being able to bring it to fruition due to opposition or a lack of recognition elsewhere.

In an unsound organisational culture, people can be inclined to cling to habits and traditions and silo themselves within their respective fields of work, regardless of how this affects the organisation and its objectives as a whole. This form of isolation may be an expression of fear of competition, weak communication and processes, indifference, and undervaluation of the environment. A key question all organisations must ask themselves is to what degree can the organisational culture be sound if key managers are unsound? To what degree can individual fields of work be sound if the leadership is unsound? It is a cornerstone of good management that those who have authority accept responsibility for an organisation and all of its constituents. Those in leading positions play a key role in determining the nature of the internal politics of an organisation. If they are self-serving and willing to promote themselves at the expense of others, this can create a bad working atmosphere where both enmity and disillusionment are likely to follow.

The impact of organisational culture on strategy and strategic planning is linked to the requirement for change, normally affecting all employees, associated with strategic planning. This in turn requires open communication and cooperation within the organisation. If strategic action plans are imposed on an organisation, rather than produced in an open and collaborative environment, they can be strongly opposed. The potential problem for anyone leading a strategic planning process is that, while organisational culture is a powerful influencing factor, it is largely intangible. There can be little to measure and control. Trying to gauge the expected resistance to imposed change as a result of recommendations in strategic action plans can be difficult simply because of its inherent unpredictability. Garnering the knowledge of people who are deeply familiar with the workings of an organisation can be essential to identify real obstacles to progress and find solutions. Timing can also be an important factor and a management team that is engaged in some form of fire-fighting or fixated on daily ups and downs of business may either ignore the benefits of proper strategic planning or be too easily influenced to change course if current circumstances are unsatisfactory, even though this may be just a temporary phenomenon.

Various analytical tools, some more complex than others, have been developed to aid the analysis of organisational culture. One such simple analytical tool called the "cultural web" (Johnson, 1987). We demonstrate this idea differently, or as a culture molecule, with different basic elements.

The molecule serves as a graphical representation of the basic components of an organisation's culture. Pa or "paradigm," at its centre, encapsulates the beliefs and thought patterns that are shared by members of an organisation and affect how they respond to given situations. Surrounding this are six key factors that influence this paradigm, and these are explained separately below.

Sy – Symbols

The first factor refers to *symbols* within an organisation – i.e. artefacts such as furniture, dress codes, and architecture, also events, actions, people, or a general way of speaking – which carry some meaning or significance beyond the obvious. A cabinet minister's car, for example, serves the primary practical function of getting a minister from one place to another, but it also simultaneously serves as a symbol of power and prominence. This is why such cars are stately and luxurious. Such symbols can be essential to the projection of an organisation's external image.

Po – Power structures

The second factor of the cultural molecule refers to so-called *power structures*. It is a well-known fact that some companies have two organisational charts – an official and documented one, on the one hand, and the real but undocumented one, on the other hand. When we talk about power structures, we mean where the real power resides within an organisation. There are many bases of power besides that associated with the authority defined in a formal organisational chart, including the power of those offering rewards, coercive power, referent power and expert power. This is discussed in more detail in our book *Project: Leadership* in this series. You must examine who makes decisions, but also – crucially – who exerts a significant level of influence over these decisions. There can be both individuals and groups within an organisation who actually exert considerable influence even though their power is neither formal nor official, nor in any way reflected in organisational governance. Sometimes those with expert power, for example, do not realise they have this power and may only come to recognise it if they threaten to leave and are then begged to stay by management who are heavily reliant on their expertise.

It is very important in relation to the whole area of power structures to look at how conflicts are resolved within an organisation. In serious cases of conflict, the option frequently taken by strategic planners might be to accept that there are intractable problems with working relationships within the organisation and to then find ways to somehow circumvent this and minimise the impact on the overall workings of an organisation. Others may feel that opening up the lines of communication to allow for constructive dialogue between opposing parties and the airing of grievances with resolution in mind may be the best option. The experience level and standing of the facilitator can be vital in these cases as difficult judgements and decisions are part and parcel of the process.

Or – Organisational structure

The third factor of the cultural molecule is the *organisational structure*. If the structure is vertical, with many layers, this might point to an organisational culture that is shaped and driven by the top executives (see Figure 3.5). If the structure is horizontal, this probably indicates more employee participation and responsibility. The difference between these two structural types can be profound in terms of how an organisation functions and the extent to which employees are willing to engage fully with their work. For example, working at a low level in a vertically structured organisation for fixed pay under a middle manager who takes any credit for good work done and apportions blame to others for their own poor decisions can be a demoralising experience. The far greater visibility and connectedness within a horizontally structured organisation mean that those directly responsible for good or bad performance will be

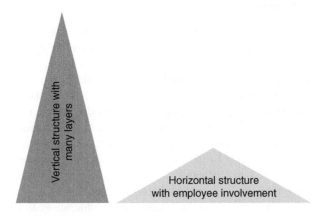

Figure 3.5

Vertical vs. horizontal organisational structure.

more easily recognised. Dealing with disenfranchised employees working at the lower levels of an organisation can be very off-putting for customers and encourage them to move their business elsewhere. Excess rigidity in approach and adherence to rules in the same situation may also be a major deterrent for customers. In order to understand the structure of an organisation fully, you need to view it from a number of different angles and see how it impacts on the experiences of customers, employees, and other stakeholders.

Co – Control systems

The fourth factor of the cultural molecule is *control systems*. These are the internal systems in use in the everyday running of an organisation and their rationale and mode of operation can vary widely. Some may be highly formalised, while others are less so, and the part of an organisation that they relate to can have a major bearing on this. For instance, the business may generate regular business productivity reports made on the basis of stringent measurement criteria and the results contained therein may, in turn, be used to allocate bonus payments and other forms of recognition. How success is measured can be an important consideration for all those working in an enterprise as well as how this information is shared with employees. Spreading the benefits of business success to all those who contributed to bringing it about is a very important aspect of retaining key staff, and having good systems in place to manage this helps to avoid any ambiguity and potential disputes.

Ri – Rituals and routines

The fifth factor of the cultural molecule encompasses *rituals and routines*. Both these elements are strong indicators of organisational culture and can shed light on attitudes, beliefs, and other important social matters within an organisation. A part of this is unconscious behaviour, e.g. how people address and treat each other and how challenges are dealt with. Routines and rituals can be reflected in the design and practice of training, employee interviews, how new employees are welcomed, how employee performance is measured, and how they are developed in their career. This may also apply to informal events, such as meeting after work on Fridays for a drink together before the weekend break. Also worth mentioning are traditions that relate to customers – such as offering them the newspaper and a cup of coffee whilst they wait for service or help – or employees – such as celebrating their achievements by the presentation of rewards at regular formalised gatherings. Conventional work methods that describe how things are done in an organisation on a day-to-day basis may be based on traditions reaching way back. It should be borne in mind that a strongly rooted work method, which has been developed and honed over decades, may be one of the cardinal reasons for an enterprise's success and its ability to be better and more efficient than others.

Or – Organisational stories

The sixth and last factor of the cultural molecule is *stories*, or how an organisation is talked about in public and private conversations between people both within and outside of that organisation. These can be based on anecdotal experience, learnt facts, company announcements, things overheard, rumours, and so on. Does an enterprise have any heroes, entrepreneurs and/or adventurers, who stand out from the masses? Are there any stories about mistakes or scandals associated with an enterprise? How does the history of an enterprise sound in the employees' own words? It is important for you to know to what degree these stories reflect the reality of an organisation and their relative importance to it. Painful events or negative information may not be talked about openly and the people responsible (if they exist) may still be at large and in key positions. Developing trust and inviting open discussion, keeping an ear to the ground, and listening to the grapevine can be absolutely necessary to find out important information that is being kept hidden. In more extreme cases, you may become aware of a situation where the management of the company have been going behind the backs of their employees (and maybe owners) and in what is known as "a conflict of agency" been making decisions and running the company for their own personal benefit. Judgement on how to proceed in those cases can be made based on professional duties and ethics and guided by experience.

Overall, the cultural molecule we have described here is a simple and useful tool for structured analysis. Each and every factor should be examined and everything that is found to be relevant and true with regard to the organisation in question needs to be documented as part of your analysis. When all six factors have been examined, a reasonably clear picture of the organisational culture should be evident to which you can regularly refer throughout the strategic planning process.

Reflection points

- How would you describe the organisational culture of an enterprise with which you are familiar?
- What aspects of its culture could be changed and how could this be done?
- Who, in this enterprise, would be likely to resist significant change? Why? How?

References

Collins, J. C., & Porras, J. I. (2005). *Built to last: Successful habits of visionary companies.* London: Random House.

Johnson, G. (1987). *Strategic change and the management process.* Oxford: Blackwell.

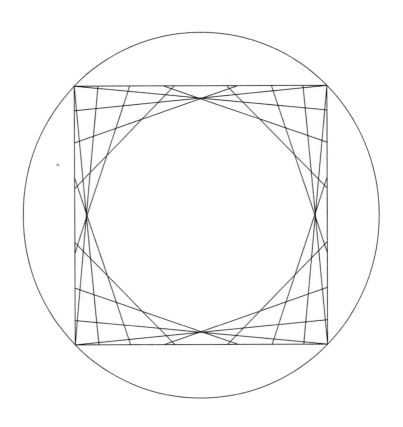

4 Understanding your organisation structure, operations, and financials

••

In the previous chapter, we focused on the human aspect of the internal organisational environment, discussing some intangible elements like organisational culture. Here we focus on the more tangible aspects of the internal environment that relate to the fundamental structures of the organisation, its management, and performance. The governance, structure, and processes of the organisation may consist of both temporary systems, e.g. projects, and permanent systems such as a project portfolio management system, financial systems, administrative systems, supporting systems, reporting systems, and systems for decision-making. We will expand our inspection by investigating the current status of the structures of the organisation, including strengths and weaknesses, which will be a vital element in your overall strategic planning.

Let's open with a brief reminder of the organisational structure we introduced in the previous chapter and provide an overview of some of the more common types of structures and methods used to manage organisations. We will discuss where the real power lies within an enterprise, something which may not be fully reflected in an official organisational chart. The next area to cover is operations including a breakdown of different elements in the value chain and supporting the infrastructure of an enterprise. The final area looked at in this chapter is the performance of the enterprise and the multitude of approaches and considerations (primarily financial) in relation to this.

Organisational structure

Most large-scale organisations use an organisational chart to represent their structure. This chart serves as a model of the authority and division structure of the organisation. By its nature, however, a model represents a simplification of what is often a difficult and complex reality. There can be a substantial gap between how decisions should be made and how tasks should be approached via official hierarchies and how these things are actually done. There are several reasons for this: (1) an organisational structure will normally evolve over time, rendering a static organisation chart obsolete; (2) the power and responsibilities of some individuals or groups are more extensive than the chart can show, e.g. union shop stewards and other influential employees; and (3) methods, work procedures, and means of communication will have evolved from since they were captured in the organisational chart. In spite of this, organisational charts remain a necessary frame of reference for both internal and external work and are important in the context of strategic planning, which more often than not brings about change to the organisational structure. The organisational chart indicates where responsibility lies for the tasks an enterprise performs and helps in analysing how information and knowledge are distributed within an enterprise.

A complex, multi-layered organisational chart implies a great distance between the uppermost layers and the bottom layers. It is likely in such a hierarchical environment that the contributions of those at the lower levels are invisible to those at the top and consequently undervalued. At the same time, much of the effort of those in the middle goes into trying to climb the ladder, sometimes at the expense of their team and other's work. Incompetence at the managerial level is far more likely in such a multi-layered organisation. This is the highly complicated and often politicised environment at which many wry commentators on management culture have taken aim. Think of Laurence J. Peter's *Peter Principle*, Archibald Putt's *Putt's Law and the Successful Technocrat* or Scott Adam's *Dilbert Principle*. The sardonic observations of these and other authors highlight the many pitfalls to progress and the stifling of talent and competence associated with overbearing organisational structures.

Another danger associated with complex, multi-layered organisational structures is that communication takes too much time and the information is corrupted on the way. It can feel like a game of "Chinese Whispers" with the added complication that some of the intermediate players may consciously decide to manipulate the message to suit their agenda. The two classic poles of a dysfunctional organisational structure in larger organisations are, on the one hand, disenfranchised employees carrying out essential work at the customer level and, on the other hand, top management and executives removed from everyday realities and operating in a bubble. In this context, an organisational chart can give a strong indication of the style and effectiveness of an organisation's structure and means of communication and information flow, as well as reflecting what kind of knowledge and competences are valued within the organisation.

Let's take a moment to review a few basic types of organisational structure. Most organisations pertain to one of these basic types or a variant. Some of the most common types of organisational structure are functional structure, product structure, hybrid structure, project structure, process structure, and matrix structure.

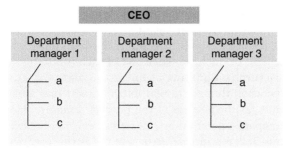

Figure 4.1

Organisational chart – functional structure.

Functional structure is sometimes called divisional structure (see Figure 4.1). What characterises this type of structure is that it focuses on the basic activity that must take place in the company, e.g. production, finance, marketing, design, and development. These essentials of the operation form the foundation of the organisational structure. Financial control is a good example of a typical support function in an organisation, providing rules, guidelines, and procedures. It also allows the organisation to monitor, manage, and report on the use of financial resources. In a functional structure, comparable or related tasks are grouped together and put in a division directed by the same party, a divisional manager, or a managing director. Functional structure is common in a stable business environment where there is little uncertainty. Against that context technical specialisation is made possible and functional structure encourages efficiency. Divisions are able to make use of economies of scale; they can leverage employees and infrastructure more effectively and so increase efficiency. The negative side of this organisational structure is that it can be ineffective when it comes to reacting to change in the business environment. Cooperation between divisions may also become difficult because the divisions are so independent and focused on their respective fields.

Product structure is based on establishing a specific operational unit for each product or product category, which embraces all the operations and infrastructure necessary for producing the respective product. The basic difference between functional structure and product structure is that product structure focuses on the product itself, while the functional structure focuses on specialisation in technical divisions. An organisation based on product structure may, therefore, be better prepared to react to changes in the business environment. On the other hand, there is always a certain danger of doing the same thing twice over since each operational unit contains infrastructure and employees that may be hard to utilise in other operational units. Each operational unit may, for instance, have their own finance department. *Regional structure* is related to product structure. This applies when a company operates in many different areas and has to organise its business operations accordingly.

Thus, a company that has facilities in different parts of a country or in different countries may develop an organisational structure in accordance with this geographical reality, establishing several business units, which need to be largely independent of the head office and of each other.

Hybrid structure is a mixture of functional and product structure. The parts of the operation that are responsible for production are assigned to the operational units, as in the case of the product structure. However, certain parts of the company operation are located in centralised departments with specialised knowledge and infrastructure, as is the case with functional structure. Typical centralised departments may include purchasing or human resources. This approach tries to combine the best of both structures. The hybrid structure's main weakness lies in a tendency towards high management cost. Furthermore, management and decision-making can become too centralised, making the organisation too slow to react to an ever-changing business environment.

A company with **project structure** has no real departments in its purest form; its operation is based rather on projects or programs, which appertain to the chief executive. Programs consist of inter-related projects that have a common vision. The projects are self-sufficient in terms of resources and each is focused on delivering its own project objectives. They may behave almost as independent companies within the parent. A pure project structure only works for companies dealing with very big projects with a clear start and finish, an example might be big engineering contracting companies. The advantage of the structure is its single-minded focus on the projects; the disadvantages generally stem from resource conflicts or dependencies between different projects. The concept of project management maturity is important for a project-oriented organisation; it is an indicator of project- and program-related organisational competences.

Similarly, a company with a **process structure** has no department and its operation is based on a set of processes that are interconnected and deliver specific outputs according to the requirements of internal and/or external customers. A core process typically encompasses the creation of a particular service or product, and it may be divided into a set of subprocesses. So-called process owners are managers who are responsible for particular core processes, and process managers are in charge of particular subprocesses. The advantage of this structure is that the operation is very much seen from the perspective of the client and care is taken to ensure continuity in the value chain, from the supplier, through the company, to the client. An example of a process-oriented company is a mass production company such as manufacturers of dairy products or aluminium smelters.

Matrix structure aims to make use of the best of functional structure and project structure and is characterised by having multiple reporting lines. This involves crosscutting relationships where employees have more than one formal boss. In terms of complexity, this form of structure can range from being relatively straightforward to complex. It follows from strategies in modern organisations where the benefits of becoming more integrated across functions and geographies have been recognised. This can stem from a desire to harmonise activities across production, marketing, IT, and HR, for example, in order to ensure efficient and effective use of resources. The impetus to integrate may also come from other sources such as: (a) global customers demanding a single point of contact for their dealings with an enterprise; (b) the benefits of streamlining supply chains that impact on different functions such as manufacturing, purchasing and distribution, and different geographies; and (c) the need for consistency of approach for global projects and products.

Matrix structure and management methods have become increasingly prevalent in larger global companies and this has entailed changes in traditional management thinking where single line organisational hierarchies are the norm. This corresponds with an increased emphasis on projects and project management in the global economy in recent years. Several types of project structures are to be found that crosscut multiple departments. In one example, such as shown in Figure 4.2, the matrix structure may be described as a table where individual rows represent individual projects and individual columns represent specialist departments or function centres with certain knowledge and defined roles or particular geographies.

In another example, the rows in the table may represent service departments or supporting departments that service the specialist departments. This situation, where crosscutting departments make all the major decisions, is referred to as a weak matrix organisational structure. An example of this would be a central purchasing department that coordinates procurement for all projects, identifies potential suppliers of resources and negotiates terms. If, on the other hand, the rows reflect discrete and largely autonomous projects, we speak of a strong matrix organisational structure. Using the same example as before, a company where the procurement is managed within the projects may be an indicator of a strong matrix.

Matrix structures may apply in companies with both recurrent tasks and individual projects and may be suitable in a complex and ever-changing

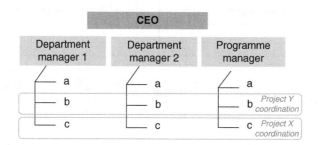

Figure 4.2

Organisational chart – matrix structure with the focus on project management.

business environment. The main shortcomings of this structure are that it can lead to conflict between managers and increase stress among the employees since they feel as if they have many bosses. The clear delegation of responsibility and an understanding of roles on the part of all participants is vital for success, as is having effective communication channels between different units and individuals. An organisational chart for a project-oriented organisation might reflect a single department or office with responsibility for project support functions, such as managing a project portfolio for the organisation (a project management office – PMO). In such cases, this office will typically define the portfolio criteria, facilitate the alignment of the projects within the portfolio, the alignment of the projects with the organisational strategy and the alignment of all projects with the reporting- and decision-making structures and define the quality requirements of the organisation. Last but not least the office makes sure that the resource use of the projects is according to the constraints of the organisation.

Organisational structures can vary widely from one organisation to the next (see the examples in Figures 4.3 to 4.5) and many different types of organisational charts can be found by examining the web pages of companies

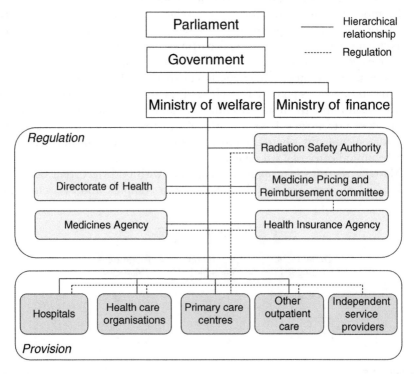

Figure 4.3

A model of the Icelandic Health Care System.

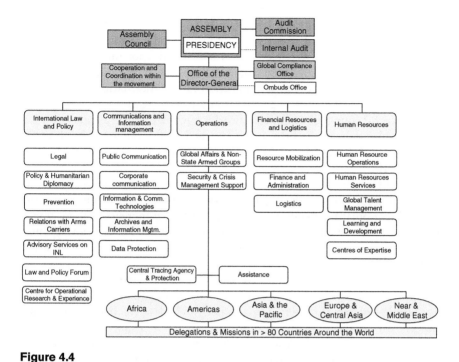

Figure 4.4

Organogram of the International Committee of the Red Cross.

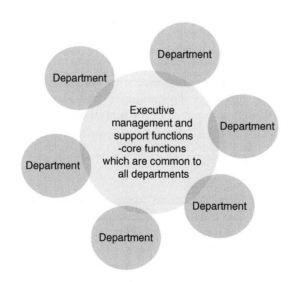

Figure 4.5

An example of a less conventional organisational chart template.

and organisations. Figure 4.3 shows a model of the Icelandic Health Care System and illustrates the organisational hierarchy for management and decision-making as well as reflects the oversight and reporting associated with external regulators (Sigurgeirsdottir, Waagfjörð & Maresso, 2014).

Figure 4.4 shows the organisational chart for the International Committee of the Red Cross. This is a huge operation, with delegations and missions in more than 80 countries around the world, but the chart illustrates how the central office is organised through an assembly, the office of the director-general and five functional units (International Committee of the Red Cross, 2018).

Sometimes the organisation charts are meant to reflect some special focus and highlight the core of the organisation's operations. An alternative to strict hierarchical organisational charts (where authority increases as one travels upwards) is to visualise an organisation as having various units (satellites) orbiting around a central administrative unit (centre of gravity) as shown in Figure 4.5.

In strategic planning, you need to examine the current organisational structure; both the official structure shown in the organisational chart as well as possible departures from it. You also need to look at the main subjects and tasks of the organisation and examine what committees, boards, and departments are active. And don't forget daily management activities, for instance how the yearly project schedule is followed and when staff meetings are held and for what purpose.

Reflection points

- How are talent and competence recognised and valued in an organisation with which you are familiar?
- Which of the organisational charts shown here would best fit your company, and why?
- Using the example of an organisation with which you are familiar, to what extent does the allocation of responsibility and use of reporting channels correspond to what is depicted in the official organisational chart?

Operations

In this context, the term "operations" refers to the steps involved in transforming resources or data inputs into desired products, services, or results that are of value to customers, employees, or other stakeholders. The combination of management methods and work processes delineates the operational aspect of an enterprise. These cover how tasks are approached and executed in line with the values and goals of an enterprise. Understanding operations is a key aspect of describing the current status of the internal environment of an enterprise. The nature of operations can vary widely depending on the sector and characteristics of the enterprise. What works for a large pharmaceutical company may not work for a local authority body charged with amenities provision and upkeep. There are a number of common elements that apply widely, however, and these are discussed further below in relation to analytical tools.

Value chain

In his book *Competitive Advantage*, Michael Porter (1985) presented ideas about how an enterprise takes a series of inputs and turns them into outputs by adding value. This added value (or margin) allows an enterprise to exist and is therefore of utmost importance. His term "value chain" describes the set of activities that an enterprise carries out in order to create value for the customer. He introduced a generic value chain that enterprises can use as an analytical tool to help them understand the nature of their operations and see how things are connected. This can facilitate prioritisation and even serve as a guide for reorganisation. The value chain template he describes is primarily geared towards manufacturing enterprises but can be adjusted to suit any enterprise type that adds value. It may be separated into primary activities and support activities as seen in Figure 4.6.

There are five primary value chain activities in Porter's basic template; inbound logistics, value-creating operations, outbound logistics, marketing and sales, and services.

- *Inbound logistics* refers to the transport, receiving and warehousing, and inventory control of material and information necessary for the production of goods or granting of services.
- *Value-creating operations* are the operations that transform input material into a final product.

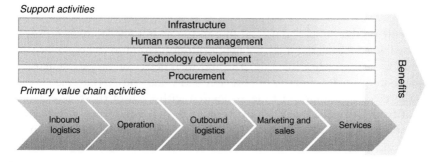

Figure 4.6

An organisation's value chain.

- *Outbound logistics* refers to the transport and handling of the product, including warehousing in intermediate warehouses, distribution, etc. These may be internal or external to an enterprise.
- *Marketing and sales* refers to the promotion of a product and providing the customer with the necessary information and platform for them to buy it and receive it. This encompasses advertising and all aspects of the sales process as well as the management and coordination of these activities.
- *Services* include the obligations that an enterprise must meet in order to maintain the value of the vended product or service, such as setup or installation, repair, training, and spare parts management.

Support activities can be divided into four generic categories; company infrastructure, human resource management, technology development, and procurement.

- *Infrastructure* includes all the supporting systems that allow for the efficient running of an enterprise. This includes accounting, legal, administrative, and general management as well as quality control, information management, and planning. Descriptions of how value-creating activities are carried out can be included here also.
- *Human resource management* has to do with the activities associated with recruiting, managing, training, developing, and compensating employees. This can be a vital element in the value chain of knowledge-based enterprises that are heavily reliant on human capital.
- *Technology development* relates to those activities carried out to manage and process information as well as protect the knowledge base of an enterprise. This can include maintaining robust data and communication systems that are compatible with process requirements and surrounding technology advances in the external environment.
- *Procurement* is all the activities carried out by an enterprise in order to get the resources it needs to operate. This involves finding vendors, developing relationships and negotiating the best pricing, and purchase arrangements.

By applying this simple analytical tool to the operations of an enterprise, it is possible to summarise a large amount of information in the one place and see in a nutshell what the strengths and weaknesses of various dimensions of an enterprise are in terms of how they add value. Various parameters such as the costs or amount of time associated with each of these aspects can identify areas for focus in the near term with a view to bringing in changes to improve overall performance. In some cases, this analysis can result in the decision to outsource certain aspects of the value chain and procure extra inputs and services.

As the structure of the organisation or the nature of its functions become more complex, the various primary and support activities can be further subdivided in order to determine more precisely where value is added (or not) as the case may be. For example, the operational aspect of an energy-intensive industry like glass-bottle manufacturing could include melting processes as a subdivision. It could be the case that investment in a much more efficient furnace system could be a vital aspect of remaining competitive in the global marketplace. Another important form of analysis using the value-chain model involves identifying links between the different elements. If, for example, the HR department is not doing its job properly in how it hires quality managers, there can be many knock-on effects such as the increased return of faulty goods and loss of goodwill. This would result in a greater need for customer services to facilitate this process and other unforeseen investments in various activities to limit the fallout from this in terms of retaining market share.

There is now an established trend to view the functionality of non-profit organisations in terms of a value-based framework. The measurement of value added (or benefits) in this sector can be much more complicated than for the simpler case of a manufacturer making products for profit. How effective is a policy-making arm of government? How effective is a publicly funded health system? How effective is a volunteer organisation in meeting its stated aims? In many cases, the only effective means of measurement in such areas is by comparison with similar bodies, either within or outside of a country. The main benefits of using a value chain model in this context are to: (1) aid strategic planning; (2) optimise the allocation of resources; (3) measure performance against various benchmarks; and (4) monitor accountability. A strategic planning consultant working in the non-profit area should have sufficient knowledge of the particular considerations that apply and how to approach the benchmarking process. When all is said and done, there is not a lot of difference between the value-based approach employed to analyse for-profit and non-profit enterprises.

Reflection points

- Describe an enterprise you are familiar with – using the value chain.
- What aspects of the above value chain would be of most interest to you to change in your role as a strategic planning consultant, and why?

Management method analysis

Every single individual is unique and applies his/her specific working styles of communicating and collaborating with other people. Management methods strongly influence everything concerning strategic planning and implementation. Therefore, it is useful for managers to get an impartial assessment of their management methods and style of management. One approach that is effective in this regard is 360° *evaluation*. This is a completely confidential assessment process that is carried out in close cooperation with the manager concerned. Co-workers, bosses, and subordinates are asked about their views and experience of the manager in question, and the results are then compared with the manager's self-assessment.

Another approach is to hold in-depth interviews with key employees using an open questioning technique so that the interviewee is given the chance to answer on their own terms. The conversation should be on a casual note, giving a sincere and true picture of the interviewee's opinions and wider views. During the strategic planning work, incidental interviews are held with certain employees as well as an in-depth interview with the managing director. As part of the assessment process, the managing director should be followed in their work for one or more days and a work meeting held between them and other employees observed. This kind of work may be carried out at a shallow or deep level. If the managing director's emotional maturity allows, a *blind spot analysis* may be carried out, meaning that they get the opportunity to hear their employees' critique of them and to process this information and reflect on it. Closely related to this is group process work where the respective individual is put in the hot seat and thus gets the opportunity to hear and react to all the things a well-chosen group of co-workers has to say. Such work can be very challenging for the facilitator conducting it and he or she will need boldness and resolve to set and maintain the right tone. 360° evaluation can be counter-productive if the person under the spotlight is not supported in addressing and processing the information it yields, for instance, if their own experience turns out to be totally different from the experience of their co-workers. If you provide this kind of personal feedback without support, it may have a lasting negative impact on their self-esteem and, consequently, general health. You need to help them to assess and understand the situation and to figure out how to react to it (see Figure 4.7).

Figure 4.7

Management method analysis.

The purpose of this work is to make all concerned conscious of their responsibilities, possibilities, and limitations in terms of management and leadership; to update them on any changing requirements for their management and leadership role; and to unite key employees and show them their importance in supporting the achievement of the objectives of an enterprise. As a part of the work, people may be encouraged to make a personal strategic plan and be coached through the execution of this plan in order to improve their performance and general wellbeing.

Reflection points

- What approaches should you as a strategic planning consultant take if it is apparent at an early stage that there is a large divergence in opinion between what a managing director thinks of themselves and what others think of them?
- How could the application of a management method analysis lead to a negative impact on and individual, and how can this be avoided?

Financials

The primary measure of the health of an organisation is its *financials* and this is consequently a key area of concern in strategic planning. The term *financials* encompass all aspects of financial history up to the present, including current and projected sales revenue, cost base, assets, shareholders equity, debts and other liabilities, cash flow, and investments. One important aspect of the financials is the different financial models for project funding applied by the organisation. Some examples of funding models are private, public, public-private partnerships, and commercial funding.

All limited liability companies, private limited companies, and other corporations and individuals conducting business activities of one kind or another are obliged to keep accounts. These should give an accurate and true picture of an enterprise's income, costs, assets, and liabilities, and are used in the preparation of formal financial statements. Financial reporting is carried out periodically (usually quarterly and/or annually) to keep lenders, owners, and the government informed of the financial situation of an enterprise, and an obvious first step when making strategic plans is to make use of the information found there. As shown in Figure 4.8, there are typically three principal financial statements, which are: (1) income statement; (2) balance sheet; and (3) statement of cash flows. Often, a statement of retained earnings is included. Financial reporting may include explanations of particular items and will also normally include a report from executive management on the activities of an enterprise including investments and approval of the financial statements as well as an auditor's endorsement that serves as a form of quality assurance.

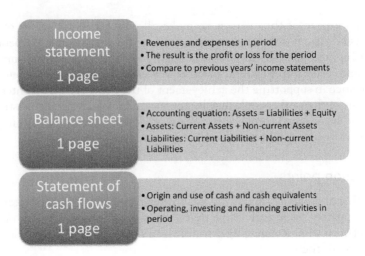

Income statement
1 page
- Revenues and expenses in period
- The result is the profit or loss for the period
- Compare to previous years' income statements

Balance sheet
1 page
- Accounting equation: Assets = Liabilities + Equity
- Assets: Current Assets + Non-current Assets
- Liabilities: Current Liabilities + Non-current Liabilities

Statement of cash flows
1 page
- Origin and use of cash and cash equivalents
- Operating, investing and financing activities in period

Figure 4.8

The structure of a company's financial statement.

In most jurisdictions, an auditor will be a certified public accountancy body that is legally bound to and liable for their statements. An auditor's endorsement may be with or without reservations. No reservations made means that the auditor believes that the financial statement gives an accurate picture of an enterprise's finances and does not invite further scrutiny. Reservations, on the other hand, can draw attention to discrepancies in the statement that invite further scrutiny. The integrity of the auditors is paramount as investors, shareholders and creditors rely on receiving factual information in order to make their decisions. The 2017 collapse of the outsourcing firm Carillion in the UK illustrates the complex and yet fundamental role of the auditor in business assurance (Rumney and Holton, 2018). Whoever intends to analyse the financial situation of a company should be aware of the subtlety and uncertainty associated with the process. Their role is to ensure that the figures make sense and show internal consistency. At times during the economic cycle, institutions such as banks can be highly profitable, but short-term profit should be seen within the context of any significant long-term risks, the negative impacts of which can take a long time to come to light. The ongoing stability of an enterprise, irrespective of one-off events and with an awareness of future risks, is the number one concern for the strategic planner.

The first part of the financial statement consists of an income statement, which is structured as per Figure 4.9.

Operating revenues represent the gross income from an enterprise's operations in the respective period, for instance from the selling of goods or services, commissions, and rental income. *Operating expenses* are the costs of operations in that period, e.g. raw materials and wages, maintenance of equipment, office costs, and depreciation (write-off). *Operating expenses* minus *operating*

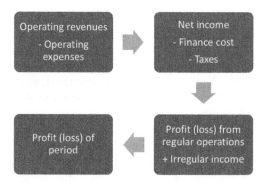

Figure 4.9

The structure of a company's income statement.

revenue gives *net income* or operating profit. From the net income *financial cost* is deducted, e.g. interest on loans and revaluation of loans. Furthermore, the tax, which has been paid in the period, is subtracted, leaving *profit from regular operations*. If this figure is negative, the company suffered a loss from regular operations in the period. To this figure *irregular income* in the period is added, which is income resulting from any other source than regular operations and which is not expected to repeat in the near future. An example here might be if a machine or even a production line from the operation is sold. Similarly, there may also be irregular expenses, which are subtracted. The final outcome from this is *the period's profit* (or *loss*, if the figure is negative).

When examining the financials of an enterprise, start with the income statement to see whether the business was delivering a profit and whether this was due to regular operations. Loss in a financial statement may be easily explainable at times by investment in development work or acquisition, which is designed to deliver greater income or lower cost in a subsequent period. Temporarily unfavourable market conditions may also account for losses in regular operations. The point is, however, that losses from regular operations call for explanations. The next step is to look at an enterprise's balance sheet and see whether the capital position is positive, i.e. whether total assets are higher than liabilities. An organisation is vulnerable to takeover, loss of investor confidence or credit risk if liabilities are higher than assets, and such a situation must be accounted for. These two factors, profit from regular operations and positive capital position, are of fundamental importance when banks evaluate companies with regard to the granting of loans.

There are various other metrics that you may find useful – specific figures from the financial statement or ratios – to assess enterprises' financial statements, depending on the relevance to or impact of this aspect of the business on your strategic plans. Ratios allow you to compare the performance and efficiency of the business from various perspectives and to measures trends over time. Measuring the performance of two enterprises, one of which has ten times the revenue of another, would not be appropriate using the actual figures for operating income alone. By dividing operating income by total revenue, we get the *operating margin*, which is far more apt for comparative purposes and judging the real performance of an enterprise. A closely related metric is EBITDA (Earnings Before Interest, Taxes, Depreciation, and Amortisation), which can be used in a similar comparative role. This type of metric provides a good measure of whether an enterprise has the ability to run its operations on an ongoing basis. Alongside these measures are other considerations such as solvency ratios, liquidity ratios, debt ratios, debt-to-capital ratios, and market value added (MVA) analysis that give an insight into the financial structuring of a company and its potential future health. Unfavourable or declining figures may be an indicator of poor corporate health and at the very least call for explanation and possibly remedy. Determining the precise nature of any liabilities is a key aspect of understanding a company's financials, particularly if they are short-term or long-term.

A very commonly employed ratio to analyse commercial enterprises is the price-earnings (P/E) ratio (share price divided by earnings per share) that can give a good indication of the overall value to be found in an enterprise from the perspective of prospective investors. Again, a number of additional considerations and caveats apply, and seasoned investors can justify decisions to invest in enterprises that have very different P/E ratios. For example: (1) where companies are on their respective maturity curves and future expectations (think of today's young internet companies' P/E ratios in comparison to those of long-established large corporations); (2) the degree to which current profits are reinvested in a company; (3) the amount of cash reserves; (4) inventory risk; (5) debt or debt-to-capital ratios; (6) the research and development pipeline; (6) currency fluctuations; (7) interest rate fluctuations; (8) accepted market cycles; and (9) unpredictable isolated events. This last factor could, for example, include unprecedented events such as oil spills or dam collapses and the subsequent fallout from these. In some cases, natural phenomena (such as the weather) or changes in the political or regulatory environments can also be very influential factors in value determinations. Operational stability must be considered. Fluctuation may be normal in certain industrial sectors, for instance in the fisheries industry, where markets can be weak over extended periods but strong in between. We will return to this general topic when we look at external environmental analysis in Chapter 6.

It can be important to study the assets and liabilities of an enterprise in more detail to gain a proper insight into what the associated figures represent. It is not always the case that the real value of assets actually corresponds to what is stated in the financial statement because assets may sometimes be given a higher valuation than is realistic. The subject of valuation could provide the material for a book in itself, not least in relation to those intangible corporate assets such as customer bases, copyrights, patents, know-how, broadcast licenses, distribution networks and rights, securities interests, supplier contracts, use rights, brands, trade names, and goodwill. The book values of tangible assets such as land, buildings, and equipment can also be subject to fluctuation in the face of changing current realities. Depreciation values in some instances may be understated for equipment, hardware, and software in sectors where time-to-obsolescence is rapidly shortening.

Likewise, the details of liabilities merit consideration. There may be *contingent liabilities*, for example, that need to be accounted for. Changes in interest rates may also affect the amounts under *accounts payable* as well as the cost of loan agreements. An organisation may face impending litigation, legal judgements, and penalties as well as outstanding taxes. There can also be opportunities to lower tax liabilities in various ways and this has been a strategic focus of many large enterprises in recent times where favourable tax terms in certain jurisdictions are secured.

Non-profit organisations will have their own particular considerations depending on their sources of funding (e.g. grants, donations, sales) and how they are spent. For example, different accounting practices apply between government departments and global charities. Nevertheless, the overall financial considerations are the same as for any business; operational and financing costs cannot exceed income over a sustained period. You need sufficient cash reserves to meet immediate and future obligations and a healthy ratio of assets to liabilities is required. Future events also need to be planned for as well as contingency allowances for the unexpected. The behaviour of a number of employees of the charity Oxfam, following the Haitian earthquake of 2010, re-emerged in the British and then International Press in 2018 (Selk and Rosenberg, 2018) and the impact that this has had on donations for the charity threatens to be very significant and may have knock-on effects on donations to the charity sector as a whole. Whether warranted or not, the perceptions of those who make charitable donations can change based on concerns they have about the ultimate use of any funds given. Another factor in the non-profit sector can be the dependence of grant funding on a particular political environment and the changes to funding that can be imposed if and when this environment changes.

Reflection points

- What are the most important financial considerations in relation to an enterprise you are familiar with?
- Find an income statement on the internet, study it and identify the main elements, as shown in Figure 4.9.
- Can you give an example of irregular income that might give a misleading perception of the financial status of a company? Explain.

Strategic planning in context

Strategic planning can be undertaken under normal or stressed circumstances. If an enterprise is either currently or about to be in difficulties and significant change is required to ensure its continued viability, this may be a catalyst for the strategic planning, where the priority is likely to be immediate survival. Whether an enterprise is in a vulnerable position may or may not be known before the strategic planning process is started. It may be the case, for example, that the internal analysis described already in this chapter identifies serious problems which had hitherto not been acknowledged, at least publicly. Once you have joined dots and understand the current situation and its implications, you can establish the focus of your strategic planning. If an enterprise is fundamentally sound, the focus will be on improving current operations, minimising risks and identifying and capturing new opportunities. The reasons and scope for change are important to keep in mind while carrying out the internal analysis. In an enterprise that operates on very tight margins, any new projects designed to bring about positive change will need to be executed with very limited budgets and this will impose certain constraints. Identifying synergies in projects can be an important aspect of making the best use of resources and motivating teams.

The outcomes of strategic planning and the implementation of strategic action plans can, in themselves, have a very significant effect on the operations and financials of an enterprise. This is particularly so where major restructuring and/or development projects are undertaken. These may include new investments or divestments, consolidation or expansion of the workforce, entrance into new markets or exit from existing ones, new or discontinued research and development programmes, geographical changes in operations and so on. In all cases, the risks and opportunities of actions need to be weighed up and detailed financial modelling and scenario analysis carried out. It is important to keep in mind the scope of changes that can (or need to) be made while carrying out the internal analysis described here. A decision by an enterprise to commit financial resources, e.g. to execute an investment project, implies that the enterprise has the necessary funds together with a contingency allowance for the unexpected. This means having both the necessary cash flow in the short term to allow the investment project to proceed and being assured that the project will deliver the desired dividends in the future. The same can also be said for decisions to remove financial resources from where they are currently employed. We will return to this theme in the closing chapters where we focus on final decision-making in the strategic planning process.

In the context of strategic planning, any decision you make, within an enterprise, whether operational and financial, should be shared with employees. It is surely in the spirit of modern administrative practices to do so. Each and every employee should understand in what way their role relates to the operations as a whole, and in what way they make (or could further make) a positive difference to overall performance, financial, or otherwise. The quid pro quo in this is that employees show responsibility for and take the initiative in maintaining and/or improving performance. Positive efforts in this regard should be recognised and rewarded by management as a follow-up to the strategic planning process.

It is worth remembering that strategic planning is not only a question of choice and decisions; it is also a vehicle to communicate a vision and aspiration to others – investors, creditors, the public, authorities – so that they may gain a better understanding of an enterprise. From a traditional business point of view, one of the key goals of strategic planning is to maximise the utility or profit of the business. A non-profit organisation, on the other hand, may have a somewhat different focus and quality time should be spent determining how the "real" value of its operations is to be measured.

References

International Committee of the Red Cross. (2018). ICRC organizational chart. [online] Available at: https://www.icrc.org/en/document/icrc-organizational-chart [Accessed 21 May 2018].

Porter, M. E. (1985). *Competitive advantage: Creating and sustaining superior performance.* New York: Free Press.

Rumney, E. and Holton, K. (2018). KPMG's audits of Carillion to be investigated: UK watchdog. [online] uk.reuters.com. Available at: https://uk.reuters.com/article/uk-carillion-collapse/kpmgs-audits-of-carillion-to-be-investigated-watchdog-idUKKBN1FI0N1 [Accessed 21 May 2018].

Selk, A. and Rosenberg, E. (2018). Oxfam crisis spreads as Haiti suggests aid workers exploited children for sex. [online] *Washington Post.* Available at: https://www.washingtonpost.com/news/worldviews/wp/2018/02/11/oxfam-could-lose-funding-over-allegations-that-it-exploited-disaster-victims-for-sex/?utm_term=.d95f3df0e2ec [Accessed 21 May 2018].

Sigurgeirsdottir, S., Waagfjörð, J., & Maresso, A. (2014). Iceland: Health system review. *Health System Transit,* 16(6): 1–182.

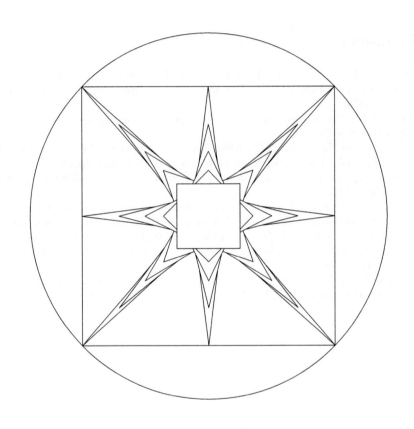

5 Understanding the business landscape: the supply chain, competitors, and regulators

· ·

Every enterprise operates in the context of a dynamic external environment. The operating environment of a business includes social, technological, and market forces as well as organisations that will influence the strategies of an enterprise in a variety of important ways that can be hard to predict. Among the principal initial tasks when you are planning any strategy is the characterisation of this external environment, surfacing the forces at work and identifying the extent to which particular elements are risks or opportunities that may influence the fortunes of an enterprise. This is a key part of defining the current status of an enterprise. In any strategic plan, recognising and dealing with the most influential aspects first is likely to be the effective course of action, although this may be easier said than done.

There is no set formula that can be applied to identify all the sources of influence in the external environment. The best approach is perhaps to hold some form of a brainstorming session with a diverse array of informed people (including external consultants, if necessary) in order to construct as comprehensive a picture of the external environment, together with associated risks and opportunities, as you can. Whether an enterprise is commercial or non-profit, the nature of its operations can have a major bearing on what aspects are important in the external environment and the kind of thinking required to ensure future success. Natural monopolies such as municipal authorities will have a different viewpoint from, say, a small enterprise operating on tight margins in a highly competitive market. Equally, the viewpoint of a small volunteer organisation with a fragile funding pipeline that is meeting an important social need will differ hugely from that of a Fortune 500 company.

In this chapter, we focus on the broad external environment and its associated entities and influencing factors. These can be regulatory requirements, political and social developments, peer organisations, fellow market participants, competitors of various kinds, suppliers, partners, investors, and assorted pioneers and trendsetters. The systematic way of analysing these different elements which we outline in this chapter can be adapted to suit the nature of a particular enterprise. The subsequent chapter (Chapter 6) also relates to external environmental analysis, but specifically focuses on customers/clients/users and the market environment and competitiveness of an enterprise.

The business landscape

There can be many factors and entities in the business landscape that can influence, or be influenced by, the operations of the enterprise and your projects. Figure 5.1 gives an overall flavour of some of the elements, which may be relevant and important, using six common perspectives. Large government organisations and small for-profit businesses can operate in markedly different landscapes.

In the centre of this diagram is the internal environment of the enterprise itself, as described in the preceding chapters, and this is surrounded by various external entities that are either in competition with, or comparable to, the enterprise in question. These can be sorted into three categories; direct competitors, indirect competitors, and comparable organisations who can be close to or far from the organisation in question. Direct competitors are enterprises that offer the same, or similar, products or services and are typically the external entities that are most commonly on the radar of profit-driven businesses. Indirect competitors can be a far wider constituency that may be harder to identify. From the viewpoint of a local football club, for example, indirect competition may come from other sporting clubs in the area, such as rugby or basketball clubs, who will also attract prospective young players. Competition for candidates will happen in any industry, particularly in times of perceived skills shortages. Thus, the highly paid financial sector has managed to attract a large proportion of bright graduates from other disciplines such as science and engineering in recent times.

Comparable organisations will have more relevance for the non-profit sector where the nature of operations means that performance and value for money can only be assessed by reference to other similar organisations. There are no direct or indirect competitors to a governmental body tasked with preserving historic monuments, for example, but their overall activities can be compared with those with similar briefs in other jurisdictions and an assessment can be made on that basis. Such comparisons can be influential in ensuring that high standards, good work practices, and value for money are achieved. Examples of this would include the regulatory impact analyses, tax policy analyses, and

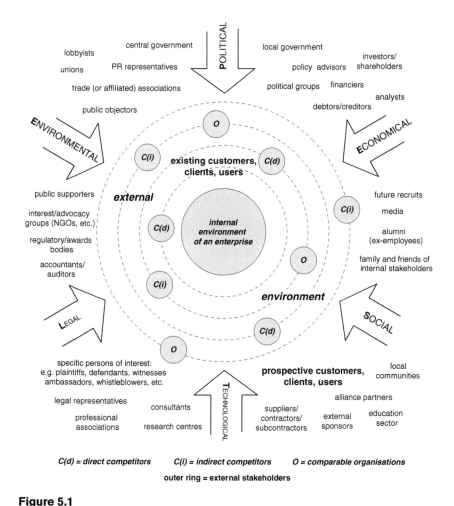

central government

POLITICAL

local government

lobbyists

unions   PR representatives

trade (or affiliated) associations

investors/
shareholders

policy advisors

political groups   financiers

analysts

public objectors

ENVIRONMENTAL

debtors/creditors

ECONOMICAL

O

C(i)   **existing customers,** C(d)
        clients, users

public supporters   **external**

interest/advocacy
groups (NGOs, etc.)

regulatory/awards
bodies

accountants/
auditors

C(d)   *internal
        environment
        of an enterprise*

C(i)

future recruits

C(i)   media

alumni
(ex-employees)

O   family and friends of
     internal stakeholders

C(i)   **environment**

LEGAL

C(d)

SOCIAL

O

specific persons of interest:
e.g. plaintiffs, defendants, witnesses
ambassadors, whistleblowers, etc.

prospective customers,
clients, users

local
communities

legal representatives

professional
associations

TECHNOLOGICAL

consultants

research centres

suppliers/
contractors/
subcontractors

external
sponsors

alliance partners

education
sector

C(d) = direct competitors   *C(i) = indirect competitors*   *O = comparable organisations*

outer ring = external stakeholders

Figure 5.1

Schematic illustration of the external environment of an enterprise.

numerous other types of comparative studies carried out periodically by the
OECD or the European Union across their member countries.

Both existing and prospective customers feature prominently as they are
of key importance in the formulation of strategic action plans. The success
of any commercial enterprise is tied to how they attract and retain customers
while earning a sufficient profit margin in the process. Taking business for
granted and not paying attention to what customer want is a recipe for failure
in the medium to longer term. Equally, price-gouging and poor experiences
can result in a lack of repeat business and negative word-of-mouth with the
same poor outlook. Tourist destinations, for instance, will have a number of
direct and indirect competitors and this is one area where word-of-mouth and
repeat business can be a strong influence. Overpriced accommodation and

restaurants and a general lack of respect and friendliness will not enamour tourists to a location and any boom in business can be short-lived as a result.

Reflection points

- Think about a large construction contractor like Bechtel or Skanska. What would be examples of important perspectives in the external environment of such an organisation? Refer to the diagram above and explain.
- Think about an international product development company like Bang & Olufsen. What would be examples of important perspectives in the external environment of such an organisation? Refer to the diagram above and explain.

External stakeholder analysis

Edward Freeman defined the term stakeholder as "any group or individual who can affect or is affected by the achievement of the organisation's objectives" (Freeman, 2010). According to Freeman, the organisation should identify any groups, individuals, or organisations that are stakeholders and need to be managed. Stakeholders may be all those that are directly involved with the organisation, investors, employees, customers, and suppliers, but they may also be governmental institutions, political parties, trade unions, different non-governmental institutions, neighbours, community groups, different interest groups, and the media. People and/or groups can have an influence for different reasons and through different means of power: legitimate, coercive, reward, expert, and relations. Paying attention to the stakeholders is necessary for any strategic planning initiative but also for practical and moral reasons, taking into account corporate social responsibility.

In the outer ring of Figure 5.1, a number of external stakeholder types are listed, only some of which may be relevant to the operations or projects of a given enterprise. *Stakeholder identification* and *mapping of stakeholder influence* are two routine analytical tools that involve identifying the full range of external stakeholders and assessing the extent to which they can influence, or be influenced by, the activities of an enterprise. Subsequent ranking of the results of this analysis can then be used to focus thinking and assist in the formation of strategic action plans. An example here might be the proposed introduction of new alcohol-related legislation by a government and the response to this by a large brewing company during the mandatory consultation period. There will likely be a lot of discussion with their trade representative body, together with joint industry approaches to external consultants, lobbyists, PR representatives, policy advisors, individual politicians, and the media to push for a favourable outcome so that business will not be impacted negatively by the new measures. On the other side of the fence, a public body or interest group highlighting alcohol-related problems will identify like-minded organisations and individuals and may commission their own independent studies by consultants to support their endeavours to bring in more restrictive legislation.

Primary and secondary stakeholders

In terms of external stakeholders, a division can be made between those that are primary and secondary. Primary stakeholders might include suppliers, customers, and creditors, while the latter might include local communities, media, and activist groups. Future recruits are an important constituency and the importance of the education sector and the potential role they play in providing a knowledgeable and skilled workforce should be borne in mind. Professional associations, trade groups, and various statutory authorities can all be influential, as can unions – acting on behalf of employees.

An important aspect of stakeholder analysis is having the ability to look at things from the perspective of others and to use this as a way of identifying opportunities and threats. For instance, a young enterprise on a steep development curve might be tempted by investment offers from venture capital funds but needs to understand that there are going to be a number of conditions associated with any offers. The venture capitalists can insist on veto rights, impose onerous sales targets, and are likely to be looking for an exit point and a satisfactory return on their investment within three to five years. Such conditions may be the cause of a lot of potential friction when the time comes, and considerable thought needs to go into investor agreements to ensure the benefits are mutual.

Creditors and other external investors are unlikely to have an emotional attachment to an enterprise, their motive is profit. But in some cases, they may be concerned about the sustainability of a longer-term relationship or share the environmental or socially responsible aims of the enterprise. Contract negotiations and the terms and conditions associated with them may represent a significant source of risk to the enterprise. You need to understand the kinds of contracts that are typical to the business, any noteworthy exceptions to these and the risk (or sometimes the opportunity) associated with these. The contracting culture of an organisation will tell you a great deal about their wider organisational culture and may offer insight into their resilience in the face of change. At the stakeholder analysis stage, though, a character judgement of external entities such as creditors and investors should include a picture of their track record, reputation, and motivations. More detailed analysis, such as their likely responses under different potential eventualities, can be done in the course of *scenario analysis*, discussed in Chapter 6.

Your project stakeholder analysis may need to extend as wide as the general public in cases where your organisation is involved with large projects that deliver citizen benefits (or disbenefits). If you are involved in public infrastructure, pharmaceuticals, and even the production of motor vehicles, understanding who is likely to support your projects as well as oppose them is a key part of the planning process, and some otherwise good ideas may be discarded if they are considered to be just too sensitive or a non-runner in the face of vocal and/or powerful opponents. A very common political tactic in such situations is to engage in *kite-flying*; leaking the details of a proposal in order to get a sense of what the public reaction will be. This form of covert activity comes with its own risks if the press or the public feel that your behaviour is manipulative or unethical. Piloting a new scheme or prototyping a new product may be a safer and better way of assessing its viability. In general, stakeholder engagement in public projects needs to be thorough. Be careful not to omit any individuals or groups that are affected by the project, whether or not they benefit directly and be careful not to give undue weight to the noisiest responders at the expense of quieter groups. Stakeholder analysis should always have a distinct purpose, and this will help you frame the structure and depth of what you subsequently do. This analysis may require significant resources. The complexity of many large infrastructure projects, such as Heathrow means that stakeholders will include obvious, immediate groups such as local residents affected by noise, air pollution, or traffic; or airlines and ancillary businesses. But it will also include businesses and organisations of all kinds who are dependent on connectivity with international markets, the UK Government who requires sustainable growth to generate taxation and fund its services and, ultimately, the UK taxpayer whose tax dollars are being spent.

A number of the potential external stakeholder types shown in the illustration above would be specific to particular organisations and their circumstances. For example, a strategic planning consultant hired in the 1970s by Johns-Manville (a large US corporation providing building products at the time) or their main insurers (Travelers Insurance) would need to have been acutely aware of all aspects relating to the company's use of asbestos and its impacts. By that stage, a large number of lawsuits were being taken by plaintiffs against the company based on asbestos-related health problems and this constituted the biggest threat to the company's future at the time (the company subsequently filed for bankruptcy in 1982). Other examples of key stakeholders in particular situations may be those currently receiving a pension from a company facing restructuring or administration. Recent large corporate restructuring and failures in the UK such as that of British Steel, Carillion and the retailer BHS have all been significantly complicated by the need to protect the interests of their pension scheme members.

The Eden and Ackermann, Power versus Interest Grid (1998) is one of the simplest ways of representing the relative nature of an organisation's different stakeholders. This two by two matrix includes the stakeholders' interests, from low to high on the vertical scale, and the stakeholders' power, from low to high, on the horizontal. In the example of the company pension fund, this then gives you four distinct stakeholder types, those with low power and low interest (perhaps other pensioners benefitting from of the Pension Protection Fund, the safety net set up to provide a level of insurance for failed corporate pension schemes), those with high power but low interest (in some cases, sadly, this can include the government!), those with low power but high interest (often the beneficiaries of the scheme itself), and, finally, those with high power and high interest (companies involved in discussions to buy the failing enterprise without acquiring the millstone of a failing pension scheme).

This simple analysis can help to determine which stakeholder's interests and power basis should be taken into account. As the example illustrates, whilst power and influence may correlate most obviously with risk and impact, less influential stakeholders should never be ignored for expediency. Social justice means that the existing and future beneficiaries of the scheme need to be represented and should have their rights protected. The grid can help to highlight different alternative approaches to a given situation, and suggest how to deal with stakeholders, e.g. to convince them to change their views or redesign the strategy by taking more views into account. As a simple example of the power versus interest grid, we have given an overview of some of the stakeholders in an on-going debate on tourism in Iceland in 2015–2018, a rapidly growing industry in the country (see Figure 5.2). This industry has been growing at an increasing rate since 2009 and in the period from 2014 to 2015 the growth reached 30%. Iceland has a population of 330,000 people and the total number of tourists visiting the country annually is fast approaching 2 million. This growth has not been supported by investment in infrastructure and while tourism has become one of the most important sources of foreign currency, a number of popular tourist attractions are beginning to deteriorate in the face of a growing weight of visitor numbers. The authorities have failed to develop any kind of strategy to deal with the situation, which seems to be

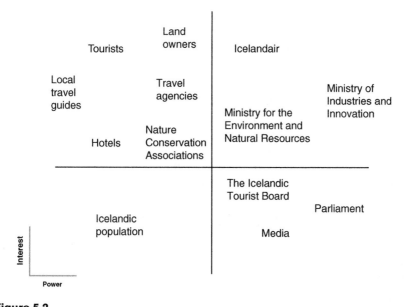

Figure 5.2

A stakeholder grid of tourism in Iceland.

getting worse, year by year. Proposed but, as yet unimplemented, solutions range from selling tickets to individual tourist attractions to a general tax on everyone flying into the country. The power versus interest grid indicates that amongst the most powerful and influential stakeholders is Icelandair, which has strongly opposed to any kind of general tax on its passengers. The Ministry of Industry and Innovation, which is responsible for tourism and should have the power to take action which thus far it has failed to do, appears powerful but disinterested. A number of other parties seem to have high interest but little real power. These include local travel guides who have expressed their deep concerns about the situation and land owners who have tried selling tickets for access to their properties but have been prevented from doing so by the authorities. The Icelandic population is shown here as a single stakeholder, with low interest and low power, which may be an oversimplification of the situation.

The Salience Model of stakeholder management is a variation of this simple model (Mitchell et al, 1997). It presents stakeholders in a graphic with three dimensions: the power of the stakeholder to influence the situation; the legitimacy of the stakeholders' relationship with the organisation; and, finally, the urgency of the stakeholders claim – or interests in the organisation. Urgency is the degree to which the stakeholder claims call for immediate attention. Power is the extent to which the stakeholder can leverage different means to impose their will. Finally, legitimacy is the assumption or perception that the actions of the stakeholder are desirable, proper, or appropriate.

The three dimensions, power, legitimacy, and urgency, are related and can overlap. Mitchell et al. (1997) used a Venn diagram to position the stakeholders in the context of the three dimensions. This approach yields seven different classes of stakeholders (see Figure 5.3) The area in the middle of the Venn diagram is where all three dimensions overlap. This class of stakeholders is called definitive or core stakeholders, who have high power, high legitimacy, and high urgency. They should be given immediate priority. In our example, the Ministry of Industry and Innovation are core stakeholders. Stakeholders in the overlapping area between urgency and power are *dangerous*. Their power and urgency can make them a threat to success, but they don't have legitimacy. In our example, we identify Icelandair and the media as being *dangerous*. Stakeholders in the overlapping area between legitimacy and urgency are *dependent*. They are typically end users, but their lack of power makes them dependent on the outcomes of the strategic planning process. In our example, land owners are *dependent*. The stakeholders in the overlapping area between power and legitimacy are *dominant*. Their power and legitimacy make them important for success, but their low urgency means that they do not call for an immediate attention. In our example, the Icelandic parliament is *dominant*. Stakeholders in non-overlapping areas of the model are called *latent*. They are considered to have low salience and no immediate actions need to be taken regarding them.

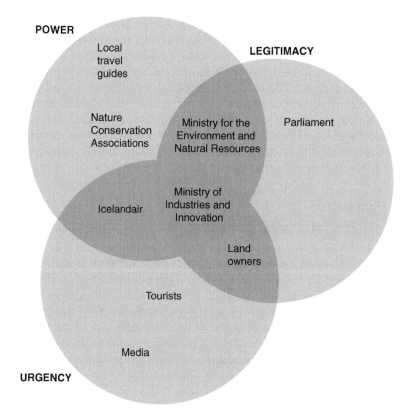

POWER

Local travel guides

Nature Conservation Associations

LEGITIMACY

Ministry for the Environment and Natural Resources

Parliament

Ministry of Industries and Innovation

Icelandair

Land owners

Tourists

Media

URGENCY

Figure 5.3

Representing the three dimensions of Power, Legitimacy and Urgency in Stakeholders.

Reflection points

- Take the Doctors Without Borders association (or any international help organisation) operating in any war stricken country as an example and use the salience model to map the major stakeholders.
- Use a Venn diagram to map the same organisation. What is special and what is common with these different models, based on this example?

PESTLE analysis

The final aspect of the external environment is the different viewpoints associated with PESTLE analysis. This is a tool for characterising the external factors that can influence an enterprise in its normal operations or if it plans to introduce a new project, product, or service. The overall method has evolved in the management literature and is now widely employed within the framework of strategic planning, often overlapping with the stakeholder analysis. Various letters in the acronym can be added or subtracted depending on what you feel is important. In the example given here, we have six viewpoints that comprise the acronym PESTLE. We describe each of these in turn, together with a comprehensive, but by no means exhaustive, list of associated factors. Worth noting is that you may not need to examine all of the viewpoints in this model with equal thoroughness on every occasion. Focus instead on those viewpoints (and, in turn, the different factors within those viewpoints) that are most relevant to your organisation.

P – Political

Political factors cover a very wide range and only a few of these may apply in any particular situation (see Figure 5.4). Any large global enterprise may view most or all of them as significant to a greater or lesser extent depending on the various jurisdictions and associated political environments within which they operate. Types of government and their political stability can greatly influence certain kinds of enterprises and projects, for example, infrastructure construction projects such as large hydropower dams that can impact a large number of local stakeholders. Whilst more democratic governments will want to involve stakeholders in the decisions associated with these projects, those that are less democratic may prefer to ignore or cow opposition. This also translates at the

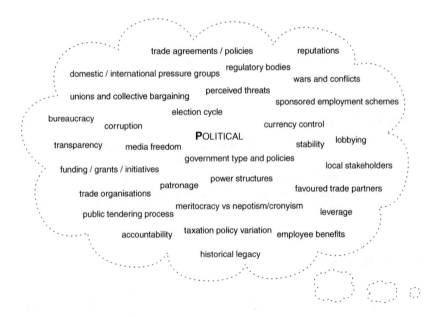

Figure 5.4

Political factors to consider in external analysis.

local government level and below. For example, a sports club in a small town may be unable to secure land and funding for development without the backing of the local town council, which is an elected body, but this may change when an election tips the balance of the council in favour of those supportive of the sports club and its plans.

It is important for all organisations to be aware that the attitudes of authorities change substantially as a result of elections. Political decisions can greatly affect the business environment for companies, both domestic and foreign. The legal and regulatory environment may soften or harden as a result of a shift in the political landscape. Access to public funds can be altered dramatically, which may represent either a serious risk or an opportunity depending on how your organisation is placed. Other strategic risks can also have a distinctively political element to them, for example: large-scale immigration, air pollution, climate change, or indeed any risks which are perceived as threatening to the indigenous population. Make sure you include a fully representative range of potential political situations when carrying out scenario analysis.

E – Economic

For many enterprises, the macroeconomic cycle (e.g. *recession*, *prosperity*, and so on) can be very important. Sentiment can be a strong influence on the economy, as expectations and risk appetite can vary widely. Large international differences can emerge as the growth rate in one region tapers off while it rapidly escalates in another. Foreseeing large-scale economic cycles and their geographical relationships can be a significant part of scenario analysis. It is often the case that companies that sell products or services need to expand internationally in order to be resilient in the face of a major domestic economic recession.

There are a number of important economic factors, either within a particular jurisdiction or more globally, that can significantly influence the fortunes of an enterprise and that can change over time. These include: (a) the tax system; (b) interest rates; (c) inflation rates; (d) commodity prices; (e) employment rates; (f) currency exchange rates; (g) property market; (h) stock prices; and (i) overall investor risk appetite. For example, the rapid increase in global steel prices leading up to mid-2008 as money flooded into commodity markets, in general, had serious implications for a large number of projects where steel price was a major cost factor. The actions of large financial institutions such as banks, insurance funds and pension funds can have a major bearing on the economic landscape with widespread knock-on effects. You need to factor these elements into your planning to limit exposure to downside risks. Timing is paramount when it comes to riding out (or benefitting from) these economic fluctuations and assuring sufficient flexibility and resources to consolidate your financial position. You may need to map trends and tendencies over years or decades to generate sufficient meaningful insight into these macroeconomic influences.

Figure 5.5

Economical factors to consider in external analysis.

Figure 5.5 includes a number of economic factors that relate to particular markets such as barriers to entry, pricing models, market efficiency, arbitrage opportunities, workforce availability, skill levels, and industry-specific industry constraints. For example, other competing companies in a particular market may be pursuing aggressive cost reduction policies by outsourcing various parts of their operations and you'll need to be aware of this and look at whether it may be prudent to follow their lead (see Figure 5.6).

S – Social

The type of society within which an enterprise operates, including general attitudes, customs, traditions, interests, and habits may influence your strategic plan. The unwritten rules and values of the society can shape the way decisions are made, how communication is executed, how variations from the common norms are judged, and so on. The culture and activities of the enterprise need to be sympathetic to, and compatible with, these different factors, and any business opportunities associated with social trends or events need to be recognised and acted on in a timely fashion. Factors such as demographics, openness, law and order, work ethos, wealth distribution, disposable income, and spending habits can be an important part of the overall picture, particularly when you are marketing new products or services or launching new products. In some countries, religion is recognised as an important influence on attitudes and behaviours and you should make it a

Figure 5.6

Social factors to consider in external analysis.

priority to study religious matters and their impact on traditions, attitudes, and views in society. With an ever-shrinking world and more international corporations, it becomes increasingly important that companies are alert to the social differences between countries, including the region's traditions. Translating a commercial interest in gaining a footing in a given market must be preceded with an examination of any potential ways in which your plans may be incompatible or even offensive to the traditions and beliefs of the country in question.

In our diagram, there are, of course, many other social factors, a number of which concern societal trends that will change over time as new generations grow up and older generations adapt to new technology to form new habits. Online search engines are now a major source of information and you need to ensure that your business models and marketing efforts reflect the significance of the digital world. The expansion of online markets at the expense of traditional markets has been an ongoing story for a number of years now. Social media is growing in prominence and increasingly replaces the monopoly that traditional media has naturally held on public information. Both news and commentary are now transmitted in real time, which is a significant source of both opportunity and risk. On the Internet, there are few checks and balances to verify facts, and unsubstantiated comments can do a great deal of damage, even if they are subsequently demonstrated to be false. It is also the case that unguarded comments by persons in high office, either written or recorded, can *go viral* and lifelong reputations can be shredded in a very short time. An oft-quoted precautionary principle is to never do, say, or write anything where it can be recorded and shared with others (e.g. on the Internet) unless you would be happy to have it broadcast to the general public. On the plus side, the potential rapid spread of information online can be used to the advantage of an enterprise and *viral marketing* campaigns are now routinely undertaken, at very low cost, to promote new ventures.

For many organisations and projects, the concept of *critical mass* (in terms of people) can be important. This represents the minimum level of interest and activity that makes an undertaking viable, in other words, the point at which the returns are greater than the effort put into development or some tipping point is reached, for example, a sustainable number of subscribers. When a group gets together to publicly object to a new development, you can reach a point when a *magic number* of objectors is reached that tips the balance. The description "magic number" reflects that this tipping point is very often imprecise and may well be unknown at the start.

Another example of critical mass might be the demand for public transport infrastructure investment initiated by a campaigning group. The support group may start small but gradually grow until public representatives take note and move to initiate a project with the necessary political support. An alternative example might be planners using future user demand projections to support a call for new infrastructure investment. These projections will typically reflect current demographic trends although a sense of realism and context is also required to guard against being unduly optimistic or pessimistic. If the views of *vested interests* come to dominate a project proposal, then the business case may include overoptimistic demand projections or unrealistic benefits and a *white elephant project* is the result: an unwanted project from which it will remain impossible to generate an economic return.

One final factor worth mentioning in relation to the social environment is *image*, which was also mentioned in relation to *customer capital*. Image describes how the general public *actually* views an enterprise and those publicly associated with it. This image may differ substantially from what is intended by the enterprise and promoted by advertising and controlled media interviews. The court of public opinion is something you should listen to and seek to understand, and your plan should include any recommendations for changes to current practices to mitigate reputational or brand risk.

T – Technological

The most important aspect of the technological perspective is that an enterprise is aware of all the relevant emerging and best technologies out in the market and understands how they relate to its field of operations (and its own technologies, if applicable) (see Figure 5.7). The fourth industrial revolution is to be kept in mind here. Technology includes those elements that: (a) constitute the current product of a competitor; (b) may constitute the future product of a (potential) competitor; (c) enable manufacturing processes; (e) allow for

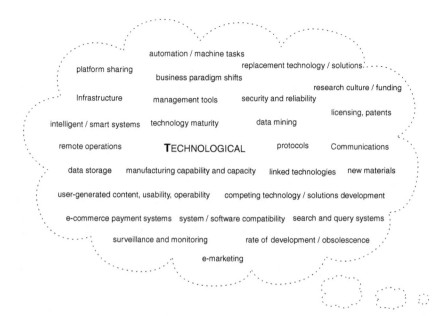

Figure 5.7

Technological factors to consider in external analysis.

new discoveries; (f) extend the limits of operations; (g) support and/or enable service providers; (e) enable data collection and information extraction; (h) increase business efficiency; and (i) serve as a marketing tool.

A broad range of questions can be asked in relation to technology and it should also be clear to those devising the strategy that the human aspects are equally as important as the technology itself. A state-of-the-art manufacturing system is of little use if there are insufficient employees who understand how to operate and maintain it. Another key consideration is compatibility. Any system that requires frequent upgrades or development work to integrate with other systems or avoid obsolescence may constitute a financial risk. From the provider's perspective, "software as a service" is a business model that requires a perspective of customers as clients, repeat, relational rather than transactional, business, and providing good overall value as the benefits to clients outweigh the costs.

An example of an industrial sector where major technological advances have opened up substantial new areas of opportunity in recent times is the oil and gas industry. The high profit margins to be found in this business (when prices are high) have enabled a sustained investment in technology, and both exploration and production methods have taken corresponding leaps forward. The older business model of having vertically-integrated large companies like Exxon or BP with extensive in-house expertise has largely been replaced by a growing industry of specialist technology subcontractors who perform a range of advanced tasks associated with field developments. This approach to the outsourcing of certain tasks involving specialist technology can be found in many other industrial sectors, for example, agriculture. Although, there is some evidence of corporations yo-yoing between outsourcing and insourcing as the endeavour to balance increasing internal fixed costs (employees) versus the ability to manage and control their projects.

Rapid advances in all forms of technology in recent decades have transformed business and many enterprises (and whole sectors) have been left behind as a result. Examples of significant disruptive technologies include the computer microprocessor, PC (personal computer), Internet, email, electronic payment systems, cloud computing, social networking, commercial networks and platforms, 3D printing, and blockchain. Numerous business models for different sectors have been challenged in recent times including those of the music and film industries, travel and hospitality sectors, retail sectors, and traditional media.

There is nothing new in this phenomenon of disruptive technology. Harvard Business School professor Clayton M. Christensen (1997) described two forms of technology in his book *The Inventor's Dilemma: "disruptive technology"* and *"sustaining technology."* According to Christensen, large corporations focus on sustaining technologies or, in other words, carrying out incremental improvements on already established technology. This involves knowing their market and staying close to their customer, but it can also mean that they are not, themselves, at the cutting edge of technology development. Consequently, there is the risk of being overshadowed by new companies with disruptive technology who threaten the status quo. A typical response strategy by incumbent large corporations who may feel threatened is to acquire the smaller companies (or just their intellectual property) at a pivotal stage in their development, subsuming their (potentially) disruptive technology in the process.

Over the last decade, *user-generated content* has proved creative and disruptive in equal measure for industries such as music or publishing as well as the news media itself. The provision of facilities to allow *amateurs* to add content on public forums and to add links as sources of reference has revolutionised communications. This socialisation of content may occur in open or closed environments and the engagement of the general public with this form of communication is unprecedented. Advertisers and publishers who want to deliver a message see this as a major area to target. Most recently the use of artificial intelligence has allowed the manipulation of this environment by paid (or otherwise motivated) agents to influence people with both benign and malign intent. This is the modern-day equivalent of *"juking the stats"* (faking success in the hope of attracting genuine support), a practice that has been present in this industry for many decades. Whilst user-generated content remains open to falsification and manipulation, genuine reviews on dedicated websites such as TripAdvisor (travel industry) can be an important source of information for potential customers. And organisations such as Feefo have grown up overnight to provide verification services to counter, in an effort to restore user-confidence.

A long-established principle that innovative enterprises should be acutely aware of is the idea of *technology brokering*. This involves taking existing technology or knowledge from one sector and applying it to another sector through whatever form modification process. Historically, this has been a very important source of innovation and examples include the electric light bulb and motion picture camera famously invented by US entrepreneur Thomas Edison in the late 19th century. More recent examples include digital photography and mobile application (*mobile app*) development and using robotics to carry out *remote operations* or having *smart systems* such as heating or lighting that automatically regulate themselves according to predetermined criteria.

For both commercial and non-profit organisations as well as various governmental bodies, a major use of technology is in the development of efficient systems for gathering, storing, and processing data. The ability to cross-reference different datasets can transform the speed, eliminate fraud error, and improve user experience. This technology has been applied with greater and lesser success to the cross-referencing of tax records, health records, or criminal records. Naturally, the security of such sensitive information is of vital importance and having robust systems with checks and balances to prevent misuse is essential for developing trust among the general population.

As a final note on the technological viewpoint, the inclusion of the term "infrastructure" in the diagram encompasses aspects such as mobile phone coverage, satellite coverage, broadband speeds, and electricity networks, which determine whether or not a particular technology can be employed in a certain area.

L – Legal

Every organisation has its formal or unformal legal policies and needs a detailed knowledge of the relevant laws and regulations that are in force in the markets in which it seeks to operate and with which it needs to comply. Compliance requirements can be informal and voluntary or formal and mandatory, and everything in between. Impending changes to legislation may, on occasion, be so significant as to require their own strategic planning. The range and volume of laws, regulations, and standards include civil, commercial, criminal, labour, intellectual property, competition, health, security, safety, and environment.

Changes to legislation and standards may have a considerable impact on the operations of an enterprise and its projects and programs. These may be signalled well in advance, but at other times the change can be quite abrupt. Legal issues, new laws, and regulations may represent both threats and opportunities. A new regulation may, for instance, cause one type of industry to disappear and another one to take its place. You need to establish an overview of valid legislation and how it affects the operations and future development of an enterprise, as part of the strategic planning process. With any potential changes to legislation in the foreseeable future, the risks and opportunities should be included in your scenario analysis. A simple matrix table that systematically documents effects and outcomes relating to the different categories of relevant laws and regulations is an effective solution. For example, an important column heading for any manufacturer of consumer products would be "labelling requirements." A good example is law and regulation regarding health, safety, security, and environment (HSSE) and organisations need to be able to balance economic, social, and environmental aspects of all their operations to meet requirements for sustainable development.

A separate but related aspect is the workings of the justice system and the process of enforcement. If, for example, a particular jurisdiction (or even a particular judge) is associated with awarding large amounts of compensation in public liability cases, then it may be advisable to try to settle any claims out of court to avoid large losses. Some laws and regulations may be rigorously applied and others less so. The enterprise needs to abide by whatever laws and regulations are applicable to them, while also maintaining a sense of perspective and priority.

Insurance requirements may or may not be mandatory. Different jurisdictions may have quite different requirements, which will also depend on the nature of the operations of an enterprise. In the UK, for example, Employers' Liability Insurance to cover workplace-related accidents or illnesses is mandatory for all businesses, while other forms of insurance such as Public Liability Insurance are only mandatory in certain sectors. The different forms of insurance cover that an enterprise will have will include what is required by legislation as well as additional considerations that reflect the overall altitude of the risk. Understanding what insurance cover is necessary and prudent to have in place is, therefore, an important concern for strategic planning and your strategic action plan may include actions to achieve the appropriate balance between acceptable risk and insurance cost.

A final mention can be given to various factors that have been growing in importance in recent times, and which reflect changes and concerns in the external environment. These include environmental legislation, data protection, discrimination law, and health and safety. Conforming to the latest requirements in these areas may require changes to longstanding approaches and policy. If you are recommending policy changes in these areas you should expect some resistance. Be prepared to emphasise the need for change and clearly explain the risks associated with failure to change.

E – Environmental

Since the industrial revolution in the 19th century, human activity has had a very significant impact on the natural environment (see Figure 5.8). Large-scale changes to habitats, overexploitation of resources, biosphere pollution,

Figure 5.8

Legal factors to consider in external analysis.

and manmade changes to the lower atmosphere and ozone layer are all examples of this. Natural phenomena such as volcanoes, earthquakes, droughts, floods, heat waves, and destructive storms can, in turn, have a major effect on human activities. The Eyjafjallajökull volcano in Iceland, which erupted in 2010, caused the closure of airspace over much of Europe for several days. This affected the operation of many international airlines as well as the plans of travellers all over the world.

It is good risk management practice for any enterprise to record any potential phenomena in the physical environment that may impact on their ability to operate, with a view to mitigating any common or rare events with substantial potential impact for business disruption. Anything that that can make the areas in which people work and live actively dangerous should be considered foremost. There are four main categories for this analysis; we will list a handful of illustrative examples against each (see Figure 5.9).

1   Environmental phenomena that are natural and have a widespread impact. Examples include major volcanic eruptions, earthquakes, floods, and droughts. These represent major risks such as loss of life and total destruction of assets. Mitigation and avoidance opportunities can be found in the form of monitoring and early warning systems, provision of infrastructure prior to an event to limit damage and post-event clean-up operations and rebuilding.

2   Environmental phenomena that are natural but only have a selective impact. Examples include weather conditions affecting horticulture growth or restricting travel, outbreaks of disease, and infestations.

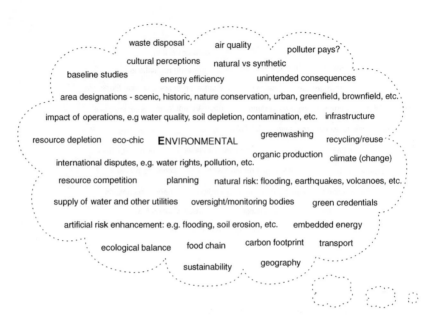

Figure 5.9

Environmental factors to consider in external analysis.

A range of distinct risks and opportunities can be identified for each specific type of event under this category.

3 Manmade phenomena that have a widespread impact. Examples include the large-scale release of highly radioactive material, upstream water resource depletion, and regional air pollution (smog). The risks here can range from temporary impacts on operations to major health risks. In the case of significant nuclear leaks (e.g. Chernobyl and Fukushima), the impact may require the total abandonment of an area for the foreseeable future. Opportunities associated with this risk can be found in providing alternative industries to whatever were the primary causes as well as providing solutions to limit any damage caused.

4 Manmade phenomena that have a selective impact. Examples include the overfishing of migratory stocks at the expense of another country, the contamination of organic crops with GM crops, an outbreak of wildfires that threatens an enterprise, local air pollution from industry, or traffic that greatly restricts operations. There can be a variety of commercial risks associated with such events and again opportunities can be found in providing alternatives, damage limitation, or in compromise.

Public awareness of and concern for the environment has grown steadily over the last 40 years. Finite resources, conservation of the natural environment, public health, and sustainability have become influential in determining consumer trends and government policies worldwide. Our attitudes have changed as our understanding of the impact of various industries and their products has grown. Those industries that are recognised as significant polluters of the environment and/or have the greatest impact on biodiversity have come under scrutiny. Increasingly, large fines and naming and shaming have been used to combat the bigger offenders. Any enterprise should have a good knowledge of how its activities affect the natural environment and the how any change in activity might alter their environmental footprint, costs, or reputation risk.

The implications of this widespread concern have also spread to the financial sector. A number of investment funds now market themselves as only investing in sustainable industries. Other growing influences include a renewed interest in organic food production methods and natural materials, maintaining a low carbon footprint lifestyle and analysing energy use associated with the manufacture, use and decommissioning, and destruction or recycling of different products. At the government level, carbon tax (in response to climate change related to atmospheric carbon dioxide) is now a reality in a number of countries and its scope is sure to widen in the near future. Being seen to be green is now a corporate strategy that can generate a competitive advantage, with the provision that the company can live up to its credentials.

Environmental risks and sustainability are complex issues. Apparently, simple solutions may introduce other, unintended risks into the system. Thus, the adoption of large-scale fish-farming, in an attempt to protect wild fish stocks, has exposed those stocks to the risk of parasites and viral and bacterial disease; all of which thrive in the conditions of factory farming.

Reflection points

- Carry out a brief but comprehensive PESTLE analysis of an enterprise with which you are familiar. If working in a group, let others do the same and compare the results before agreeing on a final version. How do individual PESTLE analyses and the one agreed upon as a group differ in this case?
- Can you mention any "gaps" in the PESTLE tool? I.e. are there aspects of the external environment that have not been included in the analysis you have done? What are those aspects?

References

Christensen, C. (1997). *The inventor's dilemma.* Boston: Harvard Business School Press.
Eden, C. and Ackermann, F. (1998). *Making strategy: The journey of strategic management.* London: Sage Publications.
Freeman, R. E. (2010). *Strategic management: A stakeholder approach.* Cambridge: Cambridge University Press.
Mitchell, R., Agle, B. and Wood, D. 1997. Toward a theory of stakeholder identification and salience: Defining the principle of who and what really counts. *The Academy of Management Review,* 22(4), 853–886.

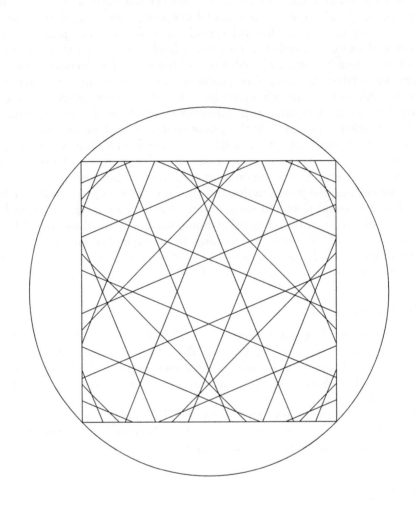

6 Market models

....

The main aim of this chapter is to explain what you need to take account of when devising strategies relating to market activities. We've tried to cover as wide a range of activities as possible whilst offering pointers to enable you to research *details* relevant to your own particular circumstances further. In this overall context, *differentiation is key* as no single "strategy" will work effectively if it is being widely copied successfully by other competitors. The concept of a market as somewhere that buyers and sellers interact and execute trades is more complex than at first sight. The commercial environment can be highly dynamic and multi-layered and it is easy for an organisation to become disconnected if you don't keep up to date with the latest developments. Imagine a buyer in a government department who tends to focus on governance and due diligence and without any effective source of ongoing intelligence is unaware that telecommunications service costs have tumbled over the last number of years; or think of a consultancy that starts to miss out on business opportunities because they don't routinely track the searches initiated by interested buyers.

Our focus in this chapter is inclined towards commercial enterprises engaged in the selling of products and services, although we will also be highlighting aspects that relate to non-profit organisations too. We start from the assumption that the underlying business model for a commercial enterprise is sound. For a young enterprise, strategy initially relates to defining a path to meet the goals outlined in the business model. As things develop, a new strategy will evolve and new goals will be identified and worked towards, and this cycle can be repeated numerous times. For mature enterprises, periodic strategic planning typically revolves around consolidating market position and making incremental gains against competitors in existing markets as well as identifying new profitable markets.

Different strategies can take many forms, but a key consideration is normally when and where to apply resources (and withhold resources) in order to ensure successful outcomes. Having good market intelligence is a prerequisite for any significant market decision. Any organisation needs to understand the profiles, needs, and motivations of customers/clients/users and we will discuss various aspects of this process along with useful analytical tools. Connecting with interested buyers is likewise critical, as is the quality of the product and service once a sale has been transacted with a view towards repeat business. You need to understand the nature of the market competition and we will cover some of the better-known theories and analytical tools relating to this. Other players with a relevance to the market are also briefly discussed including investors, speculators, and those entities that facilitate and regulate markets.

The nature of competition

Our species is essentially competitive, and this is reflected in the relationship between siblings, parents, relations, peers, neighbours, interest groups, market buyers and sellers, local villages, towns, cities, regions, nations, and ideologies. Competition exists where there is a scarcity of resources and a consequent scramble to claim these resources at the expense of others. In many contexts *"give and take"* and *"you win some and lose some"* are appropriate ways of viewing competition, such as for sibling rivalry. In tight and competitive markets, on the other hand, there can be little room for manoeuvre, and the mantra can become *"succeed at all costs."* This extreme attitude towards winning may encourage business practices that can lead to success in the short run, but ruination in the longer run. Even if they are not strictly illegal, the consequences can be sudden and dire, and the risk of litigation or reputational risk may be catastrophic. Examples from business might include the restaurant that cuts corners on hygiene practices and is served with a closure order by food safety inspectors, or the solicitor who breaches the Profession's code of conduct in relation to the handling of client monies. Restoring lost trust can be extremely difficult. Devising *sustainable strategies* in competitive environments should involve a range of practical and ethical considerations and should be transparent in relation to the court of public opinion. *Sharp practice*, if discovered and publicly aired, can be ruthlessly dealt with by the electorate at voting time, plaintiffs in civil cases, orcustomers boycotting culpable businesses.

Getting a new business from launch to profitability is always an uphill struggle. Established market players can wield a lot of power and customer inertia is a strong force to overcome. New enterprises or new commercial projects in established companies can all run out of cash before they reach profitability, particularly in digital environments where the cost of creating a sustainable business model can be complicated by the speed at which the technology is changing.

There are several distinct types of commercial environment, requiring different strategies from those working within them. These include:

Perfect competition: an idealistic notion in economics where markets that
    involve identical products are characterised as having numerous

competitors acting fairly with neither bias nor information asymmetry and a fully elastic demand curve. Profits quickly stabilise around a normalised value and there is little incentive to either raise or lower prices. Farmers' markets, with many producers selling essentially very similar agricultural produce, is an example that is often cited for this form of competition.

Monopolistic competition: a type of imperfect competition where: (a) there are a number of independent market participants who sell distinct but related products or services, i.e. not perfect substitutes; (b) market buyers typically have good but not perfect knowledge; (c) there are no major barriers to entry or exit; (d) differentiation in a range of forms is evident, e.g. product design and performance, distribution methods, customer engagement, packaging, atmosphere; (e) pricing can be independent of competitors although will typically be guided by competitors to a greater or lesser extent; (f) advertising to engage potential customers and differentiate products and services can be essential; (g) early movers can generate significant profits before other competitors enter the market and reduce margins, leading to the need for enterprises to frequently innovate; and (h) individual entrepreneurs are to be most frequently found. There are times when it makes sense for competitors in such environments to co-operate. For instance, this may involve them working together to raise the profile of a shopping area or lobbying the government for favourable tax changes for a particular sector.

Oligopoly: just a few enterprises control the majority of the market share. Examples are extremely widespread and include long-haul airline routes, electricity supply, banks, large supermarket chains, fixed broadband services, disposable nappy manufacturers, and funeral services. There is a high degree of interdependence between the main market players, and many aspects of *game theory* come into play here in relation to the benefits of either competing, co-operating, or colluding. Collusion, in this case, involves market fixing in various guises (e.g. price fixing, bid rigging, supply restriction, customer allocation) with the net result that a joint monopoly (*cartel*) is formed and high profit margins are maintained for the main players. This can occur as a result of overt, covert, or tacit agreement. Cartels are illegal according to US antitrust law and EU competition law, although, their existence can be very hard to prove in court. It is a recognised phenomenon that supposed competitors use collective lobbying as part of an overall strategy of avoiding real competition in the marketplace (Bombardini & Trebbi, 2009).

When competing in oligopolies, strategy can be challenging, and leading market players need to carefully consider every move. Deciding whether to lead or to follow can have many repercussions, with 1st and 2nd mover advantages coming into play under different circumstances. Natural barriers to entry in this market type include: (1) economies of scale; (2) restricted control of key resources; (3) high set-up costs; and (4) high R&D costs. Additional artificial barriers include: (a) proprietary market knowledge; (b) undercutting pricing strategies that deter new market entrants; (c) lengthy advertising history and brand awareness; (d) exclusive rights to trade in the form of patents, licenses, or contracts; (e) loyalty schemes; and (f) advanced infrastructure and operation efficiencies. If prices are genuinely artificially inflated for super-normal profits in undifferentiated products, there can be a lot of scope for new entrants to enter the market and offer much lower prices, highlighting the previous price-gouging as they do so. Just because customers do not have sufficient market knowledge now, does not mean that they will not have it in the near future, with consequent future actions strongly based on their historical experiences – *"I'll never be ripped off in the same way again"* or *"That's the last penny those crooks will get from me."*

Monopoly: the prefix *mono-* refers to a singular entity and a *pure monopoly* involves a single market supplier. There can be a number of reasons for this, with a prevalent one being that some activities lend themselves to *natural monopolies*. The building and operation of electricity transmission networks is one example due to the fact that there are huge *sunk costs* involved and it would be highly wasteful to duplicate such a network. Another common reason for monopolies developing is the lack of suitable substitutes for a particular product so that an exclusive market is developed, typically with very high profit margins. This may often result from original innovation that can result in the awarding of *patents* if they are applied for and maintained. These are meant to protect the intellectual property of an enterprise in the jurisdictions they cover from the actions of *free riders* aiming to benefit from the typically expensive R&D work of others. They are an integral element in encouraging enterprises to undertake technology development. Uniqueness and exclusivity can also be transferred to a range of related products. A prime historical example of this is when Microsoft packaged its Internet Explorer browser with Windows operating systems, thereby all but shutting out rival platforms in the process. A US judge found them to be acting as a monopoly in 1999 (at a time when their profit margin was around 40%), although later appeals watered down the fallout from this to a large extent. In general, enterprises are considered to have *monopoly power* where they have at least a 25% market share, but this figure can also be higher at around 40% in some cases. Competition authorities are particularly interested in analysing mergers between the larger players in a particular market to ensure acceptable individual market influence.

Monopsony: this is where there is only one buyer in the market, although it is far more often the case that an enterprise has *monopsony power* in an *oligopsony*, meaning that its buying influence is dominant in the market rather than all-encompassing. This could be a large employer in a small town that dominates the labour market, or a supermarket that has huge buying power when it comes to its suppliers – forcing them into accepting exploitative low-profit margins or even losses at times. Other cases might be the NHS and other public bodies with very large budgets who are looking for product suppliers or to outsource various parts of their operations.

From the perspective of incumbent market leaders, *disruptive innovation* can be a major cause of concern in those sectors that are more exposed to it and this is discussed further below.

Reflection points

- Give an example of a real-world market that can be characterised as an oligopoly and the notable strategic actions of the main players within it in recent years.
- Give an example of a real-world market that can be characterised as an oligopsony and the notable strategic actions of the main players within it in recent years.

Competitive positioning

Having a good overall understanding of the existing competitive environment is a necessary prerequisite for quality strategic planning work. There is also a need for a detailed focus to see what is coming down the line in terms of potential disruptive business practices. In market terms, the purpose of analysing direct competitors should not be simply to copy or imitate what they are doing (although there can be an advantage in this). Instead, the focus should be on identifying the areas where your enterprise has the resources and capability to gain a good position and recognise how you can attract new customers or make your current customers more satisfied and expand the business relationship. There can also be an urgent need to build for the future by undertaking a level of parallel development, and projects and programmes can be an important aspect of this. As Clayton Christensen and others have highlighted, complacency by large companies in the face of *disruptive new entrants* making incremental stealthy gains at the bottom of the market can lead to large problems later on as business cycles progress. Written in conjunction with James Allworth and Karen Dillon, Christensen's 2012 book *How Will You Measure Your Life?* includes a number of interesting analogies between business and personal life, with the theme being very much about *sustainable strategy*. Here, it is argued that *marginal cost thinking* – prevalent in modern business strategy – can typically lead to short-term gains, but can also send us on a trajectory away from future success. By only having a current narrow focus in decision-making and concentrating on limited criteria like cost, you can start to make decisions that eventually lead you well down the wrong path.

Strategy guru Michael Porter emphasises that competitive market strategies need to be distinctive and difficult for others to follow. *Fit* is a key concept in this, as it describes how the multifarious activities of an enterprise fit together into a logical whole. Imitation can be very hard or impossible if an enterprise has developed on the back of a unique vision, patient investment and build-up of capability, and brand reputation over a long time and/or is based on a unique technology or superior human capital that can be retained.

Five Forces

In his work, *Competitive Strategy* (1980), Porter introduced the revolutionary idea that all enterprises followed some strategy in their operations, either an explicit (conscious) or an implicit (unconscious) one. He assumed that an enterprise's strategy was not only contingent on its competition with specific rivals, but also on tension between several forces in the enterprise's environment. These forces are: (1) current competition; (2) suppliers; (3) products or services which could substitute the company's own; (4) customers; and (5) new producers or service providers (see Figure 6.1). The *Five Forces* model implied a whole new way for managers to evaluate their position and Porter maintained that the success of an enterprise within a given industry was primarily dependent on how well the company understood the forces at work in its environment. He has continued to develop this model and it has been applied not only to companies but also to cities and nations.

The model is a tool designed to give a holistic overview of a business, for instance, to assess the strengths of a market position. It works best when considering the forces at work in a whole sector or a market, rather than looking at

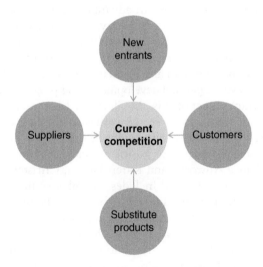

Figure 6.1

Five Forces model describing the competitive environment of an enterprise.

a singular business and its limited number of competitors. In order to explain the model better, we have used it below to describe a market with which we are very familiar – the provision of project management training.

The appeal of project management training and professional certification has been evident across many sectors for some time now, and there is an established market for the provision of such a service. The suppliers, in this case, are teachers, professionals, academics, and people with knowledge and skills and the ability to teach. We came to understand quickly that the market is essentially divided into two different sectors; firstly, organisations as clients and, secondly, individuals as clients. We soon saw that the characteristics and forces for these different market sectors are very different and, as a consequence, they must be studied separately to get any kind of a coherent result. Let's focus on the market for individuals. Traditionally, this involves a new group of students being formed for a training programme every autumn following an application process. Such programmes can be short, with a limited number of sessions, or long, with durations of one or two semesters.

Force 1 is the current competition

There are a number of competitors in various countries who offer a range of long or short study programmes in project management and who use a range of different delivery models, e.g. online lectures with periodic attendance sessions. Potential clients can assess each one on the basis of their cost, time commitments, and the likely value they will deliver in the longer run. However, information is not easily obtainable, and the characteristics of the different offerings can be difficult to discern. This is where an established reputation can be important as it allows potential clients to make an informed value assessment based on the genuine testimonials and experiences of others. Consequently, established providers of courses and study programmes have greater or lesser competitive advantage depending on the nature of their reputation and the experiences of their existing customer base and alumni.

Force 2 is new entrants

Starting a new programme for individuals requires a complete teaching schedule and a dedicated marketing effort, which are typically time-consuming and costly. Getting buy-in from suppliers in the early stages can be especially difficult, as they may have to agree to commitments without knowing that they will actually be delivered on. Building up a reputation in the business takes a long time. The principal requirements for entry into the market are experience, knowledge, and reputation, and there may be a number of consulting companies that tick those boxes. However, resources are also important. Appropriate facilities for teaching and comprehensive administration systems are needed to meet the needs of students and teachers alike, and these kinds of structures are often costly.

Force 3 is the threat of substitutes

This is an interesting perspective in the modern age of information technology. Some universities are offering open lectures, which poses a threat to the commercial model because the market may see this as a substitution. Learners can also opt for self-education based on YouTube and similar systems, and podcasts are also emerging enabling them to listen to lectures on the go. There is no doubt that there is a lot of information and training available free of charge on the Internet. However, it is not easy to see what is useful and what is not so useful. You need to make a coordinated effort to curate and then review a meaningful list of the options available, particularly where you are seeking recognised qualifications, and this reduces the threat of substitution. New training approaches are emerging such as the *flipped classroom* where students listen to a short lecture before a class and then concentrate on discussions, exercises, and projects during the class. This offers the possibility of reducing cost and increasing value for the customer, although increased complexity in offerings requires careful consideration. Traditional teaching methods and course provision may feel outmoded, but they have evolved over a long time to be the way they are and so change should be approached with caution. Take the example of perceived grade inflation which makes employers suspicious of high marks achieved in some courses or from some universities, which lack the reputation for the rigour of others.

Force 4 is supplier power

There are a large number of potential project management teachers available who possess the requisite skills and expertise in the subject and communication ability. However, excellent teachers with reputations to match are few and far between. Looking at price levels in the market, there is an unofficial rate that exists, but those trainers with the most experience and the best reputations can set their own price, within certain limits. Having a broader panel of teachers involved can lessen the risks caused by unforeseen events and the loss of individual expertise for whatever reason.

Force 5 is buyer power

Individuals are a powerful group with high expectations. Typically, they pay substantial fees for the courses or study programmes and expect to gain a lot from their participation. It is well known that long-term sustainability in the market is based on the feedback given by the buyers and it is not possible to survive in the market without positive *word of mouth*. The price range for open courses, training seminars, and longer study programmes is very wide and caters to a variety of buyers with different interests and goals. A typical concern for buyers is whether they can meet the demands of their studies while working, and this is very often a major consideration in course design.

This project management example has its own particular set of considerations and each sector and type of enterprise will each, in turn, have their own. Overall, it is important to realise where an enterprise's uniqueness and market advantage lies. What is it that the company does best and what is so special about its services or products that other firms on the market cannot offer? Porter (1980) put forward the theory that there are basically two ways for enterprises to improve their competitive position (see Figure 6.2).

The first way involves gaining a market advantage by offering cheaper products than competitors, i.e. going after volume while still retaining acceptable profit margins. This can be done by minimising unit production costs, for instance through automation, volume buying, high-quantity production, and systems/logistics optimisation. Competing on this basis can often require significant upfront investment to set up the proper infrastructure, but the gains achieved can result in a speedy recoupment of costs. Variations of this strategy for improving competitive positioning might involve simplifying design and production methods by offering a limited product range and simultaneously focusing on basic functioning. In addition, there are many ways that marketing can be done "on the cheap." For example, Ryanair's advertising route, developed over many years, has revolved around the colourful CEO Michael O'Leary who excels at getting free PR based on his unconventional, "politically-incorrect" views.

The second way involves an enterprise trying to differentiate itself from competitors by offering matchless products or services and thus gaining a unique market position, with customers typically ready to pay higher prices. An initial step towards this strategy can be to gain an understanding of the needs of higher-end customers – those that are most profitable. This can offer

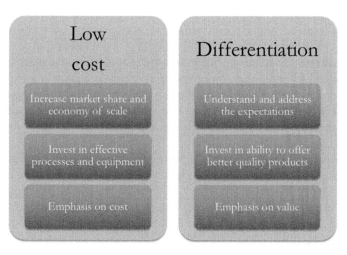

Figure 6.2

Differing strategic routes to competitiveness.

a route into other areas such as technological development around customer needs and offering the fastest and most personalised customer services.

A simple example of these two distinct strategies can be found in two segments of the grocery market in the UK. The first one is based on low prices and volume sales. Here, Asda (currently a subsidiary of Walmart, the world's largest retailer) is a leading player. According to Statista (2017b), it is the second/third largest supermarket chain in the UK, at over 16% market share. It has won the widely recognised Grocer Gold Award for "Britain's Lowest Priced Supermarket" for the 18th year running now. Asda is obviously focused on keeping production cost down so that they can offer customers products at lower prices, as can be seen by its Asda Smart Price label, which focuses on delivering basic goods in an uncomplicated way. However, Asda remains in an ongoing competition with the discounters Aldi and Lidl, which have a very different business model and are currently growing market share from a low base. Their defining strategy is to offer far fewer products in a very efficient manner, as reflected in their very low prices that typically lie significantly below Asda. As the market share of the discounters grows, though, it is also the case that their strategies are continuously evolving, and recent moves have shown their product offerings widening considerably into the higher value space.

At the other end of the grocery market is the lower volume, higher value segment. Here, Whole Foods Market, a company offering a vast selection of speciality products from around the world, can be considered to be a representative example. The first two of the company's seven core values read "*Selling the Highest Quality Natural and Organic Products Available*" and "*Satisfying and Delighting Our Customers.*" The company states that it is committed to buying from local organic producers that meet its quality standards, where possible, and emphasises their overall green environmental credentials in the form of providing assurances on the sustainable, ethical practices of their individual suppliers. The terms "natural" and "organic" are synonymous with higher prices, and their customers, who are seeking the highest value products – typically driven by health, environmental, and ethical concerns – accept this.

Here we have two good examples of different strategies companies can use in order to jostle for position in the market. Both these companies have defined their uniqueness, which differentiates them from others and makes for their competitiveness.

A general criticism of these theories and models relating to competitive positioning is that they do not fully account for what might *actually* be going on in a market. There is a tendency to simplify what may be a complex system of interacting market players, some of whom may remain unseen by the final customer. For instance, they do not account for the fact that buyers, suppliers, and competitors can interact with each other and sometimes collude, or that various middlemen and other secondary beneficiaries are influencing final outcomes. In addition, the role of governments in influencing markets is not considered, including how some market players become *too big to fail.*

In this case, extraordinary support can be offered, such as for the banking sector (although not bank shareholders) in the UK. RBS, for example, has been shielded to a great extent from the consequences of its reckless actions in the lead-up to the 2008 financial crash by the subsequent allocation of taxpayer's money by the government of the day to bail it out. This interference has upset the normal workings of capitalism to a significant degree, and there is increased recognition now that governments can choose winners and losers in certain sectors under various circumstances.

Another long-established approach that can be used to determine market positioning, and which is more product-specific, is what is commonly termed the "four Ps" (McCarthy, 1964). These stand for "*price, product, promotion* and *place*." The latter term here refers to providing the product at a place that is convenient for the customer, i.e. akin to *distribution*.

By analysing existing or potential markets under these four terms in detail, you can get a firm idea of what is working, as well as what could work in the future. If, for example, products are remaining on the shelves for a long time, it may be time that prices are lowered or that some additional marketing strategy is devised, which may be as simple as moving the products to somewhere more prominent.

Overall, a number of different approaches can be taken in terms of characterising the overall competitive positioning of an enterprise and determining future strategy. An illustrative example here might be where an external strategic planning consultant is brought in to advise a medium-sized, well-run enterprise, which has been in business for a number of years and delivers good profit. The current position is therefore strong, but those running the enterprise may be looking to the future and thinking that an experienced external viewpoint can help provide direction. Understanding the existing competitive position of the enterprise will be an important first step here, and this includes details on what exactly is the core of the enterprise's operations and what factors are responsible for its current competitive edge. The following questions, put to a representative group that includes people from all levels of the enterprise, can help in this process:

- Where, in your opinion, do the enterprise's strengths lie?
- What does the enterprise do well?
- What should be improved?
- What distinguishes the enterprise from its competitors?
- How stable is/are the principal market(s)?
- Where do you see the main threats in the future coming from?

The last two questions here are forward-looking and may produce some interesting responses that you can follow up on. The open-ended nature of the questions may encourage diverse responses and you'll need to allow time to clarify views, follow lines of thought, and summarise them in a useful way. Within the framework of the analytic phase of strategic planning, you'd also be wise to gather information from customers, particularly those considered "core." This can be done by means of interviews or surveys, and the questions may also be open-ended. Your aim is to examine and understand how customers view the enterprise, and the results should give you an idea about the prevailing levels of customer loyalty. For example, this may involve asking customers how a particular product meets their expectations and fulfils their needs, or how a particular service can be improved to encourage repeat business. Again, the results need to be analysed and condensed into digestible points, and these can then be communicated back to those working within the enterprise for their response. Such surveys should result in a fairly clear presentation of what it is that distinguishes an enterprise from other similar companies, where it performs best and why.

In the subsequent chapter, we describe many features relating to economic environments and modern markets. The main emphasis is on the scope of activities and how markets continue to evolve, together with the impacts these developments can have on competitive positioning.

Reflection points

- Chose an enterprise you are familiar with and use the Five Forces model to describe its competitive environment.
- Use the four Ps approach to describe the market for a product you are familiar with.
- Try to think of examples of hidden market players (e.g. in the oil market) who retain great influence in final product offerings and pricing.

Market environment

At the macro scale, understanding markets through the study of economics is more art than science and there are many theories on what drives business cycles and the respective roles the private and public sectors play in the overall process. A consensus view might be that it is technological advances that really lie behind market growth in the long run as they enable capital and labour to become more productive. Superimposed on this, we have the effects of demographics, interest rates, exchange rates, monetary policy, and fiscal policy as well as the significant effects of global connectivity and important events. The aggregate demand in a country is normally measured as the sum of consumer spending, capital investment, government spending, and net exports. In the UK, consumer spending is the main driver of market activity, representing about two thirds on average, although the other components (less so net exports) are nonetheless significant, and the government sector has additional heavy influence in terms of operating transfers (e.g. social welfare payments and pensions) and also contributing about 25% of capital investment. Other developed countries will have a broadly similar breakdown of contributors to aggregate demand. Therefore, the actual primary factor in market growth is the consumer, be they at the individual, household, organisational, or government level, while business investment tends to track consumer sentiment as well as government policy.

The diversity of market environments in the modern world is truly mind-boggling. While it all originally stems from bartering (which still exists at some level), we have now developed to the point where significant market activity revolves around fully computerised high-frequency trading based on millisecond advantages, facilitated by large market facilitation companies such as Intercontinental Exchange (e.g. NYSE) and NASDAQ OMX Group. This highly specialised activity is based on algorithmic programming and has been linked to a number of different business strategies, not all of which would be considered ethical, e.g. facilitating front-running large trades. The details surrounding this type of market activity are beyond the scope of this book, but we include it here as an example to illustrate the diversity that we see today, and it is worth remembering that it also competes with traditional market players and extracts profit at their expense.

Taking a step back, it would appear that bond markets and stock markets, traditionally the domain of the cautious and shrewd long-term investor, have developed an unstable life of their own. Some explanations for this increased volatility might include important changes to financial regulations and markets including: (a) the ease and speed at which money can be moved and trades completed; (b) information asymmetry; (c) skewed incentives for leading market players who speculate with other people's money; (d) individual lack of accountability; as well as excessive government interference in propping up failed institutions and business models. Deliberate complexity in investment products (e.g. structured products based on derivatives) has become commonplace, often leaving regulators struggling to keep pace; and there are also now many different ways that people can become involved with market speculation. At the more conservative end are products such as index tracker funds that follow the stock prices of a portfolio of leading companies (e.g. FTSE 100), while at the more adventurous end are activities like spread betting, which can appear to share similarities with gambling. In all cases, these market activities provide fees to a range of market service providers and facilitators who often profit from the volume of trades rather than the outcomes.

While it is usually argued that such financial innovation and market activities provide much-needed liquidity, their effects (in conjunction with government activities) on real-world commerce can be very disruptive at times. For example, price spiking in commodities like oil, steel, gold, copper, platinum, rare earth elements (e.g. neodymium used in gearless wind turbines); or indeed in currency exchange rates can wreak havoc with the business models of certain enterprises and the budgeting of their projects. Hedging risk by a variety of means such as futures contracts is a way to counteract this inherent volatility, but this can also be costly and may have been possible to avoid if speculators did not potentially have such a large influence.

Aside from this specialist market activity, mainstream commerce still retains many familiar characteristics of the past, i.e. businesses still buy in materials, equipment, and services from other businesses in order to produce goods and provide services, we still go to the local shop to buy commodities and we still periodically visit the high streets for specialist goods.

Market disruption

But much has changed in the last few decades. For instance, electronic payments through whatever means (e.g. debit and credit cards, direct debits, standing orders, IBAN payments, ApplePay, or various e-commerce platforms) have replaced cash to a great extent. Governments tend to favour these financial flows as they offer far greater oversight and taxation control, although it is also true to say that many people have strong feelings about the privacy and flexibility that cash affords. Elsewhere, the increased complexity of systems and products means that the business-to-business (B2B) marketplace is now far larger and more complex than it was in the past, particularly in relation to business services. In retail, customers may have become more frustrated with the range on offer in their local shop, high prices, and lack of parking and have decided to do most of their weekly shopping in new out-of-town shopping complexes, which large supermarket chains typically anchor. While there, they may have decided to venture into the surrounding shops and purchased goods at the expense of shops on the high street. Alternatively, they may have just sampled some goods in those shops without purchasing them and then gone home to purchase them cheaper online for home delivery.

There are now multiple avenues available to purchase most things and we have vast amounts of price comparison information at our fingertips. According to the National Statistics Office (Ons.gov.uk, 2017, Internet use by those 16 years of age or over in the UK was at 89% during the previous three months during Q1 2017. The average weekly spend online for 2014 was almost GBP 720 million (close to GBP 40 billion per year). According to UK Barclaycard (2014), online credit and debit card transactions in 2010 accounted for 16.1% of total consumer spending, whereas, by Q3 2014, that figure was 21.4% (see Figure 6.3).

Online retail sales have been growing steadily in Europe, as shown in Table 6.1; the data is from Retailresearch.org (2017).

A microcosm of this overall trend can be seen in the fashion retail sector where a number of former high profile high-street businesses have had to go into administration (e.g. Morgan, Kookai, Jane Norman, Barratts, Principles). Typical reasons include high commercial rents, declining sales, and competition from specialist online retailers. At the same time, As Seen on Screen (www.asos.com), the online fashion retailer, has expanded globally and seen annual sales grow from GBP 17.8 million in 2006 to GBP 1,120 million in 2015. Notable casualties to online rivals in other sectors and jurisdictions include Weltbild, a large German bookseller with previous sales of around

Figure 6.3

Four Ps, to determine market positioning.

EUR 1.6 billion that filed for bankruptcy in 2014; and Vroom and Dreesmann (V&D), a former leading department store chain founded in the Netherlands in 1887, which filed for bankruptcy in 2015. In some cases, though, bricks and mortar retail is still very much a viable prospect as evidenced by Swedish fashion retailer H&M (Hennes & Mauritz AB) who continue to grow sales with 400 new stores planned worldwide for 2016.

Another example of disruption in marketplaces is the taxi sector where the traditional model of queuing at taxi ranks, ringing cab companies, or flagging down one on the street and paying with cash has come under a lot of pressure from taxi-app companies that match supply and demand and facilitate easy electronic payment for smart-phone users. Uber, founded as recently as 2009, leads the way in this transformation and was recently valued at over USD 60 billion in its latest funding round in 2015. Direct competitors to Uber in different jurisdictions include Lyft, Gett and Hailo, and they each have different strategies in place to grow their markets, although all rely on commission as their main revenue source. The commission rate appears to be around 20–25%

Table 6.1 Online retail sales and growth rates in Europe

	Online sales (£bn) 2016	Growth 2015–2016	Online sales (£bn) 2017	Growth 2016–2017
UK	60.43	12.6%	67.38	11.5%
Germany	54.21	18.3%	63.09	16.4%
France	37.00	16.7%	42.11	13.8%
Spain	9.94	18.8%	11.85	19.2%
Italy	7.62	16.9%	8.78	15.2%
The Netherlands	7.11	16.5%	8.32	17.0%
Belgium	4.83	15.3%	5.46	13.2%
Austria	4.77	13.5%	5.41	13.4%
Switzerland	5.78	11.6%	6.38	10.3%
Sweden	4.98	11.6%	5.70	14.5%
Poland	5.23	17.8%	6.14	17.2%
Europe	**201.90**	**15.6%**	**230.62**	**14.2%**

on average, which these companies describe as a fee to license their technology. In a number of countries, Uber's policy of using drivers other than traditional unionised taxi service providers has been a major source of contention, most notably in France where 2016 has already witnessed nationwide strikes by unionised taxi drivers and counter-protests from Uber drivers. Changes in regulations by governments represent a risk to the current business model but it would seem that the sector is irrevocably changing at the same time. Other variants in strategy include the use of "surge" pricing by Uber, which means that prices for a journey rise during times of increased demand. Gett, on the other hand, currently operate flat rate pricing regardless of demand and they emphasise this in their marketing campaigns against their main rival Uber. This is an example of a very dynamic market environment and it is very likely that the current strategies employed by the companies mentioned will not remain static, but rather continuously evolve.

Similar disruptive business practices are to be found in the travel accommodation market where companies like Airbnb, Wimdu, and VRBO match supply and demand on online platforms and have made a big impression. In the case of Airbnb, their current main revenue comes from charging guests a commission fee of between 6–12%, while hosts are typically charged a 3% commission fee.

Changes in household spending patterns

In more macroeconomic terms, household consumption expenditure is very much tied in with discretionary income and this has a direct bearing on the markets for luxury items, holidays, and non-essential goods and services. In the UK and other places, recent economic developments have meant a very mixed picture is emerging. For those homeowners with affordable mortgages, reliable employment, and no other financial drain, the past few years have been relatively easy in terms of household income and expenditure. Other households, without reliable well-paid employment and with less affordable mortgages or high rents, are struggling. While unemployment rates may be largely the same, the conditions of employment for unskilled jobs appear to be worsening on average in the UK and elsewhere. This phenomenon, combined with stealth taxes and increased basic living costs including accommodation, utilities, and foodstuffs, means that a very significant percentage of the population have little discretionary income. Paying attention to trends in spending power provides valuable market knowledge, and the Office of National Statistics in the UK and Eurostat for the EU provide a useful service in this regard (Armstrong, 2018). A diagram showing the median salary in selected countries is shown in Figure 6.4. Such information can be very helpful, for example, in deciding where to set up particular types of businesses.

There are now many options for companies researching their market environment. Companies now have huge amounts of internal data that can

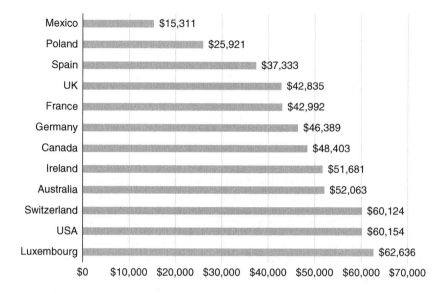

Figure 6.4

Median salary in selected countries in 2016 in USD.

be used for statistics, data mining, multi-dimensional analysis, trend analysis, and reporting. The foundations of this approach involve tailored data warehousing and database management systems, and nowadays much information comes from AIDC (Automatic Identification and Data Capture) sources. These include barcodes, RFID (Radio Frequency Identification), biometrics, magnetic stripes, OCR (Optical Character Recognition), smart cards, and voice recognition. Another large data source in more recent times is web analytics. This can be either off-site (e.g. related to wider internet trends) or on-site (e.g. *landing pages* and purchase decisions). Google Analytics is a widely used application, while new more sophisticated tools such as *heat maps* and *session replay* are also becoming available. In the background, larger external data aggregation companies such as Statista, Nielsen, or Gartner continuously gather the most up-to-date data from numerous different sectors and sell it to customers in a range of ways. In addition, individual sectors typically have a few recognised market intelligence companies that compile the latest industry data and sell it to market participants. Examples include: MEPS – steel industry; GHX – healthcare; JEC Group – composites industry; Douglas-Westwood – oil and gas industry.

Government agencies, as well as companies, now make frequent use of geographical information systems (GIS), which are systems designed to capture, store, manipulate, analyse, manage, and present all types of spatial or geographical data. Such systems have the ability to store many layers of data and so can be used for sophisticated multi-dimensional analysis relating to geographical considerations. A police force, for example, may use a GIS system to record the locations and nature of crimes and any other relevant information. This combined information can then be used to decide on the best allocation of resources to reduce crime in the overall jurisdiction. The use of this and similar technology has now spread to many sectors where spatial planning is significant, and the possibilities should be examined by any enterprise that might benefit from having such spatial knowledge.

Information (or knowledge) has now become a major commodity in the age of computers and this was recognised early on by leading thinkers such as US economist Fritz Machlup. His 1962 book *The Production and Distribution of Knowledge in the United States* was a harbinger of things to come in this regard; no need to look any further than Google or Facebook to see how user-derived information is being monetised to generate a major source of *competitive edge* in the modern market environment. *Big data* and the data monetisation of the *Internet of Things* (IoT), which has been described as a network of embedded sensors in everyday "things," are hot topics in the current business environment. Until recently, designers of IoT hardware have not conceived of the value of user contextual data, but their mindset is changing and software development focusing on capturing data from this perspective is growing rapidly. Geolocation is an obvious early example of this new direction, as are "smart" appliances. The boundaries between the physical and digital realms may be dissolving but there are also huge considerations in this that revolve around privacy. Countries like Germany take citizen's privacy very seriously and there is a major tug-of-war currently going on between regulators and companies as well as other government agencies over this topic worldwide. In other countries, it is well understood that online information is very closely monitored and that Internet censorship is a reality with non-conforming websites blocked.

Alongside information gathering, connecting businesses with customers is a major source of online revenue. According to Statista (2017), the total advertising spending in the UK for 2017 was GBP 22 billion, of which almost 50% related to digital advertising. As increasing numbers of people use their mobile telephone to connect online, the tailoring of user experience by marketers needs to adapt and the traditional ways of designing sites for desktops need to be revisited. This includes looking at landing page content, speed, and functionality from the mobile user perspective as well as a number of other user experiences such as mobile content delivery. Overall, the surge in digital advertising expenditure comes at the expense of more traditional advertising such as print media, which has shown a steady reduction in recent years.

The rise of the Internet and social media is something that traditional enterprises have been gradually adapting to. Recognised areas of relevance include HR, communications, sales, marketing, services, branding, community engagement, innovation, and development. Major platforms used in a European context include Facebook, Twitter, Google+, Wikipedia, LinkedIn, YouTube, Instagram, Tumblr, Reddit, and Pinterest. Web syndication (e.g. RSS feeds) allows for the widespread dissemination of a source site's information (including licensing opportunities) as well as benefitting user content through-flow for receiver sites. Some trends in this general area include video and other content; storytelling – showing the back story to a product; bringing existing content into new countries; personalisation – including *calls to action* on websites that engage the user very quickly; retro styles such as email newsletters; live streaming; and experience design.

There are now large numbers of digital media start-up companies that focus on offering many different forms of marketing services that can prove highly cost-effective. This area requires considerable tailored research, as the particular circumstances and needs of one enterprise may differ greatly from another. Take the example of sports where the main stars are increasingly having their back-story told and light shone on their off-competition lives such as training regimes. YouTube videos would be a popular medium for doing this and there are many production companies that help provide content. This can help generate lasting interest in the people concerned and a loyal following.

The business-to-customer (B2C) environment is undergoing a lot of change, but it should also be noted that a large percentage of businesses still operate very successfully in a more traditional fashion. They may incorporate some of the latest technologies in inventory control, production processes, billing, and accounts, for example; yet their modus operandi continues to rely on "old-fashioned" values that translate into such things as quality, exceptional customer service, personal experience, friendliness, and community engagement.

The transformation of B2B markets

In the business-to-business (B2B) world, there is now far greater complexity in offerings and in the means of engagement between buyers and sellers. In saying this, established trade shows and industry-relevant conferences and events retain a centrally important role in many sectors. New products are showcased in front of many potential buyers and the business media while networking, sales deals, and other negotiations may be carried on in the background. The degree of professional organisation of such events has typically risen with improved targeting now possible by both buyers and sellers given the greater number and specificity of events. Attendance at these events can represent a significant investment decision that may or may not pay off. In the meantime, the event management sector has witnessed impressive growth in recent times.

Globalisation has left few sectors unaffected and the range of market suppliers in the B2B world has grown exponentially, particularly in China and other prolific Asian economies. The phenomenal rise of Alibaba Group – a Chinese e-commerce firm founded by Jack Ma in 1999 and valued at around USD 200 billion as of Q4 2015 – is one clear example of this trend. Low labour cost has been the differentiating factor underpinning this development. There may also be other influencing factors like less stringent regulations (e.g. health and safety, environmental, labour) and economies of scale.

In transactional terms, there are significant differences between the B2B and B2C. The nature of purchases and the means by which they are executed is usually different between the two worlds. Developing networks, identifying/following leads, and developing lasting customer relationships with local contacts are all of prime importance in a B2B context. Technology can assist these processes but there must be real substance behind any undertakings.

You may provide potential buyers with substantial amounts of information via websites and their associated content, but how you do this needs to be carefully thought through. Demonstrating capability and emphasising reputation to potential buyers in a short space of time (no slow-loading pages) should be key objectives for the websites of companies engaged in selling complex products and services. Potential customers will quickly continue their search elsewhere if any website is too slow. The preceding step of guiding potential buyer traffic to your website may be done in many different ways. Writing articles in prominent publications linking to your website, paying for traditional advertising, exploiting social media links, generating online video content with links, paying for inclusion in lists of suppliers in prominent publications or websites, paying for keyword search prominence, search engine optimisation (SEO), and so on.

Where the complexity of products or services is high, price information is rarely provided online. Take the example of a large concrete U beam for a bridge. Detailed engineering and other information are needed. Once a potential buyer is satisfied that the capability and reputation of a given supplier look promising, they will make contact either by phoning, emailing, or submitting query forms. A representative of the company then takes the process from there and will be primed to handle price queries (or objections).

Where complexity is lower (be careful not to confuse complex with large or complicated), products and prices can be displayed in a clear systematic fashion with shopping cart links so that purchases can be made quickly and efficiently whilst retaining customer interest. The process may involve the customer filling in a certain amount of detail about what they are seeking to buy before receiving an instant quote. Even if a purchase is not the outcome, this submitted data can be useful for market research purposes. These types of sites can often meet the needs of both the B2C and B2B customer. Let's look at the example of a rapidly developing SME, MicksGarage.com, which was set up in 2003 and originally specialised in supplying car parts to the UK and Ireland but has expanded and ships 18,000 orders a month to 70 countries. It has grown to become a major stockist of all the most commonly required car parts. With 48 employees and a turnover of around EUR 11 million in 2015, it is still in the rapid development stage. Their site serves both individual customers and professional garages.

To conclude this discussion on the nature of the modern market environment, let's move onto two final dimensions, which may overlap. The first involves situations where the buyer is a government body or other public organisation, and in the second the buyer is a company looking to enter foreign markets.

Public tendering processes associated with central government and public authorities can vary from country to country, although within the EU there are strict procedures and rules in place for contracts over a certain value that brings consistency to the process. There can also be onerous requirements to comply with quality procedures and various standards. Pre-qualification can be used to whittle down the bidders to those most capable on the basis of appropriate initial eligibility criteria. These may include financial standing, quality standards, capacity and competence, and track record. While notable for its transparency, fairness, and the potential for cost-savings when properly applied, public tendering processes can also be overly bureaucratic and a major obstacle for SMEs who do not have the requisite contract management specialists nor the resources to divert for the tendering process. In addition, greater importance can be attached to process over substance, or cost over value, in the tendering process and these systems struggle to accommodate uncertainty and the need for innovation.

Each year over 250,000 public authorities in the EU spend around 14% of GDP on purchasing services, works, and supplies so this activity represents a very large market (ec.europe.eu, n.d.). Across different sectors, there are different thresholds, above which cross-border rules apply, and below which national rules normally apply. At present, cross-border thresholds generally start around the EUR 150,000 mark, although that figure can be significantly higher in some sectors. All public procurement tenders above the requisite threshold need to comply with strict cross-border guidelines, which may include the basis on which you should alert potential bidders and the provision of relevant pre-bid information, including the criteria upon which final awards will be made. Any enterprise with an interest in supplying to the higher value public procurement market should familiarise themselves with whatever process is applicable. At both national and cross-border levels, this can involve attending official events and making connections with representatives of the relevant public bodies as well as gaining acceptance onto lists of approved suppliers.

Publications such as the *Official Journal of the European Union* (OJEU) and various websites (e.g. www.ted.europa.eu) provide tender information at the EU level. In the UK, you can start searching at the URL contractsfinder. service.gov.uk and follow up on the relevant information and opportunities from there. There are also numerous private companies that provide tendering information and consultancy services for a fee. Millstream Associates, for example, have been operating in this space since 1989 and operate the www.mytenders.org website which includes a variety of services for buyers and sellers alike. One such service is Tenders Direct, which enables you to filter substantial quantities of public tendering information down to what is relevant to a particular enterprise and delivers concise information in the form of daily custom email alerts.

In the case of an enterprise looking to do business in new markets abroad, there are a variety of considerations, a number of which have already been mentioned in relation to PESTLE analysis in Chapter 5. These include: (a) the business culture to be found in that country; (b) the political and economic environment; (c) all trade regulations, customs, and standards; (d) the investment climate; (e) trade and project financing; (f) business travel; and (g) contacts, market research, and trade events. Particular areas of interest may include tax incentives, inflation, and currency exchange rate volatility. In some countries, it may be worthwhile to use local agents that handle the importation, distribution, and marketing of products. Alternatively, you may choose to open a local office to look after such things and provide sales- and customer-support. Many companies operate internationally using the franchise model while others undertake joint ventures and licensing. Each of these approaches can limit risk by leveraging local knowledge and resources. Pricing will be just as important in international markets as it is at home and you need to understand how your marketing-, distribution-, and sales channels might be adapted to international business in order to comply with local tax and trade agreements, import restrictions, and even data protection law and to be culturally sensitive to the countries with which you are trading. Just because your e-commerce system enables international transactions, don't assume that the documentation and processes associated with international orders will be unchanged from your home country.

Reflection points

- Describe the current market environment of an enterprise with which you are familiar.
- To what extent do you believe disruptive innovation will change this environment in ten years' time?
- How is disruptive innovation changing the travel accommodation market around the world, and how does this impact the housing markets? To what extent was that impact foreseen?
- Give an example you know of a technology company that operates in a B2B market, and another example of a comparable company that operates in a B2C market. Comment on the difference between the markets.

Procurement by tendering

Formal procurement or tendering is usually carried out where public money is being spent above a particular threshold amount, ostensibly to obtain the best overall value encompassing quality and price. Similar processes can also be followed by private enterprises when making large purchases of products or services. Examples may include utility companies building power plants and electrical infrastructure, or large road-building contractors looking for tarmac suppliers. This form of competitive procurement is also common when private enterprises are carrying out projects (e.g. R&D) involving a substantial component of public funding.

Figure 6.5

Successful tender.

The main approach in public or private contexts is to issue a request for tenders (RFT), which is a document made available to all potential suppliers through recognised channels and on an equal basis. An RFT invites suitably qualified entities to bid and outlines in sufficient detail the nature of the products and/or services that are required. Variations can be used in different ways during the procurement process. A request for proposal (RFP) outlines basic information on what is required of bidding suppliers and is typically circulated during the preliminary (pre-tendering) stage of procurement. If the work being undertaken is uncertain by nature or technologically complex, then additional pre-bid informative meetings may take place in those cases as part of a *competitive dialogue procedure*. Other documents that can be used in the overall process include a request for quotation (RFQ) price information for supply of a commodity or finished product and a request for information (RFI), which is primarily used to decide on the eligibility of a given supplier or contractor and/or the next steps to be taken. An RFI process can be part of a *restricted procedure*, with the second stage involving only selected applicants in the invitation to tender. Eligibility, in this case, includes providing evidence of enterprise history, tax compliance, financial ability to carry out the work, technical capability and customer references.

The value of contracts awarded under Competitive Tendering is huge. Public contracts falling within the scope of the European directives represent EUR 425 billion annually or 3.4% of the EU's GDP (EU, 2011). The EU has detailed and evolving regulations in place related to procurement by tendering MEAT (*most economically advantageous tender*) is a recent development which enables the contracting authority to take account of criteria that reflect qualitative, technical, and sustainable aspects of the tender submission, as well as price, when reaching a decision to award. The relevant EU legislation includes the following criteria:

- Quality.
- Price or cost using a cost-effectiveness approach.
- Technical merit.
- Aesthetic and functional characteristics.
- Accessibility.

- Social characteristics.
- Environmental characteristics.
- Innovative characteristics.
- After-sales service and technical assistance.
- Delivery conditions such as date, process, and period.

A contracting authority may also decide that a contract is to be awarded at a fixed price, meaning that bidders will compete on quality criteria only. Overall, recent changes in EU procurement regulations represent a significant change in approach, with an emphasis on making things more straightforward, greater environmental awareness, and greater SME involvement. In the case of the latter, awarding authorities are encouraged to split large contracts into smaller sub-contracts and are required to explain any reasons for not doing so. In addition, the minimum turnover required to take part in a public tender is to be capped in principle (at a maximum of double the estimated value of the contract).

Submitting bids in a formal tender process can be a time-consuming process and it is important to be methodical in providing all the necessary information in the best manner possible. This means that: (a) all stipulations are complied with – having the requisite accreditation is a big consideration and may need to be strategically planned for, e.g. by committing resources well in advance to improve competence or increase capacity; (b) the submission is easy to read and sufficiently concise and clear; (c) all submission requirements are addressed; (d) detailed evidence of competence is provided; (e) pricing and outline of delivery is realistic and competitive; and (f) all submissions are made on time according to the schedule. Where detailed information is given in RFT documents, this should be studied carefully and well understood. An RFT may include information that describes different evaluation stages, weighting models, and award criteria along with "notes" and "remarks." Providing a detailed breakdown of cost estimates can convey the right level of experience and leave assessors with a good impression. Estimates may include a realistic figure for a contingency based on prior experience and the details of the current tender.

If an enterprise considers that it will need particular goods or services on a continuing basis but is not yet certain about details or timing (for example, food or stationery), they can decide to set up a "framework agreement." There are four basic types: (1) single user/single supplier; (2) single user/multi-supplier; (3) multi-user/single supplier; and (4) multi-user/multi-supplier. Once the framework agreement is in place, the next step is to invite potential suppliers to apply to be part of the framework before choosing the most eligible applicants. Once the framework is in place, individual contracts can be made throughout the period of the agreement. Where there is more than one possible supplier, a "mini-competition" can be set up to decide between them. Such framework agreements usually last for a maximum of four years.

Equitable treatment for all is the backbone of the tendering process and competition law in the UK and elsewhere is explicit in what it allows and disallows. It is illegal for those awarding the tender to have inappropriate contact with any bidder where sensitive information is divulged in relation to the process. No one bidder can be given preferential treatment and bidders must not collude to ensure a particular outcome. Examples of activities viewed as bid-rigging include: (1) agreeing with your competitors how much you will bid for a contract or sharing information about your bid; (2) taking turns to win contracts; (3) asking other businesses to bid at higher prices when they do not want the contract – called *cover pricing*; (4) paying other businesses either not to bid or when you win a tender; and (5) agreeing with other businesses not to bid or to withdraw your bid. According to the former Office of Fair Trading, which issued fines totalling GBP 129 million to 103 construction companies in the UK from 2000 to 2006, by far the single biggest infringement in the construction sector was "cover pricing" (Webarchive.nationalarchives.gov.uk, n.d.).

Enforcement in all cases is very much down to assigned powers and manpower, and these can vary substantially between countries. Government agencies have a leading role but there is also a growing private fraud investigation industry. The increased outsourcing of products and services and contract management has led to a corresponding increase in procurement fraud. Individual contracting officers can have a lot of power at all levels, and enterprise owners should be vigilant and keep an eye out for red flags that would merit further investigation. This also applies in the case of competing bidders who see anomalous patterns emerging over time in sectors where their bids are repeatedly unsuccessful. In a 2012 article entitled "Finding the bid riggers," private investigator Charles Piper describes the following red flags for indicating possible bidding fraud in the US, which can merit further investigation:

- Repeated awards to the same entity.
- Competitive bidder complaints and protests.
- Complaints about quality and quantity.
- Multiple contracts awarded below the competitive threshold.
- Abnormal bid patterns.
- Agent fees.
- Questionable bidder.
- Awards to the non-lowest bidder.
- Contract scope changes.
- Numerous post-award contract change-orders.
- Urgent need or sole source.
- Questionable minority/disabled ownership.

Problems don't end with a successful tender. Contractor underperformance following the awarding of a contract does arise and, if this is prevalent, those overseeing the procurement process should look at ways in which competence and ability can be assessed properly, for example, through a "right to audit" clause. If a given contractor's bid is significantly lower than a group of similar bidders, it may not be an indication of greater capacity and competency but rather of poor quality.

Reflection points

- Put yourself in the position of a contracting authority and discuss the design and award of tenders from a strategic perspective, e.g. by using the general strategic planning process presented in this book (Chapter 2).
- Do you know examples of bid-rigging in your environment? How did this happen and what were the consequences?

User analysis, data, and marketing

There may be subtle differences in mean or appropriateness of terminology when we talk about customers, clients, or users, and different sectors or industries may be sensitive to this. The most remote group from the perspective of the seller are usually the "users." Users rarely pay for goods or services directly (if at all). The term "user" might encompass a citizen accessing services for the homeless, paid for out of general taxation, or an office worker using software paid for by their company. The successful and repeat use of goods and services from both groups can nonetheless be essential for convincing funders to continue to fund a product or service and, consequently, their user-experience can be important, and their influencing power should be respected. Let's take the example of the large numbers of people who browse through different websites that contain sponsored ads. If there is little worth looking at, or if the whole set-up is configured and policed badly, then current users will migrate elsewhere, and sponsorship money will dry up. The 2018 data protection storm that has engulfed Facebook is an excellent example of the risks businesses face if they neglect or exploit their users.

Where money is paid directly, such as to purchase a ticket for a bus or train, the term "user" becomes very closely associated with "customer," with the latter term usually suggesting a greater level of interaction and expectation of quality. The traditional notion of a "customer" is someone who makes standard purchases from an enterprise that do not require more from the transaction other than basic empathy and professionalism. A "loyal customer" generally indicates those who engage in significantly profitable repeat business in a marketplace where they may choose their provider. In a B2C environment, these are the kinds of customers that loyalty cards or reward schemes are aimed at, or who may be the target for email and other marketing campaigns. In the B2B environment, organisations may invest time and money in assuring a close relationship with a loyal customer. This may involve offering an exclusive level of service or sales channel or inviting them to pay for networking events.

A client is usually considered to be someone purchasing a bespoke level of service, such as that offered by a professional service provider, where consultation is part of the transaction. An environmental consultancy, for example, will only have "clients" as each of their work projects involves a unique complex set of considerations and tasks. The same is true for other professional service providers like lawyers, accountants, auditors, engineers, and doctors (although the term "patient" is normally employed where medical treatment is involved). In the B2B environment, there are many enterprises providing uniquely tailored solutions to others on a repeat basis and so the term "client" is typically used in this context. For example, a software-as-a-service (SaaS) provider such as Salesforce would naturally view those business customers with whom it has an ongoing dynamic relationship as "clients."

Clayton Christensen emphasises the need to *"understand the job that a product or service is being hired for"* (2012). Let's take an example, a successful executive may subscribe to a selected group of leading daily business newspapers and, by doing so, influence subordinates to copy their behaviour. A competitor who becomes aware of this lucrative market may try to enter it by offering a news subscription service via an online aggregator site. However, there may be several difficult barriers to overcome here to convince the target market to switch. Examples include: (1) the perceived value of aggregated content – newspapers associated with informed and probing journalism will have a strong reputation for providing unique knowledge, insight, or analysis; (2) information display – the size and crafted layout of a newspaper allows for quick scanning of content that can cover very diverse subjects, a number of which may interest readers in peripheral ways; (3) image – reading a clearly visible and branded form of printed media in public makes a statement about your status, intelligence, and aspirations in a way that is not possible with electronic content devices, where typically what is being read is invisible to those around you; and (4) a newspaper can act as an extension of body language and a comforting physical statement of personal space.

Analysing customer behaviour is something that you can undertake for individuals and for groups. In the case of groups, you will normally aim to build up a series of representative *customer archetypes* to guide the testing of design and marketing ideas. In a B2C environment, the overall process often begins with demographic profiling (e.g. on the basis of age, sex, level of education, and so on) along with behavioural analysis. Specific data may be gathered by dedicated observation, through representative surveys, or simply by asking employees with the greatest customer exposure for their views. From the results of these approaches and reviewing sales data, an enterprise can build a reasonable picture of its customers and how they change over time. A variation of this process can be done in a B2B environment, with an appropriate awareness of differences between customer types that we have already highlighted in this chapter.

The following stage looks at the different needs of customers and how products or services, as well as follow-up customer service (if applicable), are fulfilling them. In their 2007 book *Professional Selling: A Trust-Based Approach*, Ingram et al. break down different customer needs into the following five categories:

- *Situational needs*: these relate to specific requirements at a particular time and/or place. For example, in contrast to a low-cost supermarket, a petrol station in a more remote area could sell smaller packets of higher-priced nappies due to the typical emergency situations customers would be buying them in.
- *Functional needs*: these are where items are purchased in order to get a specific job done. An example here would be an enterprise buying hardware and software to better manage their customer support systems. Another example would be where one funds a training qualification in order to be eligible for a particular job type.
- *Social needs*: these relate to the need for acceptance from others, or being associated with others. A person wearing an expensive suit can be seen by others as belonging to a select group of successful people.
- *Psychological needs*: these can be multifarious, with examples being related to feelings of: (a) security; (b) assurance; (c) self-contentment; (d) excitement; (e) joy; (f) escape; and many others. Watching comedy on TV at home in the evening after a stressful day is but one example.
- *Knowledge needs*: these relate to various kinds of information that should be known in order to understand events, and so that we can apply ourselves to bring about desired outcomes. Examples include factual subject books that deliver the right information in order to be able to fulfil a particular task.

Once the needs profiles of customer archetypes have been identified, there are two main additional areas of consideration: (a) the degree of commitment to a particular organisation or brand; and (b) the initial means by which customers become aware of the organisation or brand and what influences them to subsequently engage further with it. In terms of brand commitment, this relates to additional factors such as a customer's perceived level of affinity to a particular brand and his or her attitude to alternatives. *Authoritative influences* can be significant in a customer's choice, for example, what are the "coolest" group in a school wearing? Or what are the recommendations of a trusted car mechanic in terms of vehicle reliability? If the views of a customer are ambivalent towards a particular organisation or brand, they may normally shop around and look to fulfil their needs while focusing on other criteria such as immediate availability or price. These types of customers are most receptive to *point-of-sale stimuli*. If, on the other hand, their outlook towards a brand is unequivocally positive, they will then be willing to pay a premium price and wait, if necessary. In terms of brand awareness and engagement, this initially relates to how the product is marketed and the extent to which others have had positive experiences. In order for engagement to occur, however, the new customer needs to feel that they are valued and that what was promised was delivered.

Since its inception, the global e-commerce leader Amazon and its founder Jeff Bezos have been obsessed with understanding the needs of customers and working backward from there in order to make sales conversions and ensure repeat business. Originally developing in the B2C and C2C space, but now venturing into B2B, Amazon basically operates as a facilitator, being an aggregated marketer, matchmaker, and distributor for goods made or owned by others, and size is a critical factor. The types of things it has to do well to retain customers are few as a result, so customers (e.g. buyers and sellers) will be happy to engage in repeat business provided that it: (1) covers a sufficiently wide range of goods to meet demands; (2) offers competitive prices through economies of scale and retail models; (3) markets items sufficiently well; (4) has acceptable commission fees and transaction fees; (5) vets sellers and their products; (6) facilitates buyer payments in a secure fashion; and (7) guarantees prompt delivery of a product in satisfactory condition within a wide geographical area.

In order to understand their customers, Bezos asks thousands of Amazon managers to join him and attend two days of call-centre training each year. This constant customer focus and the matching collection of sophisticated data using advanced customer relationship management (CRM) systems enables Amazon to take innovative business risks based on convincing evidence. The overall message is that customer retention is a vital aspect of building a stable loyal customer base, from which further growth comes organically.

The type of market an enterprise is engaged in and the degree of market saturation can be very influential in customer behaviour and there are a number of ways this can be analysed. A classic B2C market model in this sense that can apply to many products where peer influence is important is Roger's Bell Curve (Diffusion of Innovations), described by US statistician Everett Rogers in 1962 and shown in Figure 6.6.

There are five main customer types identified on the curve. Those at the left-hand end of the curve, the *innovators*, are crucial in convincing sceptical executives to invest and make what was merely an idea into a reality. This group may be used to provide extensive customer feedback to iron out any issues and guide business decisions such as pricing. They can be a very important constituency for enterprises who seriously engage in *empathic design* (i.e. user-driven) for their products and services. From a market perspective, the *early adopters* are a vital group as they are the ones that build the required momentum to get the product noticed and talked about. In conjunction with innovators, they serve as brand/product ambassadors and, where applicable, can be very influential in attracting larger market players to the product, e.g. convincing supermarkets and other large footfall stores to stock the product. From there on the focus can be on reaching a wider audience by marketing the product and ensuring that the supply and distribution network is functioning properly. By the time of the *late majority*, customer experience

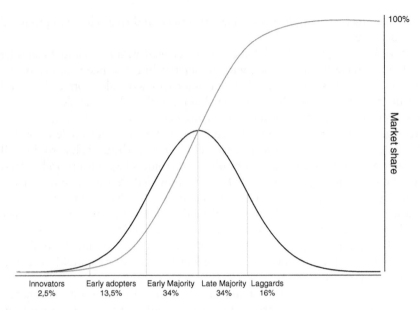

Figure 6.6

Roger's Bell Curve market development model showing progression up to saturation point and the different customer types within this.

should be a major focus as the most important issue switches from customer growth to customer retention. This means converting satisfaction into loyalty and commitment.

It is a natural process for enterprises and individuals to evaluate their purchases in terms of perceived quality of product or service and perceived value against their prior expectations. A company that overpromises and under-delivers can be viewed harshly. Customers may feel that a salesperson did not sufficiently address their needs and spent too much time talking rather than listening, or that calls and emails were either ignored or not responded to satisfactorily. Both brand engagement or ingrained dislike can often stem from key interactions with frontline staff. For instance, an airline check-in attendant might have shown genuine unscripted empathy in the face of a customer in clear emotional distress, while another may have shown impatience and exacerbated what was already a delicate situation. According to McKinsey, over 70% of customers reduce their commitment to an enterprise on the basis of bad experiences (Beaujean, Davidson and Madge, 2006).

Enterprises that are simply focused on building market share can lose their connection with higher margin customers as competitors start to see niches to exploit. Cumulatively, poor customer treatment and lack of engagement over a period by an enterprise can eventually boil over with customers pulling the plug, never returning, and telling as many people as they can about their experiences.

It is generally well understood that the cost of acquiring new customers can be many multiples of the cost of holding on to existing ones (e.g. Coyles & Gokey, 2005). In addition, it is clear that some customers contribute significantly more business than others and it may prove difficult to keep all customers satisfied. Given that these statements can be made in relation to countless enterprises operating in most sectors, it makes sense to prioritise areas where resources should be applied to address issues and influence customer retention. The value gained can be substantial. An important first step in this process is to determine which customers are the most important, and which of their needs the company should seek to fulfil first.

In market terms, the Pareto principle is a rule-of-thumb that says that 80% of an enterprise's sales value comes from 20% of its customers. The principle is named after Italian economist Vilfredo Pareto who in 1906 found out that 20% of assets in Italy were owned by 80% of the nation. Pareto was captivated by this ratio and believed we could apply it equally to most things in his life. The Pareto principle does not have a strong scientific foundation, but it can be useful to guide thinking in analysing an enterprise's customer base and realising which customers count the most. An example of such an analysis for a financial company is shown in the chart (see Figure 6.5) where you can see that a large majority of their sales is concentrated in just a few industry sectors. These are the clients that trust the company, are satisfied with the products and services, and are likely to buy again and again. Based on this information alone, efforts to retain customers in these few sectors should be prioritised given the stiff market competition. There can be other important considerations such as the rate and direction of change for the individual sectors shown. If, for example, the current rate of individual sales (5%) was 0% just two years previously, this would indicate that the market is currently expanding rapidly, and the individual market will also react more smoothly to economic cycles. Prioritising this sector in terms of the allocation of marketing and operational resources should then also be a logical path to take (see Figure 6.7).

Pareto analysis is also useful to help understand organisational change. In this context, 80% of problems relate to 20% of causes, and so the priority becomes identifying these strong causal factors and finding ways to eliminate them first, rather than simply applying resources to deal with all identified causes at once. The input into such analysis may be a combination of stakeholder surveys, data mining, and looking at the internal workings of an enterprise. In order to get to the root of the problem, it can be useful to think of the varied nature of stakeholder complaints as mere symptoms of underlying causes. Using inference can lead to recognising patterns and may enable you to identify systemic problems such as lack of training or insufficient staffing levels.

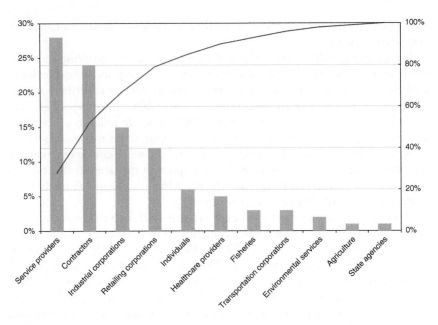

Figure 6.7

Pareto analysis of clients of a financial corporation showing their percentage contribution to sales revenue.

Marketing and sales

We have already described the fast pace of evolution in the market environment in recent times. Change encompasses the increasing diversity in marketing and sales channels. Perhaps the single biggest impact is the increasing difficulty in getting your voice heard amongst the proliferation of suppliers, channels, and content. For instance, where a TV advert for a popular broadcast show in the past might have had several million views in the UK, it now faces competition from subscription channels, online content, and computer games. Where a European yacht builder may have previously relied on a handful of local fibreglass suppliers, they can now purchase quickly online through Alibaba from a broad range of Chinese suppliers whose takeover of this particular sector has been dramatic in the last twenty years. The apparent growth in speed, access, and availability of everything from information to bespoke services has encouraged a growing mindset of expectation in people from all sections of society. If you or I want to book a foreign holiday, we can have the necessary price comparisons and transactions completed in minutes. It is naturally a key capability for all kinds of enterprises that people are able to do this as delays are likely to lead customers to take their business elsewhere. The same people are also faced with buying decisions in a B2B environment and will be looking for quick price comparisons and purchases there too. This is more likely at the SME end of the market where individuals have greater autonomy and flexibility than is the case in large enterprises with dedicated purchasing departments.

As touched on in the previous chapter, the more fundamental aspects of customer engagement remain largely unchanged for enterprises and essentially revolve around generating positive feelings, managing expectations, and meeting needs. In reality, these needs are often a complex mix of the functional, social, and psychological, and good marketers and salespeople will have a strong insight into their relevance in the sectors they operate within. When customers spot a recognised brand in a sales environment which is associated with positive feelings (trust, desire to own), this is an effective shortcut to a sale. The buying decision simply becomes a question of affordability. An unfamiliar product and/or an unfamiliar sales environment requires a lot more time for customer reflection and, hence, is already much less likely to result in a purchase unless there is some other big draw such as price or convenience to compensate for the lack of familiarity. Where a recognised brand is associated with negative feelings, price and convenience can be significant decision factors that overcome any reluctance, particularly if the purchase involves something the customer needs, rather than just wants.

Reputation also plays a part where products are marketed according to "Country of Origin," i.e. Made in Britain. This can send a message to customers based on hard-earned reputation (but also national pride), and national brands are rigorously managed to maintain their appeal. Examples of particular reputational association include "Made in Switzerland" for luxury goods, "Made in Japan" for electrical goods and "Made in France" for food and beverages. Where this reputation is tarnished, there can be major fallout for those directly impacted and major PR and technical assurance programmes may be required to recover the position. When bovine spongiform encephalopathy (BSE) or "mad cow" disease was first detected in British cattle in 1986 and then throughout the early 1990s, the phrase "British beef" came to be associated with fear of contagion, and the EU (along with many other jurisdictions) banned British beef exports between 1996 and 2006. Successive British governments applied considerable resources in a concerted eradication programme that saw cases drop from 37,000 at its peak in 1992 to just 90 by 2004. While the overall episode has severely impacted many individual farmers, the industry sector as a whole, together with its national brand, has now largely recovered.

Other examples of associative brands that are widely adopted by enterprises are "Fair Trade" and "Organic." Both appeal to the health- and environmentally conscious customer and are associated with significantly higher prices, sometimes dramatically so in the case of organic products. As with any brand, erosion of quality standards is of concern. For example, vocal advocates of pure organic methods, who are often small producers themselves, are uneasy about the recent wide-ranging takeovers of many smaller original producers of organic products by large multinationals and the pervasive influence of large retailers. Customers of such products might be surprised at who ultimately owns different popular organic brands. This is viewed in some quarters as the takeover of the industry sector by stealth, and the overall portfolio of brands that these large companies own, and the means by which most of their ingredients are produced, do not sit well with the "organic" ethos. A leading voice, the Organic Consumers Association, was formed in 1998 in response to a perceived proposed downgrading of US organic food regulations. In the UK, the Soil Association aims to maintain the high standards to go along with the certified organic brand.

Branding is arguably of even more importance in the consulting and professional services environment where clients will typically be paying high fees and have high expectations in return. Here, brand association with success is a key message to convey to existing and potential clients. Word-of-mouth, combined with visible advertising, such as *article marketing* in prominent publications, or attending and sponsoring key events, are amongst the successful methods employed. Informative websites offering short case studies to illustrate the scope and success of previous engagements are also common. Three interesting examples are: (1) IDEO (www.ideo.com, n.d.) – the largest product design consulting firm in the US focusing on mechanical engineering and industrial design; (2) Moz (www.moz.com, n.d.) – a leading US company specialising in online marketing software and analytics; and (3) Marel (www. marel.com, n.d.) – an Icelandic company with a strong global presence specialising in food processing solutions.

The key question that marketers ask themselves when trying to market a product is: what problem are we trying to solve and for whom? Answering this question will help frame the key impact messages and explain how to go about the process of connecting with people and convincing them that particular products and services can deliver. The value proposition and differentiation from others in the market needs to be made explicit, and careful pricing is invariably an important element. Getting this right requires good market intelligence and insight and may be done initially on trial and error within test markets prior to wider release. Production values and presentation can be important, as are all aspects of labeling and branding, with all of these different elements designed to convey a sense of brand. Appropriate and consistent communication style can also have an important impact.

The range, type, and diversity of channels for connecting with people have grown exponentially with mobile content and social media leading the way in redirecting marketing spend in recent years. SEO (search engine optimisation) and PPC (pay per click) are now key marketing tactics which act as a funnel to guide the searcher towards particular sites offering products and services. In order to maximise their potential, enterprises need to concentrate on customer search experience. This can involve optimising such elements as title tags (what is seen in browsers) and meta description tags (brief visible descriptions that convey informative content). A large and growing percentage of customers today are researching heavily online and engaging with social media – praising or denouncing as they do so. Leading enterprises all need to maintain a strong online presence and they will need a credible, ethical, and transparent plan for dealing with bad reviews, if and when they arise.

CRM systems are now standard software tools used by enterprises to manage their customer-related data in the most efficient manner and allowing them to react in real-time. The four main CRM suppliers are Salesforce, Microsoft, SAP, and Oracle. The principal goal of CRM systems is to gather data and automate sales, marketing, and customer support. This can be a complex process, as efforts need to be coordinated between different areas of an enterprise such as centralised sales, marketing, call centres, and retail outlets. The main aim is to avoid duplication of effort, inappropriate contact with customers, and an improved customer experience (e.g. query or complaint follow-up). It can also enable increased accountability, i.e. identifying when and where a problem occurred in customer service provision.

Whenever possible, customer information based on a unique identity is input into a CRM system from the first engagement of a customer with an enterprise, and all subsequent information, including past sales, and previous marketing, is linked to this so that a coherent customer history is documented. Done well, CRM helps to preserve enterprise knowledge in the face of employee departures. Once hosted in a cloud system, the information can be viewed and amended by any enterprise employee, or the process may also be fully automated. Customer relationship management through time is an important consideration for any enterprise. In a properly functioning system, the most loyal and valuable customers can be readily identified using scoring systems which, in turn, are very useful tools for targeted marketing in the form of automated emails or social media posts. Collated data is typically used for statistical market analysis, which provides business managers with the wherewithal for their decision-making. Analytical CRM systems can automatically produce user-friendly information for management based on common recognised business concerns; imagine a bar chart showing the percentage distribution of customers within a set of predetermined age ranges. Such information provides useful market intelligence for product design and advertising campaigns, with different approaches in each case identified for different age brackets. Another role of CRM is to incorporate input from a broad range of stakeholders such as suppliers, distributors, overseas agents, and technical support staff. This information can assist in helping an enterprise to find its strategic direction and to identify tactics to achieve existing strategic goals.

Alongside marketing, sales models are also undergoing significant change in the modern environment. We have already discussed Uber and Airbnb, which operate on commission. Another online sales model that is becoming more common is the "freemium" model, in which one layer of content is available for free, while successive layers with premium content are paid for. Most online academic journals employ this form of sales model, as do software providers and online books (e.g. the "Look Inside" function from

Amazon and "Preview" from Google). From the customers' perspective, it enables them to get a good feel for the product and its suitability before agreeing to pay for it. A useful aspect of this sales approach is that the customer is typically required to fill in a certain amount of information about themselves and/or that their movements and choices are trackable. The Freemium approach, therefore, can be an excellent tool for generating detailed market intelligence. However, increasing customer impatience at barriers to access, growing concern about personal data footprints and changes in data protection regulation means that this is no longer an unfettered source of data. Companies such as Skype (communications) and Dropbox (data sharing and management) have managed to convert a large portion of their initial "free" customers to paid services, with Dropbox also cleverly offering greater data storage space for existing users who recommended its services to new users.

Reflection points

- Think of a common product and try to analyse the job(s) it does for customers.
- What market is currently solely made up of innovator-type customers?
- Give examples of key positive moments in your dealings with different organisations. Did they have lasting impacts?
- Give examples of key negative moments in your dealings with different organisations. Did they have lasting impacts?

Benchmarking

Benchmarking is the process of comparing one company or industry's processes and performance to those of others. The term "others" here can be very broadly defined, and examples include: (a) the same entity in the past; (b) a different division or place of business within the same organisation; (c) another external entity; and (d) multiple other entities with shared characteristics, e.g. whole sectors. Singular or multiple parameters can be compared, and dimensions typically measured are quality, time, and cost. Norms and/or best practice can be looked at as well as current innovative approaches and solutions adopted by others and the results of these to date. Special care needs to be taken to ensure that the figures used are indeed comparable. Usually, some numerical processing of absolute data is required to allow for more direct comparisons, e.g. using percentages, incorporating weighting factors, or employing statistical representation (see Figure 6.8).

Overall, benchmarking is an effective, disciplined way to position an enterprise in the competitive environment, to determine what products, services, processes, or actions are successful and to identify the key performers

Figure 6.8

Benchmarking.

that you might emulate. Benchmarking can be seen as a process of continuous improvement by comparing the organisation's practices with generally accepted good practices; one example might be the project management competences of an organisation. Useful organisational comparisons can be made on which ERP (enterprise resource planning) systems enterprises employ, and how these compare to what is available on the market and being used by competitors. In general, comparative information can be extracted from focused observations, various sources of official data, the financial statements of competitors, and press reports as well as professionally from market intelligence providers. External strategic planning consultants and management consultants are naturally strongly inclined to employ benchmarking in their work given their typical broad range of dealings within a sector and consequent multiple information sources. Other potentially important sources of comparative information are people who have newly joined an enterprise having previously worked for competitors or comparable organisations. This can occur naturally or as a result of a deliberate headhunting strategy. In such cases, you need to take care that neither your organisation nor the individuals concerned transgress prior contractual obligations or ethical boundaries in divulging information about their former work.

Nowadays, benchmarking is widely adopted across all public and private organisations and examples of questions the process attempts to answer are given below:

- How do particular service delivery costs compare with their equivalent in other jurisdictions?

- How long are our current waiting times in comparison to those in our old operational regime?
- How do particular staff turnover rates compare to industry norms?
- What are our average operational load factors and how do they compare with industry bests?
- How successful are patient treatments for a particular disease in relation to the equivalent elsewhere?
- How do the levels of pollution from a particular industry compare with others?
- What is an acceptable rate of return on a particular type of investment?
- How do the pay and conditions in one sector compare with others?
- What constitutes safe practice in a particular industry?
- How does the raw material consumption of our manufacturing process compare with industry best practice?
- How does the lifespan of our product compare to that of our competitors?
- What is an appropriate staff/customer ratio for our enterprise?

Michigan-based Truven Health Analytics is a consultancy that employs benchmarking at the forefront of its offerings in the health industry. The company, a leading provider of cloud-based healthcare data, analytics, and insights, has recently (early 2016) been taken over by IBM Watson Health in a USD 2.6 billion deal. Before that deal, Truven worked with 8,500 clients including US federal and state government agencies, employers, health plans, hospitals, clinicians, and life sciences companies. Following the acquisition, IBM's health cloud will now house one of the world's largest and most diverse collections of health-related data with wide-ranging benchmarking capability relating to many different types of cost, claims, quality, and outcomes information.

In the UK, the Institute of Customer Service produces periodic reports from 13 different industry sectors that highlight a range of information relating to customer satisfaction (UKCSI) that can be used for benchmarking purposes.

Reflection points

- Choose an enterprise that you know. How would benchmarking benefit this enterprise?
- How could such benchmarking be undertaken?

References

Armstrong, M. (2018). Infographic: The countries with the highest salaries. [online] statista.com. Available at: https://www.statista.com/chart/13093/the-countries-with-the-highest-salaries/ [Accessed 23 May 2018].

Beaujean, M., Davidson, J. and Madge, S. (2006). The "moment of truth" in customer service. [online] McKinsey quarterly. Available at: https://www.mckinsey.com/business-functions/organization/our-insights/the-moment-of-truth-in-customer-service [Accessed 23 May 2018].

Bombardini, M. and Trebbi, F. (2009). *Competition and political organization: Together or alone in lobbying for trade policy?* NBER Working Paper No. 14771.

Christensen, C. M., Allworth, J., & Dillon, K. (2012). *How will you measure your life?* (p. 87). New York, NY: Harper Business.

Contractsfinder.service.gov.uk. (2018). Contracts finder. [online] Available at: http://www.contractsfinder.service.gov.uk/ [Accessed 23 May 2018].

Coyles, S., & Gokey, T. C. (2005). Customer retention is not enough. *Journal of Consumer Marketing*, 22(2), 101–105.

ec.europe.eu. (n.d.). Public procurement. [online] Available at: https://ec.europa.eu/growth/single-market/public-procurement_en [Accessed 23 May 2018].

Ideo.com. (n.d.). IDEO. [online] Available at: https://www.ideo.com/ [Accessed 23 May 2018].

Machlup, F. (1962). *The production and distribution of knowledge in the United States* (Vol. 278). Princeton, NJ: Princeton University Press.

marel.com. (n.d.). Marel. [online] Available at: https://www.marel.com/ [Accessed 23 May 2018].

McCarthy, J. E. (1964). *Basic marketing: A managerial approach.* Homewood, IL: R. D. Irwin.

Micksgarage.com. (2018). About us. [online] Available at: https://www.micksgarage.com/ [Accessed 23 May 2018].

moz.com. (n.d.). MOZ. [online] Available at: https://www.moz.com/ [Accessed 23 May 2018].

Mytenders.co.uk. (n.d.). mytenders – eProcurement made simple. [online] Available at: https://www.mytenders.co.uk/ [Accessed 23 May 2018].

Ons.gov.uk. (2017). Internet users in the UK – Office for National Statistics. [online] Available at: https://www.ons.gov.uk/businessindustryandtrade/itandinternetindustry/bulletins/internetusers/2017#main-points [Accessed 23 May 2018].

Piper, C. (2012). Finding the bid riggers, 12 red flags of contract and procurement fraud. *Fraud Magazine*, 27(4), 31–37.

Porter, M. E. (1980). Competitive strategy: Techniques for analyzing industries and competitors (Vol. 267). New York, NY: Free Press.

Retailresearch.org. (2017). Online retailing: Britain, Europe, US and Canada 2017 – Centre for Retail Research, Nottingham UK. [online] Available at: http://www.retailresearch.org/onlineretailing.php [Accessed 23 May 2018].

Rogers, Everett M. (1962). *Diffusion of innovations.* Glencoe, IL: Free Press.

Statista. (2017a). Market share of grocery stores in Great Britain from January 2015 to March 2017. [online] Available at: https://www.statista.com/statistics/280208/grocery-market-share-in-the-united-kingdom-uk/ [Accessed 23 May 2018].

Webarchive.nationalarchives.gov.uk. (n.d.). Bid rigging in the construction industry in England – The Office of Fair Trading. [online] Available at: http://webarchive.nationalarchives.gov.uk/20140402154534/ [Accessed 23 May 2018].

www.statista.com. (2017b). Topic: Advertising in the United Kingdom. [online] Available at: https://www.statista.com/topics/1747/advertising-in-the-united-kingdom/ [Accessed 23 May 2018].

www.home.barclaycard. (2014). Where's Britain spending? The Barclaycard Consumer Spending Report Q3 2014. [online] Available at: https://www.home.barclaycard/content/dam/bcardpublic/FinalContent/NewsandViews/2014/q3spendreport/Barclaycard_Spend_Report_Q3_2014.pdf [Accessed 23 May 2018].

www.ted.europa.eu. (n.d.). TED home: TED Tenders Electronic Daily. [online] Available at: http://www.ted.europa.eu [Accessed 23 May 2018].

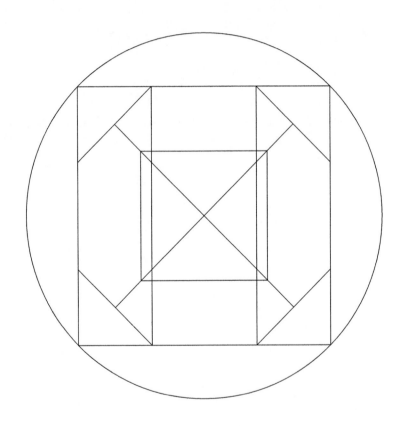

7 Direction finding

··

In the previous chapters, we have discussed many aspects of the current status of an enterprise and drivers of change. Strategic planning is a complex process that operates on many levels and relates to the past, present, and future of an enterprise. For this reason, it is good to stand back and view the process from a distance before engaging in detailed analyses in order to understand the full scope of what you are undertaking and to help you to prioritise the areas on which to focus and the projects you subsequently initiate. Let's open this chapter with an overview; bringing together the different strands of what has already been covered and explaining how strategic action plans are finalised. Once you have properly established the context and main strategic considerations for an enterprise, you can then undertake detailed focused analysis to outline key opportunities and threats and provide directional guides to future actions. This work is closely tied in your use of feasibility studies, business case development, and PPP (project, programme, portfolio) planning.

Once the implementation phase begins, the focus switches to reviewing actual results and how they compare with expectations. You'll benefit from having a firm understanding of initial conditions in order to allow for accurate comparisons and inform your judgements on the strategic effectiveness of different options. At times, the speed of action can be very important in order to grasp fleeting, time–bound opportunities and you'll need to limit yourself to only cursory analysis where this is the case. Timing is often more important than detail but, no matter what is being considered, it is essential that you understand the extent of potential risks before committing to any action. Keep in mind the risks associated with the unintended consequences of any decision and remember, you may "*Act in haste and repent at leisure.*"

Overview of the process so far

Strategic planning usually involves the accumulation of large amounts of information and this needs to be analysed intelligently in order to see what is of most importance and to establish a *future vision*. Each time strategic planning is carried out it represents a unique undertaking with typically many levels so, while the various analytical tools we describe here can be repeatedly used, they can only ever act as broad guidelines and you'll need to adapt them to suit particular needs at a particular time.

With this in mind, we give a generic example in Figure 7.1 that shows where the synthesis of information and direction finding fits into the whole strategic planning process. Knowing what has gone before and what is likely to come after puts things in context and will guide your subsequent work. In this example, we show the connections between the past, present, and future and the iterative nature of the process of developing a strategic action plan and continually revising it in the face of real circumstances as time progresses. May we stress again how implementing change in an enterprise can be viewed as (part of) a project (or programme) in itself. We've also illustrated the different stages in the process to which the different chapters of this book primarily refer. Defining overall success criteria and project planning are integral aspects of the different analyses covered in this chapter.

Three initial distinct project plans (PP1, PP2, and PP3) are shown in the above diagram, which together define a programme of works. This programme is the outcome of the initial strategic planning process and a series of progress review dates should be agreed upon in advance, with the first review being

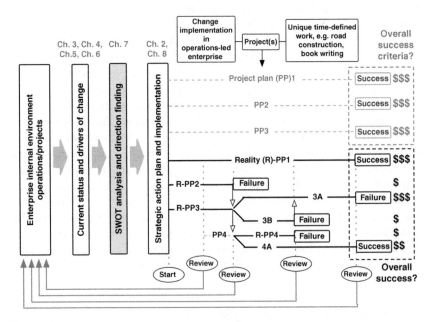

Figure 7.1

Schematic illustration of an overall strategic planning process with the synthesis of information and direction-finding stage highlighted. Different initial project plans are shown as well as how things might progress in reality through consequent iterative reviews.

undertaken shortly after the start of the implementation phase. Let's imagine that the enterprise in question here is a small-to-medium enterprise (SME) currently supplying components to a number of large domestic manufacturers within a particular industry sector, and the overall success criteria are defined as "continued profitability in the face of competition from new market entrants and the maintenance of a reputation for excellence." In this case, then: (a) PP1 relates to upgrading to a new state-of-the-art manufacturing system; (b) PP2 relates to a complete overhaul of the enterprise website to allow for product displays and online ordering as well as improved online marketing to increase exposure; and (c) PP3 relates to expanding into the market of a neighbouring country. The success criteria for PPP planning can naturally vary widely but in this example, we highlight cost ($) as a key performance indicator alongside project completion.

In the lower right of the diagram, we show how things might pan out if successful. PP1 is carried out exactly as planned, i.e. the new manufacturing system is installed and works as expected. Elsewhere, the initial review reveals that PP2 is not progressing as planned – the early website changes were made without consulting existing customers and have not led to any increase in business. On the other hand, online marketing changes have resulted in companies from another domestic industry sector becoming aware of the capabilities of the SME and making sales enquiries. As a result, PP4 is initiated, which involves designing and marketing products for this potential new market.

By the time of the second review, it is clear that the website modifications to allow online selling (PP2) are not a success and so these features are removed. The online marketing campaign has led to some promising queries from abroad, however, so PP3 is continued and split into 3A (the original target neighbouring country), as well as other countries (3B). Meanwhile, PP4 (new product development for a different sector) is continued, but another potential sector is also identified and development work in this area is carried out separately (4A). As it turns out in our example, this last project is the only one of the remainder that is successful and so the SME is left with a mixed set of outcomes, the overall success of which needs to be judged against their profitability and reputational expectations.

None of the details are important in the broader sense and we included it merely to provide context and understanding. The main reason for including this example is to emphasise how analysis and direction finding is carried out each time a significant strategic decision is made. In our example, the other industry sectors referred to may have been little known to the SME before the process started, but the consequent sales queries led to the recognition of potential significant market opportunities. In order to exploit these opportunities, the company needed to undertake careful analysis and planning to tailor their product development and marketing projects for these new sectors.

The context of strategic planning varies hugely, but the process of structuring the resulting strategic action plan is common to most situations.

The different elements of the strategy and the projects or programmes that may be adopted to deliver them provide the constituent elements of your enterprise portfolio. Within this, you should locate your range of products and services (your product portfolio). You may then classify different product or service offerings within the portfolio as being any of the four designations shown in Figure 7.2. Please note that the BCG matrix (Morrison & Wensley, 1991) does not define what constitutes each of the four categories so you will need to establish what each means in the context of your business and your industry and define the boundaries between them. *Stars* are products or services that have a relatively large market share in a growing market. These products/services are likely to be profitable, to have the potential for further growth and to become an important part of the enterprise portfolio as their market matures. With this in mind, you should focus tie and resources on *stars*, perhaps investing in building up further capacity and increasing market penetration, as they have the potential to become *cash cows*. The natural lifespan of a *star* can be very short in certain markets, so you need to understand the market and capitalise on success while it lasts without compromising the sustainability of your business in the long-term.

Question marks are characterised by high growth but low market share. Products and services in this category offer some opportunities and it may be sensible to invest in them in order to increase market share and consequently increase revenue. However, you are less certain of success (hence the question mark) and therefore you'll need to analyse your various options carefully to determine which are worth the investment needed to increase their market

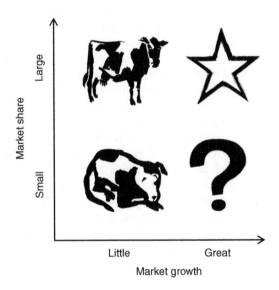

Figure 7.2

The Boston Consulting Group product portfolio matrix.

share. *Dogs*, on the other hand, are products and services with low profitability; they have a low market share in a mature, slow-growing market. According to the BCG matrix, you should not invest in these areas. Aim instead to exploit them for profit using pricing and careful cost management depending on the current circumstances and consider selling them off to others who may be able to better maximise their value.

Such portfolio analytical tools can help you to focus discussions, but the results will only ever represent a crude representation of reality where many additional factors will add complexity and may prove very significant. There may be particular, temporary circumstances that lie behind the reasons for individual constituents being within certain brackets, and small changes in the external environment could have a major impact. Some products or services could have disproportionately greater success in a different market. For instance, when Pfizer scientists were developing and trialling Sildenafil in the early 1990s for heart problems such as angina, the poor performance of the drug made it non-cost effective (a *dog* in the above terminology). What was observed, though, was that it had a noticeable impact on improving and sustaining penile erection in men and by 1998 Sildenafil was being marketed as Viagra, which has since become a major *cash cow*.

The BCG matrix has been criticised for oversimplification and there are indications that those companies that slavishly follow portfolio-planning models such as the BCG matrix have lower shareholder returns than rivals (S.F. Slater & T.J. Zwirlein, 1992). However, we have included it here as one of many possible analytic tools; all useful, each in its own way, in overall strategic planning work. Final decisions on whether to invest in or divest yourself of, or abandon specific products or services, should be taken on the basis of the perspectives offered by a range of models and measures and in the light of the direction you have chosen for your strategy.

Reflection points

- Think about the outcome of a strategic planning effort by a company you know. Was this a project or rather a program? Explain this difference and what it means.
- Think about your industry. Look at the Boston product portfolio matrix. Can you find examples of dogs, stars, cows, and question marks? Explain.
- Explain the difference between projects, programs, and portfolios by taking an example from your own organisation.

Synthesising information, trend analysis

At any particular moment in time, the future environment of an enterprise or any of its constituent business units or projects will typically be clouded in uncertainty, and the only means to discern potential opportunities or threats is to extrapolate based on existing trends. To do this properly, you need to have a good overall awareness of the main influencing factors in any particular set of circumstances and an appreciation of how these vary over longer time spans. In the case of a novel phenomenon – say a property bubble in a previously poor country or rapid growth in a new technology market – there may not be a direct precedent and you will need to look for potential analogues in other areas to analyse how events might unfold. Past trends elsewhere may indicate several possible scenarios and we refer to this further in the next section.

As part of the PPP framework structure, we have described, the remainder of this chapter is essentially about identifying opportunities and threats and developing a business case for pursuing particular strategic action plans. This is not just confined to initial plans, but also to any subsequent proposed changes made on the basis of reviewing performance once you have set your plans in motion.

The key questions are: 1. What is likely to happen in the future in a "do-nothing" scenario? 2. How can we influence the future by our own strategic actions? 3. Once the implementation stage starts, the question then becomes: do early measured trends indicate likely success? To answer these questions, you'll need to collect and analyse baseline data to determine underlying trends, and you'll need to set and monitor key performance indicators (KPIs) once a strategy has been implemented to monitor its ongoing effectiveness and general impact.

There are many different types of trends that individually share distinctive patterns with others, and that can also be strongly time-dependent, varying in characteristic ways over different time scales. While rarely smooth in reality, they can often be broadly described in mathematical terms, at least in part. At the more straightforward end, an example of a strong positive trend in evidence is shown in Table 7.1 in relation to the number of foreign travellers entering Iceland at Keflavik, the international airport of Iceland, Seydisfjordur seaport and other airports (Icelandic Tourist Board, 2018)

Table 7.1 International visitors to Iceland by point of entry: Keflavik International Airport *, Seydisfjordur Seaport and other airports

	2015	2016	2017	Change between years	
				2015–16	2016–17
Keflavik Airport	1.261.938	1.767.726	2.195.271	40,1%	24,2%
Seyðisfjörður Seaport	18.540	19.795	22.353	6,8%	12,9%
Other airports	8.661	3.859	6.450	−55,4%	67,1%
Total	**1.289.139**	**1.791.380**	**2.224.074**	**38,9%**	**24,1%**

* Data from Keflavik International Airport shows that the number of departing foreign passengers in April 2018 is 3,7% lower than in April 2017.

The data indicates current rapid sustained growth in Icelandic tourism and is being used by a range of enterprises to support new investment decisions; everything from new and upgraded hotels, cafes, restaurants, shops, museums, swimming pools, and health spas, along with a broad range of supporting tertiary service industries and increases in administrative government sector support. Of course, the current trend is not guaranteed to continue – as the most recent data from Keflavik International airport indicates – and macroeconomic and other factors will play their part in the future. Currency exchange rates, in particular, can be influential; as can jet fuel prices which impact on air travel costs and the risk of volcanic ash which can ground aircraft. Those promoting any tourist destination need to pay attention to visitor experience and pricing if the industry is to be successful in the longer term.

Such data may also be looked at from the perspective of those who are reviewing the effectiveness of their strategy to entice tourists to Iceland. The eruption of the Eyjafjallajökull volcano in Iceland in April–May 2010 had an immediate 20% negative impact on Icelandic tourism. In response, a number of leading stakeholders in the Icelandic tourist sector, which represents a significant portion of the total Icelandic economy, met urgently to agree on a range of efforts to salvage the tourist season. These included the Ministry of Tourism, leading airlines, Reykjavik City, the Export Council, and the Iceland Tour Operators' Association. An initial campaign was launched that ran from mid-May to mid-July that aimed to convey the message that Iceland was open for business. What followed was a more concerted effort to build a lasting marketing campaign that would also extend the tourist season into the winter months. The multiple award-winning "Inspired by Iceland" campaign was born, which aimed to convey the uniqueness of the country and enjoyed the firm backing of both well-known and lesser-known Icelanders as well as a number of famous international celebrities who acted as "brand ambassadors." The campaign was delivered both through traditional channels such as the tour operator and newer channels such as social media, allowing it to be targeted at a very wide audience. Largely thanks to these efforts, there has followed a consistent rapid upward growth in Icelandic tourism. Those responsible for overseeing the marketing of tourism in Iceland can look at the clear upward trend shown in the graph and see it as confirmation that they are doing many things right at the present time. The challenge, of course, is to continually adapt strategy and maintain appeal in the face of international competition.

A different set of data is shown in Figure 7.3, with a set of data series from the period 2006–2017 portraying some of the eminent challenges of Europe and Africa. The figure conveys the general uncertainty associated with environmental factors, population, refugees trying to enter Europe and GDP over this limited period of time. It is not possible to show statistical correlations between the variables but based on the graph, some of them seem to be linked. It is, for example, tempting to assume that the increased number

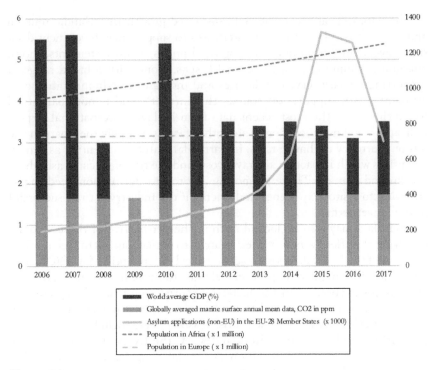

Figure 7.3

Plotted data sets, showing trends in GDP, population, CO2 concentration and asylum applications.

of asylum applications in the EU member states (Eurostat, n.d.) is somehow related to the increased population in Africa (Worldometers, n.d.), but the fluctuations in the latter half of the period cannot be explained by any data shown in the figure. Global climate change is happening on a longer time scale and the increase in globally averaged marine surface annual mean carbon dioxide (Earth System Research Laboratory, n.d.) can hardly be noted in the figure. World average GDP fluctuates (Wikipedia, 2018), and we know that the figure from 2009 (below zero) was caused by the international financial crisis. Data is important and no matter what sector you operate in, you need to understand the historical context of data and the range of factors that influence your market before making strategic decisions. But care should be taken in interpretation; fixating on trends in the most recent data and ignoring the range of historic variability can lead to protracted problems over the longer term.

Depending on the nature of the sector and the data in question, there are various elements to look out for in trend analysis including: *up-trends, horizontal trends, down-trends, positive feedback, negative feedback, seasonal variation, inter-annual variation, cycles and sub-cycles,* and any other type of pattern that appears coherent. Remember to consider the potential time lag between cause and effect, which can lead to flawed conclusions if not properly understood. You'll need a full range of the most influential parameters in any given situation and an understanding of how they are plotted to draw any worthwhile conclusions. You may find a variety of approaches useful: ratios, inflation-adjusted figures, or well-defined indices for proper comparisons between different datasets. A good working knowledge of statistics and the presentation of data should be part of the skill set of any strategic planning consultant if you are going to have any hope of extracting meaningful information from any dataset and/or present compiled data to management in a way that will influence the decision-making process.

Both our examples involve *true complexity*. This means that there is a great deal more going on than is suggested by the individual, discrete parts and/or components. They interact in a way that cannot be explained through reductionist and linear thinking. In *complex adaptive systems*, multifarious components that typically have no set properties interact in ways that defy simplistic modelling. Systems need to be understood in the context of emergent outcomes derived from the evolving and interconnected behaviour of all the constituent influencing factors (Lichtenstein et al., 2006). Thus, all biological, ecological, social, and economic systems demonstrate *emergent properties* to a greater or lesser extent. Hence, an empirical study carried out over a sufficient length of time is really the only way to come to have some understanding of the overall behaviour of such systems. Due to the inherent evolving nature of such systems, however, the standard caveat applies: *"Past performance does not guarantee future results."*

One approach to charting how more complex systems develop over time is the use of *system dynamics*, *agent-based modelling*, and *phase plots*. These can illustrate more complex relationships between variables and are useful for discerning trends in a dynamic system. An example is shown in the world-famous book *Limits to Growth* by Meadows, Randers, and Meadows (2004). This was the 30-year update of a book that was originally published in 1972. Figure 7.4 presents an overview of some of the outcomes of system dynamics modelling and illustrates the development of the world population. More specifically, the figure shows four different scenarios. Scenario 1 is "business as usual." The scenario is conservative on the abundance of non-renewable resources, but nothing is done to change the course of events. Scenario 2 is also "business as usual." No action is taken to take the course of events, but this scenario assumes plenty of non-renewable resources. Scenario 4 is "sustainable growth." We continue growing the economy and in the medium term, it looks better since the improvement in the productivity of, for example, agricultural land and pollution control, allows us to grow even more. The growth of industrial production and population continues to pace. Scenario 9 is "the steady state" scenario. It shows the results of applying corrective policies such as population control policies, improvements in food production, stabilisation of industrial production per capita

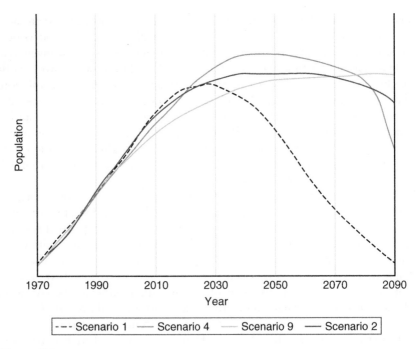

Figure 7.4

Example of the outcomes of a system dynamic model to forecast the development of the world population, four different scenarios are shown, based on different assumptions regarding application of corrective policies.

and control policies for pollution, soil erosion, and depletion protocol of non-renewable resources.

The general message of the book was that with no changes, the limits to growth would become evident already by 2072, with an uncontrollable decline in population and industrial capacity.

International investors widely adopt the strategy of studying a broad range of trends across various sectors of interest in different countries or regions with a view to identifying underdeveloped markets and allowing them to become involved in the early rapid growth and expansion phase. The property market is a typical example. Gentrification of an area is a recognised phenomenon that allows early movers to realise large investment returns, but the process presents a dilemma for urban planners and communities alike. The rundown urban area attracts a bohemian community who seek cheap living. Gradually, the new community livens the area up and more people and businesses are drawn to the area, leading to upwards pressure on the previously low rents and housing prices as well as on other living costs. This is the opposite process to that of urban decay, which we mentioned earlier in relation to Pruitt-Igoe.

Reflection points

- Describe three current trends with which you are familiar and how they may influence future strategic investment decisions in your organisation.
- What can be the benefit of building and applying a system dynamics model in the context of strategic planning?

Scenario analysis

Scenarios, in the general context of this book, offer *"plausible alternative views of how the business environment of an organisation might develop in the future"* (Johnson et al., 2008). Planning for uncertainty means properly accounting for a range of different outcomes, both in relation to singular events and sequences of events, so as to better realise where threats and opportunities lie. A logical next step, once you have completed stakeholder analysis, PESTLE analysis, market analysis, and trend analysis, is to convert the results into a restricted number of key scenarios that together encompass the full range of uncertainty that might be anticipated and document the associated opportunities and threats.

There are a number of steps involved in scenario analysis and it is advisable to carry out dedicated studies to try to quantify those aspects that are quantifiable. Take, for example, the financial risk to a large airport of having to ground all flights in snowy weather. Specific economic analysis carried out may indicate that each day of the closure means the loss of 100,000 passengers, and so further financial modelling may be used to ascertain what level of investment in new systems might be justified in order to ensure that the airport can remain operational at all times.

The universal benefits of undertaking scenario analysis are that it encourages people to ask probing questions and provides a structure for those with contrary views to voice their opinions in a way that is politically less threatening. The process also helps to uncover any predetermined outcomes that strategic planners should be aware of. For example: is there a predictable demographic shift on the way? Is some important event such as a scheduled bond repayment or expensive litigation on the horizon? Is the writing on the wall for our current business model? These questions, in turn, feed into the determination of the potential consequences associated with specific decisions before you make them.

In most circumstances, it makes sense to restrict scenarios to between two to five different narratives that are easily differentiated from each other and have the greatest potential impact. This avoids making things overly complicated but should also genuinely reflect the real potential risks involved. Depending on the nature of an enterprise, different time scales might be employed, for example: what will the environment be like next year? In five years? 20 years? 100 years? Such scenarios can then be used to stress-test different strategic action plans to predict whether successful outcomes can be delivered under a range of circumstances and which are more sustainable in the longer term. Having a default number of scenarios in mind (say four) can automatically encourage critical thinking and the exploration of many influential factors, while the final number will depend on the nature of the area in question.

Situations that can be foreseen are the only ones that can be assessed with some degree of accuracy and thus form the foundation of scenario analysis where the emphasis is on the predictable. Enough detail should be included to be able to guide strategic thinking and to assess potential outcomes based on decisions made. For example: will our current design wall height be sufficient if the sea level rises by more than 0.5m in the next 50 years? Does our plan make economic sense if oil prices will be consistently over 100 USD per barrel in the coming years? Will TTIP (Transatlantic Trade and Investment Partnership) become a reality within the next few years and how will it affect us? Will we be able to maintain our current level of exports if Britain were to leave the EU?

Experience generally shows that unforeseen circumstances can also have a significant impact. Standard approaches to mitigating risks involve: (a) maintaining a flexible strategic framework of action; (b) allowing for contingency in planning schedules and budgeting; (c) aiming to avoid systemic risk factors; and (d) building redundancy into systems. At the systemic level, US Sociologist Charles Perrow (1984) wrote the very influential book *Normal Accidents* where he talks about the risks associated with systems that are "*complex, tightly coupled and have catastrophic potential.*" In his view, there is a statistical inevitability about accidents occurring in complex systems and worst-case scenarios (i.e. total loss of control) should be looked at closely to identify the real risks involved in projects, rather than being overly reliant on safety systems. He also argues for caution in the use of system redundancy as this strategic approach has inherently associated risk factors that may, on occasion, actually increase overall risk. These include increased modes of failure, operator complacency, and production pressure with associated corner cutting.

It is important not to become overconfident when predicting the future and to ensure that potential scenarios are rigorously examined with the aim of ensuring that they are truly representative. This can include low-probability but high impact events such as geopolitical conflicts. Being prepared for a range of outcomes in this way while focusing on one likely "base case" scenario empowers executive teams to act decisively and can enable them to strike the right balance between risk and return. If, on the other hand, executives are solely reliant on a single envisaged "official" future, they can become paralysed and incapable of action when faced with unanticipated circumstances. Scenarios in which risks have been artificially constrained, for example, by excluding extremely high or low predictions of passenger numbers for large transport projects such as the UK's High Speed 2, can lead to scenarios that encourage complacency and, counter-intuitively, increase the risk of the endeavour.

As mentioned above, the past is not always a useful guide for the future and negative impacts can happen at great speed, potentially catching you completely unaware and unprepared. Scenarios are most useful when the influencing factors are few but big and when the uncertainty about the consequences is high. As careers progress, enterprises mature and experience accumulates; you may find it useful to review previous scenario analyses and compare them with reality to see if, and how, mistakes were made.

At both the individual and enterprise level, carrying out proper scenario analysis can help guide current actions that may be later brought into focus by subsequent events. For example, politicians in the run-up to elections have a habit of painting themselves into a corner through the pre-election pledges they make. Embarrassing U-turns can follow such pledges shortly after they form a government, and this can have major reputational repercussions. A broader example might be where the material that we put up on social media now is viewable later and in a very different context by others who can play an important role in determining our future circumstances. How will your social media profile look to a HR team considering you for a future role?

As a final word on scenario analysis, it is worth mentioning the potential impacts that evolving complexity in business arrangements and operations can have. For example, the currently prevalent outsourcing business model, whereby specialist contractors and subcontractors are employed to perform major tasks that typically require advanced technological expertise, can be severely tested when major accidents occur due to negligence by one or more parties or other unforeseen events.

The Deepwater Horizon oil spill in the Gulf of Mexico in 2010 is a prime example. This is the world's largest oil spill to date and involved BP as the platform owner and also large contractors Transocean and Halliburton, who provided the ocean drilling rig and much of the well expertise (BOEMRE/US Coast Guard, 2011). The incident occurred when an exploration well 5,600m deep and in 1,600m water depth experienced a catastrophic blowout followed by a fatal explosion and fire on the rig in which 11 workers were killed. The rig sank shortly after and very substantial amounts of oil leaked into the Gulf of Mexico in the ensuing months. The fallout from this disaster and the controversial clean-up operation afterward has been enormous in terms of health, environment, and reputational and financial cost.

While BP, with a current market capitalisation north of 60 billion USD, is a very long-established energy company that has operated very successfully and survived many economic downturns in its time, the Deepwater Horizon incident seriously threatened its entire future. The CEO at the time memorably demonstrated his poor grasp of the situation in various post-disaster car-crash interviews and the share price roughly halved in the period following the accident. An original small leak in one of the thousands of its drilled wells had cascaded into a disaster of monumental proportions while the whole world watched a number of fruitless well-plugging attempts. This was well outside the scope of any scenario planning that BP might have undertaken and the litigious relationship with its contractors and subcontractors only served to exacerbate the situation. In July 2015, *The Economist* reported the pre-tax costs for BP related to the whole incident as being 53.8 billion USD, which is many multiples of all previous benefits derived from the cost-cutting measures that led directly or indirectly to the incident occurring and its severity. This has led to a fundamental change in how risk is assessed by companies such as BP in scenario analyses for the US oil and gas industry.

Reflection points

- Explain the possible benefits of doing scenario analysis in the context of strategic planning by taking a real example.
- Write down four scenarios relating to the operations of an enterprise you are familiar with. What strategic measures can be taken to ensure successful outcomes in all cases?
- What can be learned from the Deepwater Horizon oil spill case in terms of scenario analysis?

SWOT analysis

Throughout the course of this book, we have already made references to SWOT analysis, which is a widely adopted analytical tool that can be applied at all levels from individuals through to products, services, locations, business units, and whole organisations. Some internet sources claim that the originator of the tool was Stanford University professor Albert Humphrey, who used SWOT analysis in a research project he was leading in the 1960s and 1970s. Other names have also been mentioned; it has for instance been pointed out that Harvard academics used the term SWOT in the 1960s. But regardless of who coined the term, SWOT is a well-known concept in strategic management and a fundamental tool in strategic planning (Helms & Nixon, 2010).

SWOT analysis provides a structured way of compiling information, extracting the essentials, and presenting these results in a readily understood matrix format (see Figure 7.5). Strengths and weaknesses relate to the internal environment of an enterprise, while opportunities and threats relate to the external environment.

In Figure 7.6, we give an example of an overview SWOT analysis for a knowledge-based SME. The analysis captures and expresses the most important considerations and provides a key directional guide for deciding on a new strategic action plan.

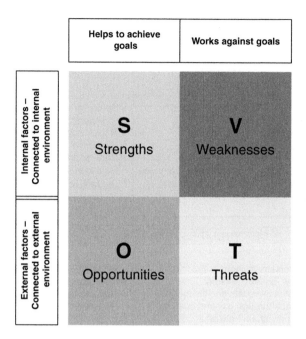

	Helps to achieve goals	Works against goals
Internal factors – **Connected to internal environment**	**S** Strengths	**V** Weaknesses
External factors – **Connected to external environment**	**O** Opportunities	**T** Threats

Figure 7.5

SWOT analysis – overview.

The basic matrix shown in Figure 7.6 can be used to frame the most important elements under each category and as part of the structure of brainstorming sessions during the analysis stage in conjunction with a range of guiding questions. For example, *intellectual capital* might provide a useful focus for capturing the competences of employees and the capability of the organisation under strengths and weaknesses. For instance: in which field(s) is knowledge invested and what are the skills to be found there? Are there knowledge gaps or qualification/certification gaps? Will key employees be available to work into the future? Are the right people doing the right jobs? Is the organisational culture a positive one? Is employee retention an issue? Is information such as business process knowledge properly recorded and readily available for reference? (see Figure 7.7).

An appropriate next step would be for you to look at *finances*, including both cash flow in the short term and budgeting in the longer term. Is there enough liquidity to continue operations if there are missed or delayed payments or a temporary dip in sales? Does our current budget for the next year leave us exposed to a change in circumstances? Will we need to return to investors for funding? You can then look at the *processes*, of which there can be many, that together constitute a key aspect of the internal environment. For example, these can be processes relating to: (a) value-adding activities;

	Helps to achieve goals	Works against goals
Internal environment	**STRENGTHS** S > Good all round financial health > Unique abilities > Diverse team experience > Established track record > Latest technology/methods > Flexibility to suit customer demands > Close proximity to main market	**WEAKNESSES** W > Behind on certification > Experience being underutilised > Reluctancy to expand horizons > Over-reliance on key personnel > Poor record keeping > Replacement of staff due to retire > Old facilities costly to modify/expand
External environment	**OPPORTUNITIES** O > Overseas markets > New industry sectors > Increased sustainability focus > Leads through existing customers > Supply chain networks > New strategic alliances > Business cycle upturn	**THREATS** T > Imminent legislation changes > New market entrants > Costs to penetrate new markets > New employee pipeline > Externally-imposed bureaucracy > Changing customer demands > Cost of living rise for employees

Figure 7.6

Overview SWOT analysis example for a knowledge-based enterprise.

	STRENGTHS	WEAKNESSES
OPPORTUNITIES	Take advantage of opportunities	Have an eye on the competition
THREATS	Build up internal strengths	Turn things around

Figure 7.7

Summary of a SWOT analysis.

(b) customers; (c) suppliers; (d) partners; (e) other external stakeholders; (f) compliance; (g) data storage and usage; (h) innovation and productivity; (i) technology use; and (j) communications. Finally, the *market* should be considered using customer analysis data: what is the current customer profile and how satisfied and how loyal are they? How strong is the value chain from beginning to end and what is the worth of the products or services being supplied?

In Chapter 5 and Chapter 6 we discussed many different aspects relating to the external environment including those associated with PESTLE analysis and a range of market considerations. From the perspective of an enterprise, these can be viewed as being either opportunities or threats, and the purpose of formal SWOT analysis is to summarise the most important factors under each category and the necessary level of detail required in each case.

Let's take the example of the impact of existing regulations, and their proposed changes, in the areas of competition and data protection law and right to privacy in the EU, and how these (will) impact Internet companies such as Google, Facebook, and Twitter. In Google's case, the EU Commission has recently been closely studying its business practices in terms of compliance with competition rules and it could face potential fines of up to 10% of annual sales. With so much at stake, this has become a very hotly contested and technical area. One of the principal areas of contention relates to Google's Android-OEM contracts and app-install requirements, while other areas include issues related to search results and various other services provided as well as a range of aspects relating to data protection. The online search market has grown enormously in value in the last 15 years, with Google well out in front, but new and existing competitors are constant threats who are looking to increase market share and targeting the sweet spot in user search journeys where solid purchasing ideas are being formed. We can differentiate between *initial searches*, *specific searches*, and *revised searches*. Google is very likely to be used for an initial search based on a generic description (e.g. East London builders' merchants), but this may direct the user onto topical sites where *vertical search* is possible and specific searches may be done through one of these leading to product choices. If no purchasing decision is made then the user may return to Google with a much more specific revised search (e.g. BG 45A DP Switch & Neon Flatplate Brushed Stainless Steel) or they may abandon the search. Advertisers, of course, are interested in where and when they can have maximum influence during the overall funnelling process, which has meant online marketing strategy has become an area of rapidly growing complexity.

Porter's five forces competition theory model described before is a useful structural guide to identifying opportunities and threats in the external environment together with other specific market factors. For example: how large is the current market? Is it growing or declining? Are there any possible new markets that have significant potential? Who are the principal competitors (direct and indirect)? What are their strengths and weaknesses? What are their main policies and goals? What choice of suppliers is there and what power do they hold? What power do buyers hold?

SWOT analysis can be aimed at digging a little deeper, whether in relation to the internal or external environment, in order to evaluate the different factors using the right level of detail required (Olsen, 2007). Let's return to the topic of *intellectual capital* in relation to an organisation's strengths and weaknesses in the internal environment. In this context, we should ask how good an enterprise is in relation to:

- Its level of in-house expertise.
- Leveraging knowledge-based resources.
- Communicating the enterprise's vision and strategy.
- Team building and collaboration.
- Retaining existing talent.
- Hiring new talent.
- Supporting innovation.
- Managing knowledge originating in the company.
- Communicating this knowledge throughout the company.
- Implementing strategic action plans.

Different topics relating to the internal environment of an enterprise such as finances, processes, marketing, and innovation might also be addressed in equivalent detail using a tailored range of the most appropriate questions. Chapters 5 and 6 provide source material for this process. The results can be shown in the form of an evaluation matrix (see Table 7.2). In this example we again refer to the same knowledge-based enterprise we referenced earlier. The use of four measures (excellent, good, ok, and poor) allows for a more accurate portrayal of strengths and weaknesses and the "comments" column can be important for adding enlightening details.

Other columns can be added such as "ranking" to highlight the most influential factors as well as "timing" to prioritise and schedule when things should be improved/fixed. The simple analysis provided by this table shows that, in the context of a largely healthy picture of enterprise intellectual capital, there are also some red flags. For instance, there is due to be a *changing of the guard* as a number of key staff are set to retire and smooth succession is always of concern in such circumstances. The enterprise is also weak when it comes to managing information based on previous experience and communicating it throughout the company. Management, in this case, have identified the problem and reacted by initiating research on ERP options. Other simpler approaches may also help such as more frequent cross-disciplinary meetings and formal reporting.

As each enterprise is different, so will the nature of the topics and questions that are most relevant to the internal environment be different, as will the opportunities and threats in the external environment. The material in Chapter 5 and Chapter 6 will provide you with much source material for formulating your own question sets. Threats and opportunities lurk in many places, the most important being the environment, market, and competition. Consider an example of a simple method to implement the analysis using an evaluation matrix for threats and opportunities for the industry. Factors to consider include: competition in the industry, new competitors, products that can replace current products, the bargaining position of suppliers and

Table 7.2 Intellectual capital strength/weakness analysis for the knowledge-based company. The information is presented in the form of an evaluation matrix built on a series of focused questions

Topics being assessed	Strengths		Weaknesses		Comments
	Excellent	Good	OK	Not OK	
Having the right in-house expertise	X			(X)	(X) Refers to the fact that a number of key staff are due to retire shortly
Leveraging knowledge-based resources			X		Experience without qualifications is holding back potential
Communicating the enterprise's vision and strategy		X			Vision is clear but strategy not so much
Team building and collaboration	X				Excellent team leaders across all operations
Retaining existing talent	X			(X)	See above regarding retiring staff
Hiring new talent	X			(X)	(X) Good candidates are applying and being hired – just not enough
Supporting innovation			X		Tendency to rely on tried and tested methods
Managing knowledge originating in the company				X	Better enterprise resource planning (ERP) systems needed
Communicating this knowledge throughout the company				X	As for above
Implementing strategic action plans		X			Level of commitment good rather than great

the bargaining position of customers. Here we refer to Porter's five forces competition theory model, which we have already discussed. Table 7.3 illustrates just such an implementation. Items from the five forces model are in the first column. The example uses the same knowledge-based company as was previously discussed.

You could, of course, find more items for the first column, using a brainstorming session, with a focus on threats and opportunities in the environment in general. Or you could use other analytic tools, such as PESTLE analysis. Finally, it is worth mentioning that these are items that have come up in interviews with customers, employees, and suppliers. For each of the items in column one, the question is asked of whether it will affect the company immediately, in the next few years, in the next 5–10 years or never. Respondents are asked to indicate whether the item involves a threat or an opportunity and are invited to draw conclusions and propose actions.

Table 7.3 Implementation of a SWOT analysis – threats and opportunities in a knowledge-based company

Topics being assessed	Impact on the company				Threat/ opportunity?	Comments
	Immediately	1–4 years	5–10 years	Never		
Increase of competitors		X			Both	Further study necessary
Possibility of products emerging that could replace the organisation's main product				X	Opportunity	To continue being a leader in the field
Stronger position of suppliers				X	Opportunity	
Stronger position of customers	X				Threat	
More competition on the market	X				Threat	

You should always examine the results of SWOT analysis in the context of what you are trying to do and be careful to draw integrated conclusions, in other words, take account of how different elements are interrelated and how the likely consequences of decisions and actions in one area of the business affect the related areas.

Note that the SWOT analysis can give good input into the formation of a future vision. If strengths have been recognised within an enterprise, they can be used to react to threats and to exploit opportunities. If you detect a weakness, which is related to a threat, it may be time to make a strategic decision, for instance in relation to discontinuing some specific product or activity. You may also find that you have detected opportunities, for instance, new and exciting possibilities in the market, but that some organisational weakness currently precludes you from pursuing them. If that is the case, keep a good eye on what the competition does and explore ways to overcome the weaknesses.

Our knowledge-based SME identified that customers were in a stronger position and, as a result, there would be more competition in the market. This was seen as a threat. On the other hand, the company is doing a great job in hiring competent employees and communicating to them the company's vision and strategy, which is a strength. The opportunity exists for the company to make use of these strengths to mitigate the threats associated with increasing competition.

Sometimes, thinking about threats can actually lead you to opportunities as events may turn out to have a silver lining, or proposed solutions may develop into valuable ideas that have broader applications than originally intended. There are plenty of successful businesses (and projects) that began by trying to find solutions to a particular problem (which they may or may not have solved) but ended up expanding into all kinds of different areas as the work took on a life of its own and led down unexpected paths.

Reflection points

- Explain the difference between weaknesses and threats by using an example.
- Can SWOT analysis be a way to compile the total outcome of all analyses of internal and external environments in strategic planning? Explain by using an example.
- What are the pitfalls of SWOT analysis? Can you explain by using a concrete example?
- How can SWOT analysis be used to pave the way to a future vision? Explain with an example.

Path finding, feasibility analysis, and business case development

Synthesising different sources of information and wayfinding typically involve several layers of activity, a number of which we have already discussed. As you progress, you will identify and quantify existing problems and potential risks as well as highlight opportunities that require active pursuit. From a project management perspective, you are now in the "initiation" phase of the strategic action plan where objectives or needs are being defined and solutions/approaches sought. You can form ideas either individually or collaboratively and further filter these down during group brainstorming sessions where their respective merits and pitfalls are outlined and decided upon. The two main question types guiding this stage relate to feasibility ("Can we…?") and justification ("Should we…?"). Resources might only stretch as far as being able to complete a portion of what is initially planned, so you'll need to prioritise which elements to pursue. It would also be normal at this stage for a project sponsor to be appointed to oversee development of a strategic action plan and drive the process forward. In the *Execution* book in this series, we discuss at length many different aspects relating to best practice at this stage of project work.

As the typical final deliverable here is an ambitious but grounded strategic action plan, you will need to carry out detailed feasibility analysis and business case development at the proposal stage, both for each individual planned element and for the plan as a whole. For simpler elements, it may be sufficient to make final decisions on straightforward actions to take. Where things are more complicated and/or complex, you may need to carry out dedicated studies that can be significant projects in themselves. Remember, we are moving towards identifying targets that are specific, measurable, achievable, realistic, and time-bound (SMART).

Let's take an example. Imagine a port authority wants to develop a new pier. Assessing the feasibility of this project will involve a broad range of considerations including user studies, physical constraints, rough costs, legal issues, environmental aspects, and stakeholder views. If the proposal is deemed as being broadly feasible after initial studies and consultations, then a more comprehensive economic study can be undertaken to better determine both direct and indirect costs and benefits. In this case, the strategic action plan needs to present clear objectives and the principal means by which these will be achieved in order to capture the attention and effectively address the concerns of investors, authorities, and the public alike. Alongside these elements, a strong business case is required that highlights the likely return on investment and all-around benefits. It is also necessary to account for all probable eventualities and address the relevant concerns of key stakeholders.

This is not always achievable, however, and feasibility and business case studies can at times be inconclusive, even if a lot of money has been spent on them. In the UK there tends to be public uproar when it snows and critical infrastructure such as airports is forced to shut down. While highly disruptive at the time, the overall frequency and length of these events are very low, so it can be difficult to justify expensive investment such as an increased number of snow-ploughs and other specialist equipment and supplies. The opportunity costs can be high and investment to counter a more common threat, involving greater numbers of people and with greater impact such as river flooding, might be viewed as being more justified. Again, though, there are numerous considerations in determining the best overall outcomes. For instance, effective containment defenses upstream can lead to greater flooding downstream. Thus, knock-on effects are important to understand but often difficult to foresee.

As we have already referred to in the case of Pruitt-Igoe, it makes sense to implement a strategy on a step-by-step basis, learning from projects that have already started and not over-committing limited resources at too early a stage. Model testing, pilot studies, and pilot projects are good ways to manage risk, but they also need to be of sufficient scale to enable meaningful observations and deliver in a timely fashion. Such work is closely tied in with scenario analysis already discussed.

Reflection points

- You have taken over as the CEO of an IT company and you are planning to do strategic planning. Why and how can feasibility analysis be a part of this process?
- Is feasibility analysis sufficient as a tool to prioritise the resources? Give examples of when it is not enough.

References

BOEMRE (Bureau of Ocean Energy Management, Regulation and Enforcement)/U.S. Coast Guard Joint Investigation Team (2011). Deepwater Horizon Joint Investigation Team releases final report. [online] Boem.gov. Available at: https://www.boem.gov/BOEM-Newsroom/Press-Releases/2011/press0914.aspx [Accessed 1 April 2016].

Earth System Research Laboratory. (n.d.). Globally averaged marine surface annual mean growth rates. [online] esrl.noaa.gov. Available at: https://www.esrl.noaa.gov/gmd/ccgg/trends/full.html [Accessed 30 June 2018].

Eurostat. (n.d.). Asylum statistics. [online] ec.europa.eu. Available at: http://ec.europa.eu/eurostat/statistics-explained/index.php/Asylum_statistics [Accessed 30 June 2018].

Helms M. M. & Nixon J. (2010). Exploring SWOT analysis – Where are we now? *Journal of Strategy and Management, Emerald,* 3(3), 215–251.

Icelandic Tourist Board. (2018). Numbers of foreign visitors – Icelandic Tourist Board. [online] Available at: https://www.ferdamalastofa.is/en/recearch-and-statistics/numbers-of-foreign-visitors [Accessed 24 May 2018].

Johnson G., Scholes K. & Whittington R. (2008). *Exploring Corporate Strategy.* 8th edition. Harlow: Prentice Hall.

Lichtenstein, B., Uhl-Bien, M., Marion, R., Seers, A., Orton, D. & Schreiber, C. (2006). Leadership in emergent events: Exploring the interactive process of leading in complex situations. *Emergence: Complexity and Organization,* 8(4), 2–12.

Meadows, D., Randers, J. & Meadows, D. (2004). *The limits to growth: The 30-year update.* Milton Park: Earthscan.

Morrison, A., & Wensley, R. (1991). Boxing up or boxed in?: A short history of the Boston Consulting Group share/growth matrix. *Journal of Marketing Management,* 7(2), 105–129.

Olsen, E. (2007). *Strategic planning for dummies.* Hoboken: John Wiley & Sons.

Perrow, C. (1984). *Normal accidents: Living with high risk technologies.* Princeton, NJ: Princeton University Press.

Slater, S. F., & Zwirlein, T. J. (1992). Shareholder value and investment strategy using the general portfolio model. *Journal of Management,* 18(4), 717–732.

Wikipedia. (2018, June 28). Gross world product. [online] Wikipedia.org. Available at: https://en.wikipedia.org/wiki/Gross_world_product [Acessed 30 June 2018].

Worldometers. (n.d.). Population of Africa (2018). [online] worldometers.info. Available at: http://www.worldometers.info/world-population/africa-population/

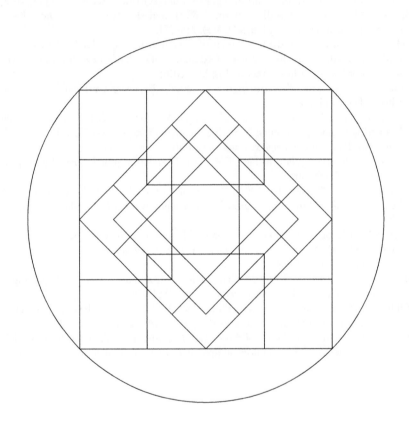

8 Bringing it all together

· ·

We have described many different levels of strategic planning in this book, ranging from large-scale corporate restructuring to more straightforward projects with well-defined outcomes. In Chapter 2 we introduced a generic strategic planning process that combines *strategic thinking* and *planning* that can be tailored to suit the particular circumstances of an enterprise and its undertakings. In the subsequent chapters, we described several stages in the process by which data is gathered and analysed to support making decisions. At this juncture, when the nature of the internal and external environments of an enterprise should be reasonably clear and you have gathered the results of various targeted analyses, it is time for you to form the future.

There are various routes you may take to do this, and your final choice may be determined by a broad range of factors such as experience, abilities, level of complexity, and available resources (e.g. people and money) as well as other factors such as the organisational culture (particularly relating to risk) and level of drive and ambition. The primary aim of this chapter is to describe how a structured approach can be used to produce a strong strategic action plan that delivers results. In the course of this discussion, we also describe and illustrate various kinds of strategies together with common pitfalls.

While the nature of strategic action plans may differ widely, a common element that is essential to them all is that your future vision and any subsequent undertakings to achieve set goals are consistent with the values and mission of an enterprise. Where there is inconsistency, the resulting conflict can have serious repercussions, sometimes irretrievably so. For leaders of the enterprise, this process may present them with tough decisions. High-pressure and conflicting demands on time and resources or for specified results may incrementally threaten to compromise the organisational values. This may be almost imperceptible at first, and unintended or negative outcomes may not be apparent for some time, but reality has a way of bursting even the most well-planned of bubbles (see Figure 8.1).

In practical terms, a strategic planning report should present a clear case for action, which will involve summarising key information relating to the current status and aspects that are driving change. When it comes to detailed planning and implementation, you need to designate responsibility, focus on

Figure 8.1

Strategic thinking, strategic planning.

realistic deliverables, and determine carefully what approaches are best taken to achieve set goals. We will discuss a variety of practical approaches and the general application of project management methodology to deliver results.

Round up

Let's start by returning to the process diagram first introduced in Chapter 2. By committing to this structured approach for your strategic planning, you are much less likely to overlook important considerations, regardless of scale and circumstances (see Figure 8.2).

Let's take a few moments to go through the different elements in the process model and provide a more in-depth exploration of each in terms of finalising strategy as well as commenting on a range of general strategic approaches

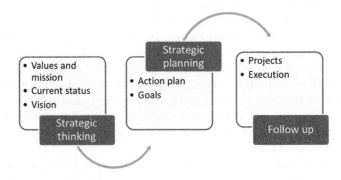

Figure 8.2

Strategic planning process diagram – simplified version.

and their relative merits and pitfalls. The desired outcome in all cases is a robust strategic action plan that has been thoroughly thought through, and which has the necessary support and resources for its implementation.

As we also discussed in the opening chapters, participation in the overall process of strategic planning is key, and it is vital that you build up a strong representative team to carry this out. Those tasked with delivering results need to be on board with the overall vision and the best way to achieve this is through ensuring their genuine involvement in the decision-making phase. All aspects of the status quo approach should be reviewed with an open mind and the opportunity given to challenge fixed mindsets. What is presently good and works well should be recognised as such, but it also needs to be assessed to check its continued relevance and suitability in the face of new challenges. On the other hand, if radical changes are made, they are more likely to unbalance an enterprise that has developed its own internal dynamic stability over time. Sometimes with market disruption, this can be unavoidable, but if a previous strategic planning exercise had anticipated such events, then the transition may have been made smoother.

For individual projects, you need to assess overall risk in conjunction with separate risk elements and account for a number of different scenarios fully. Keep in mind Murphy's Law or *"whatever can go wrong will go wrong"* in doing this. It can take great courage to take a stance against a particular activity in a pre-emptive fashion as it may be some time later, or even never (at least with any accuracy), that you can say it was the right approach to take. During the Spanish Flu pandemic in 1918, for example, American Samoa operated a strict quarantine protocol for visiting vessels, while nearby Western Samoa (under the authority of New Zealand) did not. The results of letting the ship *S.S. Talune* dock in Apia without quarantine restrictions rapidly led to the deaths of around 22% of the population in Western Samoa, while there were no corresponding deaths in American Samoa. Another very tragic example is when Chinese hydrologist Chen Xing recommended that 12 sluice gates be installed during the design phase of the Banqiao Dam in eastern China. This was considered to be far too conservative by those directing the project and only five were eventually installed when it was completed in 1952. Xing also had many other issues with the entire river management programme includ-ing the specifications of a number of other dams. The subsequent catastrophic failure of Banqiao Dam in 1975, during unprecedented rainfall and a consecu-tive series of other structural failures in the enormous deluge that followed, led to all his worst fears being realised. In total, an estimated 171,000 people died as a direct result of the flood and some 11 million were displaced from their homes and livelihood.

Strategic goals usually take the form of straightforward statements; e.g. build a dam to store 100 million cubic meters of water in four years, increase revenue by 50% in three years, reduce employee numbers by 10% in two years or complete the acquisition of GBP 10 million worth of properties for subsequent rental within the next 12 months. There will be more than one way that a particular strategy can be delivered, however, and the attitude and culture of an enterprise as a whole (but particular its leaders) is important in determining what approaches you take. This crosses over into the discussion on values that follows and covers the approach taken e.g. in terms of quality, risk, employees, customers, suppliers, stakeholders, the environment, laws/regulations, and so on.

In relation to employees, for example, if there is a perceived requirement to reduce numbers, different organisations will have a different cultural approach. Some enterprises – particularly those in industries involving sensitive commercial information or client relationships – will give people 20 minutes to clear their desk after being served notice and have security personnel see them to the door. Other less draconian enterprises will work with those affected, e.g. by giving them plenty of notice and generous redundancy offers, trying to offer them alternatives such as reduced hours, facilitating retraining, or helping with finding work in other places. Different market sectors reflect their own realities and consequent managerial mindsets but, in general, high staff turnover should be viewed as an indication of poor management and is not something that is readily associated with the sustainable strategy. Remember the power of reciprocity: employees are most likely to mirror the level of respect given to them by management. Treat your employees with respect as they are important to you and they will be more likely to reward you with loyalty and support; don't and they will think nothing of leaving.

Another important dimension in strategy is the extent to which customers and other external stakeholders are genuinely valued or respected. Are suppliers kept waiting for months to be paid for no valid reason? Are emails left unanswered leading to irate customers on the phone? Are customers being given the proper information about products and services? Has there been a proper level of engagement with protesters and should their opinions have been proactively sought? There are many complex issues here that require extra focus, planning, and effort and yet, by not doing these simple things, relationships can be needlessly damaged.

Reflection points

- Why is it vital to build up a strong representative team to carry out the strategic planning? What is the risk of not doing this?
- Do you have examples of Murphy's law in the context of strategic planning? Explain.

Values

As described in Chapter 2, *values* are those principles or standards that are fundamental to an enterprise, reflecting its philosophy and approach, and acting as fixed guides in relation to decision-making. Values describe how an enterprise is different from others and they should not be subject to compromise. The values of an enterprise reflect what it represents and what it is that connects it with the employees. They represent the focus in an enterprise's operations and projects, what it is known for, and therefore they have a fundamental effect on all of its operations and attitudes as well as behaviour within the company.

Values reside deep within the organisational culture and are typically strongly influenced by the founders of an enterprise as well as other historic and current influential leaders. They are important in the sense of what influences everyday decision-making rather than what is written down, i.e. what matters are *real* values rather than *stated* values. In corporate literature, considerable emphasis is placed on stated values, which will normally have their genesis in widely accepted ethical practice. It is assumed that all those directly associated with an enterprise will have internalised these values and that they guide their decision-making. So, for instance, when an enterprise is known for meeting the demands of customers, for being a good employer, and for professionalism – to mention but a few things – anyone who has dealings with this enterprise, regardless of who they are dealing with, should have similar positive experiences.

When values become strong and deep-rooted in the consciousness of an enterprise, they unite all the employees, no matter where they find themselves in the hierarchy. In this way, values can function as the invisible ties that govern how things are tackled; they become the outward hallmark of an enterprise. For example, when the American engineering and construction company Bechtel came to Iceland to build Alcoa's aluminium plant in Reydarfjördur, the great emphasis they put on security and very detailed risk analysis were unusual in an Icelandic work context, but simply reflected how they routinely operated worldwide (see Figure 8.3).

For the strategic planning consultant analysing current status, grasping the real values of an enterprise in their entirety is not always a straightforward task. Using the iceberg analogy, the explicit, written values represent only what is visible above the surface, while what is unwritten or tacit exists below the surface and can be difficult to penetrate, but very real nonetheless. For example, we can all probably agree that the following values signify good intentions:

- Integrity and Honesty (or "*think straight, talk straight*").
- One Firm, One Voice.
- Training to a Shared Method.

The above values are actually key ones drawn up by founder Arthur Andersen in relation to the auditing/consulting company of the same name and provide the backdrop to a classic tale of the clash between values and aggressive strategy (Squires, 2003). Below is a shortened account, highlighting key developments in this story that led to the company's sudden demise in 2002.

Figure 8.3

Values of an organisation.

Arthur E. Andersen was an accounting professor at Northwestern University in the US who started a small auditing practice in 1913. Soon after, the president of a local railroad approached him to approve a transaction that would have falsely lowered the company's expenses and boosted earnings. While being in a precarious financial position himself, Andersen famously told the president that there was "not enough money in the city of Chicago" to make him do it. This approach bolstered his reputation as the client subsequently filed for bankruptcy shortly after. Andersen's personal values were summed up in the above values and a reputation for probity was carefully nurtured by his next few successors that ran the firm, most notably Leon Spacek. From an early stage, though, it was recognised by Andersen and others that the potential conflict of interest between the auditing and consulting work of the company needed to be carefully managed to avoid damaging credibility.

Over time, however, the consulting side of the company rose in prominence and, as anticipated, their role differed very much from the auditing side. Their focus was on bringing about change in the companies that they consulted for and early developments in this regard included installing some of the first computerised accounting systems for large companies such as General Electric in the 1950s. Over the next few decades, tensions built up in the company as the consulting side, which grew rapidly as IT specialists, resented having the auditing side running things (as clearly demonstrated in a key splitting vote in 1979), and the requirements of audit independence did not sit well with developing close business consulting arrangements.

Things came to a head in 1989 when the auditing and consulting divisions split, but still remained part of an umbrella organisation with a complex profit-sharing agreement between them. 1989 was also the year of the infamous "Eye of the Tiger" stunt at a gathering of audit partners in Dallas that set the tone for what was to come in the 1990s. To this rousing rock anthem, a live tiger was brought on stage, a strong representation of the new aggressive strategy to bring in extra business from clients that the audit partners were expected to fully embrace. What followed during the next decade was driven largely by bravado as the consulting side continued to grow its revenue per partner and resented having to transfer some of their profits to the other side. For their part, the auditing side underwent a major strategic change of direction, ditching a high percentage of experienced partners in a purge in 1992 and pitching themselves for a much broader range of business. A typical change that was noticeable at this time (but that had started some years earlier) was that, instead of becoming partners, Andersen employees would leave and go to work for big clients while maintaining close links to their former employer. Opportunities outside of traditional auditing such as advising on tax strategy and advice on corporate-finance issues were pursued.

The next major structural development came in 1998 when Andersen Consulting broke all links with Arthur Andersen (who were also developing a distinct consulting side to their business aimed at smaller enterprises known as AABC), eventually renaming themselves as Accenture in 2001. This resulted in a large loss of revenue for Arthur Andersen and the pressure grew to aggressively pursue new business opportunities. After being named top partner in 1998, Steve Samek introduced the "2X" strategy, which meant, for example, that a partner bringing in USD 2 million in audit fees had a performance target of bringing in USD 4 million in consulting fees. Increasingly, the company was decentralised, and partners focused on individual targets while cultivating deeper relationships with their clients, employing increasingly questionable methods to account for peculiar transactions. This overall strategy provided the backdrop to a number of high-profile Arthur Andersen auditing scandals that came to the surface up to the year 2002. These included Waste Management, Enron, and WorldCom.

There are many different aspects to the Arthur Andersen story that illustrate the realities of the modern business world and the inevitable negative consequences of pursuing a strategy that conflicts with established values. This theme is not unique to the auditing/consulting world and many other examples can be given from other areas. For example, academic medical journals are expected to provide a high standard of peer review and weed out poor quality scientific articles or those based on dubious research before they are published. But they undertake this role against the backdrop of receiving advertising revenue (or other sources of revenue such as for reprint orders) from pharmaceutical and medical device companies. According to Richard Smith, who edited the prestigious *British Medical Journal* for 25 years, this conflict in the academic publishing world is very often settled in favour of increasing revenue and supporting the marketing machine at the expense of delivering quality information (Smith, 2005). The very basis on which such publications are bought, however, is that customers trust them to contain the best available information. If it subsequently turns out that this is not the case, then the foundations of the entire enterprise are unstable.

Another prominent example of divergence from stated values is the 2015 diesel emissions scandal at Volkswagen. The fallout from this episode is likely to rumble on as the activity that was undertaken to cheat the environmental regulatory tests was so clearly at odds with the stated values of the company. Enterprises should operate on the basis that all knowledge comes out into the public arena eventually and, as a result, should think very carefully about pursuing strategies that clash with their stated values.

Leading culpable individuals in such cases can often ride the wave, personally doing very well financially, while their company or organisation is being driven towards the rocks. They can then deny responsibility and plead ignorance or jump ship at the opportune moment, continuing to pursue a successful career in the same role or elsewhere provided that they can avoid the legal or other consequences of their actions. This refers back to the *principal-agent problem* discussed before that can represent a major dilemma for enterprises that are seeking to pursue a sustainable strategy with foundations based on trust. For the vested owners of an enterprise and those it employs who do their work, the consequences of pursuing a strategy that diverges from established values are very likely to be negative as the impact of decisions made in the short term become reality over the course of time. Imagine a town council in which a few corrupt individuals gain financially by taking bribes to subvert the town planning process. The town in question will earn a reputation for poor governance and corrupt planning and will be avoided by potential investors or employers, leading to boarded-up main streets and financial decline. This can also happen at a regional or national level. As another example, consider a local authority that issues a tender for the construction of social housing. They may choose the winning bid on the basis of lowest cost, but if the standard of construction is subsequently very poor and the assumed values of *integrity* and *dedication to quality* are sacrificed on the altar of profit, the projects that follow will be fundamentally flawed. In the time it takes for this to come to light, however, the construction company may have moved on out of reach or folded and taxpayers may be left to foot the reparation bill.

It should be clear that a sustainable strategy that is focused on customer satisfaction and repeat business over the longer term should be in harmony with the stated values of an enterprise. This also applies to all activities undertaken in the execution of such a strategy. Despite the cautionary tales outlined above, a high percentage of established enterprises choose their values wisely and stick by them.

So how are values to be dealt with in terms of strategic planning? If you collate all the available information and invited responses, you should be in a position to get a good handle on the real values of any enterprise. To start with, invite representatives from different levels of an enterprise from the grass roots through to management to answer the following questions:

- What is the enterprise known for? What should it be known for?
- What currently shapes enterprise culture? What should shape it?
- How is the work of the enterprise conducted? How should it be conducted?
- How does the enterprise rate against competitors? How should it rate against them?
- How are the clients, suppliers, and community respected? How should they be respected?

The first question in each case is supposed to reflect current enterprise values, while the second question reflects personal values. You can gather and compare all the responses against each other as well as against stated enterprise values. In fact, by asking these questions and soliciting considered responses, you should be able to ascertain views on *values, mission, current status,* and *future vision.*

Given that there may be a significant divergence in how people at different levels within an enterprise answer these questions, or even within different subgroups at the same level, use your judgement as to what the most appropriate approach is. At times, confidentiality and anonymity may be required, while, at other times, an informal brainstorming session mixing all levels can work well. In cases where you feel that potential contributors may be afraid to state their real opinions for fear of reprisal or how others may view them, you need to consider carefully how to overcome this. Inviting confidential submissions or using anonymous questionnaires may help in a number of cases although sometimes even these can lead to the complainant being identified, purely by the nature of their contribution. For more complex cases, face-to-face meetings with the ensuing discussion held in strict confidence can be the best way to get the true views of others, but great trust must be required. Sometimes an imaginative approach may help to provide a solution such as picking up on nonverbal communication from people and taking the initiative in confronting issues in a roundabout way that cannot be traced to anyone in particular. Experience is a very important asset to have when faced with delicate situations and those who are new to such situations should be extra careful about the approach they take.

There are different types of authority and it is very often the case that charismatic individuals, who may or not be at the managerial level, are most influential in setting the behavioural example that others follow. As we saw with the case of Arthur Andersen, however, various prevailing internal and external circumstances can also be strongly influential. On the one hand, the competitive relationship between the auditing and consulting divisions of the company in that case drove a culture of one-upmanship, while, on the other hand, financial deregulation and the rise of dubious financial engineering in the external environment encouraged a new breed of aggressive managerial performers with lower levels of empathy, risk aversion, and loyalty to become more prominent in decision-making.

By holding up a mirror to an enterprise, you can encourage both management and employees alike to question the prevailing values, but any significant directional change of values has to come from the group as a whole. Writing down a new set of values or reiterating the importance of existing values counts for little if they are not representative of reality. At the end of the day, prevalent values tend to percolate down through the different levels of an enterprise from those in positions of leadership and can have deep roots that strongly influence attitudes and behaviour. If individual employees cannot identify themselves with the values of an enterprise, then there can be ongoing tension and a rift may develop between them and their colleagues. This is a prime cause of work-related stress with a common enough example being a conscientious and ambitious worker who recognises systematic failings being faced with the prevailing unwritten attitude of "*don't rock the boat, this is just how things are done around here.*"

The best way of synchronising the values of individuals with those of an organisation is to give them the opportunity to take part in defining the values of an organisation in an overall environment in which those in leadership positions take such engagement seriously. A fun way to accomplish this can be to have employees define their values for themselves and discuss them with each other in a group, and then discuss the organisation's values as a whole and determine what they should consist of. A variant of this process is to start with examining the values of individuals, followed by the values of work units, the values of interested parties, and at last the values of the organisation as a whole.

Considering the essential values of an enterprise, you might ask: what should it be known for? Should the emphasis be on the maximisation of profits? Quality? Showing ethical responsibility? Complying with all relevant sustainability principles? Creating new knowledge? Being family-friendly? Chosen representative values will be part of the preamble involved in making decisions and characterise enterprise culture. In tandem with this is ascertaining what are the dominant values of employees, management, and owners, which is something that cannot be automatically answered. The overall job of drawing up the values of an enterprise requires preparation and needs to be carried out with care in order to guarantee that the values go deep enough to matter and that they reflect reality.

Clear values can endorse a powerful corporate culture, which in turn can lead to a stronger feeling of solidarity within an enterprise and consequently better performance. However, experience shows that strong values and cohesion within groups increases the probability of *groupthink*. This term is used in the negative sense, describing defective decision-making whereby individuals forming a group are solely concerned with reaching a consensus decision, being unwilling to challenge the prevailing wisdom and thereby excluding any critical evaluation of alternative ideas or viewpoints. A basic requirement to counteract it is that there is always a *Devil's advocate* in any decision meeting and contrarian viewpoints are given a proper airing.

Values form an organisation's culture and they can be used as instruments to affect the culture. This culture – which often consists of unwritten benchmarks, ideas, and rules – is reflected in key employees' conduct, who may be considered as exemplary heroes within an organisation of whom tales are told. For example, we can imagine the culture within a rescue team where the core values are most likely to invoke a sense of courage, team spirit, skill, endurance, and confidence. Those individuals that best illustrate the core values in this instance will stand out and their colleagues will inevitably look up to them. The culture in such a team will also be influenced by various customs and traditions, such as the welcoming of new members and how incremental successes and heroic achievements are celebrated. Much of this happens automatically or informally. It is, however, a useful exercise to identify the values that team members want to honour and the methods they want to use to share these values.

When it comes to consciously defining predominant (or corporate) values, various interested parties should be kept in mind including customers, suppliers, users, clients, employees, owners, sponsors, creditors, families of employees, authorities, etc. In the end, there is always compromise involved in agreeing on the right value statements that convey the right message to all parties. Care should be taken though not to just say any old thing to keep the credulous public happy. The court of public opinion has been shown to be hard on enterprises who do not operate according to their stated values and, as stated already, it should be assumed that any such nefarious activity will eventually become public knowledge.

Values are in many ways a complex phenomenon although there is also a certain tendency to unnecessarily complicate the definition of their conceptual meaning in strategic planning. In essence, they reflect the belief that certain attitudes and/or forms of behaviour are more desirable than others. Values tend to be expressed in terms of a statement of intent with the terms "we" and/or "our" present in each case. Avoid setting values that are too general as they will be essentially meaningless. The foundations of strategic planning as a whole are based on such statements (usually between five to seven in number as a general guide) that, under normal circumstances, conform to reality. Regretfully, experience shows that the professed values of an enterprise are not always in keeping with the values reflected in their operations. It is, however, imperative to have faith in the integrity of strategic planning and to recognise the importance of values in this process, i.e. that the values described and expressed are as much in keeping with reality as possible and refer to the intellectual and moral valuables which function as guiding lights in the organisation's operations. For this reason, they should appear prominently in strategic planning reports and be adequately referenced when decisions are being described.

To conclude, below are two examples of sets of corporate values that illustrate somewhat different approaches, but nonetheless, give a strong sense of what the enterprise in each case is about:

British Broadcasting Corporation (BBC) – The world's leading public service broadcaster (Bbc.co.uk, n.d.)

- *Trust is the foundation of the BBC: we are independent, impartial and honest.*
- *Audiences are at the heart of everything we do.*
- *We take pride in delivering quality and value for money.*
- *Creativity is the lifeblood of our organisation.*
- *We respect each other and celebrate our diversity so that everyone can give their best.*
- *We are one BBC: great things happen when we work together.*

Moz – A US search-engine-optimisation (SOS) company founded in 2004 (Moz.com, n.d.)

Our TAGFEE Code. The core values of Moz – Transparent, Authentic, Generous, Fun, Empathetic, and Exceptional.

Reflection points

- What is your own experience of the extent to which corporate values influence the operation of a company during difficult times?
- How do corporate values influence strategic planning? Explain by using an example.

Mission Statements: creep, neglect, and erosion

The *mission* of an enterprise describes what it uncompromisingly aims to do on the basis of its values. The mission is usually conveyed in the form of a short and concise descriptive statement that is indicative of the operations of the enterprise on a day-to-day basis. It may sometimes be referred to in other ways such as "*What We Do*" or "*Our Role.*" The mission should state the fundamental purpose or point of the organisation and it should be a guideline for decision-making at all levels. It should answer such questions as: what does the enterprise make? What are its activities? What added value does it provide? What are the needs it fulfils? For whom does it exist? What does it aspire to achieve, and with whom? For profit-driven enterprises, making money by selling products and/or services is automatically assumed to be part of the mission so this does not need to be highlighted. For non-profit organisations, the mission is a particularly strong element in their identity and often rigidly guides their activities. For example, an organisation may state that their work is aimed towards children, those with disabilities, refugees, cancer sufferers, victims of natural disasters, and so on. It is also common for the mission statement to include information on the geographic scope of the organisation. The government of other official institutions usually base their mission on the relevant laws and regulations that guide their area of operations. A well-written mission statement can be a source of strength for those who work within an organisation and so it should be written in a way that is instantly memorable and that conveys desirable attributes, e.g. competence, responsibility, and enthusiasm (see Figure 8.4).

During the overall process of strategic planning, you'll want to make frequent reference to the mission statement to guide your decision-making as it really sets the tone for what the enterprise is aiming to do. The objectives and critical success factors (CFS) of the enterprise should be emphasised, as should the needs of customers, users, or clients. It is also good practice to include what it is that makes an enterprise (or brand) strong and to get the views of customers and others in this regard. Given its significance, any changes to the current mission statement should be widely consulted on amongst employees, managers, and owners and receive broad-based approval. A simple way of doing this visually in a work session is to begin by drawing a circle on a piece of paper. Individuals may then, in turn, submit singular specific statements that express the mission on post-its, following which the group decides whether they belong inside or outside the circle. Once final consensus agreement is reached, what is left inside the circle is considered to constitute the overall mission of the enterprise, while everything that is outside can be ignored. Since the Mission Statement goes to the core of the organisation's purpose, you'll need to keep the final statement focused and relatively brief.

This exercise can be especially beneficial for new enterprises that are still exploring their business rationale and have not settled on a firm mission statement. Defining the mission may require some time for development and

Figure 8.4

The mission.

refinement of your initial ideas before the final result is made public. It should begin with a draft form of words and allow the text to develop and mature during the strategic planning period. Various sources should be consulted in this process including what is declared in the articles of association, legal objectives, market considerations, and core competencies. If a newly defined mission is not in line with the articles of association, you'll need to decide whether the mission or the legal documents should be adjusted. In the latter case, the requisite changes must be made according to the legal process and reported formally to the relevant authorities. Remember, the mission must be compatible with the values and culture of an enterprise. It should be phrased in terms that are general enough to allow some flexibility but, at the same time, never vague or unclear.

When looking at the activities of an enterprise, part of your work involves reflecting on the details of the mission statement (or draft) and comparing them with reality. Is it your view that the enterprise in question is fulfilling their stated roles in what they practice? Aside from making direct changes to the mission statement, you may come across three common issues while carrying out this exercise. These are *mission creep*, *mission neglect*, and *mission erosion*. Let's look at some examples of these concepts.

Mission creep: when operations or projects expand beyond their original goals, those responsible may lose focus and begin to concentrate more on peripheral activities of limited value, at the expense of core activities, or step on the toes of others and provoke a response. What is and isn't part of the mission can be a grey area, and those activities that could be identified as mission creep may or may not be adopted in revised mission statements. Strategic choice implies both what you decide to do and what you decide not to do. Circumstantial success, owing to good fortune rather than clever strategy and perseverance, can often encourage mission creep as it provides a misleading signal about your organisational capabilities and can lead decision-makers towards risky expansionary investments. Unchecked mission creep can lead to resources becoming "stretched too thin" with the result that the overall system of operations becomes vulnerable to changes in circumstances and external shocks.

In the sphere of public services, many countries have opted to consolidate their strategic decision-making and administration in areas such as transport or infrastructure into new powerful public authorities, often through the amalgamation of a number of previously separate entities. The Swedish Transport Administration has a mission that now extends far beyond projects such as road building to the extent that they are developers of Sweden's plan for the holistic integration of the entire transport system including road, rail, shipping, and aviation. Another example is Transport for London (TfL) that oversees the running of all the main aspects of London's transport infrastructure as detailed in the mission statement included at the end of this section. While competent and experienced people may be in charge of running these kinds of organisations, an important part of their role is to provide a voice for the general public who may have strong views on certain topics and wish to be seen as significantly influential in the decision-making process. Such decisions often have a considerable political dimension and are not just the realm of the engineer or other relevant expert. Democracy implies more than an opportunity to vote on the make-up of a parliament or administration and input into local decision-making is important. Citizens may, therefore, be wary of what they perceive as the mission creep associated with a power grab by new authorities.

For instance, a particular area of concern in the UK has been changes to the NHS (National Health Service) and how this impacts upon the funding and provision of healthcare services and facilities at a local level. The Health and Social Care Act 2012 set up a range of new administration entities with clinical commissioning groups (CCGs) replacing former patient care trusts (PCTs). At present, there are 211 CCGs that each have their own mission statements that are primarily distinguishable by reference to a geographical area. However, there are frequent tensions between CCGs and local pressure groups such as "Protect Our NHS" that claim to represent the best interests of patients but are not at the heart of decision-making, as defined by CCG mission statements.

Many members of the public believe that *mission erosion* of the taxpayer-funded NHS is gradually occurring and that the overall strategy of those in power is *privatisation by stealth*. While such a strategy might have the aim of constraining running costs for the public purse while maintaining standards, there is always a degree of scepticism amongst the general public about the intention and likely impact of privatisation on public health services which they fear will limit access or remove some free services altogether. This concern may extend more widely to the process of privatisation for those citizens who are suspicious of public services that are managed for financial profit. Who decides on what treatment, in what facility and at whose expense amidst all the mission changes that are going on? With the dramatic rise in PFI (Private Finance Initiative) contracts to build hospitals between 1997 and 2010, which enabled the construction of additional investment out of future income rather than through additional public borrowing, there is now serious concern that the often 30-year DBO (design, build, operate) contracts entered into actually represent very poor value for money in the longer term and have been the cause of various needless problems in healthcare provision as budgets have come under severe pressure.

Examples such as these put the importance of mission in the public (or non-profit) sector into context, particularly where this interfaces with the private sector. For example, the mission of a privately owned nursing agency is to provide nursing requirements to healthcare facilities on demand, which is readily understood, but this provision is also within the remit of the NHS. In relation to ongoing nursing needs, it is significantly cheaper for a nurse to be taken on and employed through the public system than it is to have the same role constantly filled by agency nurses, who are really only meant to provide exceptional cover. This is one example where the public interest groups claim *mission neglect* on behalf of the NHS who are not fulfilling their role of providing adequate staffing on a cost-effective basis. It is a basic reality in healthcare that overspending in one area leads to cutbacks in another area, which compromises the stated mission of the NHS to provide *"health and high quality care for all, now and for future generations"* (NHS England, n.d.).

To conclude, let us look at two differing forms of mission statements. The first relates to BBC (bbc.co.uk, n.d.) and is notable for its brevity, but also for its clarity:

> *"To enrich people's lives with programmes and services that inform, educate and entertain."*

The second relates to TfL (Transport for London, n.d.), and gives a good overview of the complex functions it performs on a daily basis and how it sees its role in planning for the future:

> *"We run the day-to-day operation of the Capital's public transport network and manage London's main roads.*
>
> *No other city is as recognised by its transport system as London. Its red buses, black cabs and Tube trains are known the world over.*
>
> *Every day more than 31 million journeys are made across our network. We do all we can to keep the city moving, working and growing and to make life in our city better.*
>
> *We listen to, and act upon, feedback and complaints to constantly improve our services and work with communities, representative groups, businesses and many other stakeholders to shape transport provision in London.*
>
> *Customers are at the heart of what we do, and every journey matters."*

Reflection points

- What is the logical relationship between the mission of an organisation and its values? What happens if this relationship is lost?
- Try to think of an example of mission creep and explain any important contributing factors. Was the outcome positive or negative for the organisation in question?
- Do you know any examples of when the missions of public bodies and private enterprises clashed? What happened?

Strategic thinking – again

Pursuing a strategy requires you to act consciously towards achieving longer-term goals that signify real success. In a football match, for example, it is the final result that matters, rather than being 1–0 up at half time.

Some situations will have binary outcomes –"*We were unsuccessful in the tender and will not get any work in that area as a result;*" while others will be nuanced – "*Our sales growth target was 5% and we managed 3% which needs improvement but is not a disaster.*" As we outlined in the opening chapter, the use of the term "strategy" typically relates to situations where the future has an element of uncertainty and the actions of others or the nature of events are not entirely predictable. For much of the time, strategic decision-making can involve complex multivariable analysis, multiple scenario analysis, meticulous planning, wise allocation of resources and overall good judgement. There are also times, however, when what turns out to work well may be something as simple as consciously avoiding doing or saying anything out of the ordinary for a period of time.

Strategic thinking is typically complex and operates on a number of different levels. You and your organisation may be required to simultaneously address many different elements that each involves a distinct sub-strategy. Examples of issues to be addressed include: (1) assisting in deciding what the future vision should be and related goals and objectives; (2) detailing the tasks that need to be done to get from position X now to position Y in the future in accordance with the vision and in the best fashion; (3) deciding via scenario analysis the extent to which external forces might influence (1) and (2) on an ongoing basis; (4) setting the pace at which work is done with (3) in mind, and also deciding on milestones and final deadlines; (5) ensuring exceptional funding needs are met either by ongoing sales, savings, or creditors, or convincing potential financial backers/investors to initially commit and then maintain ongoing support; (6) ensuring that the right team is in place to execute what needs to be done and that they remain motivated; (7) ensuring that all necessary resources are available when required and that activities are executed in the most cost-effective fashion including optimising synergies; (8) negotiating with and choosing external suppliers including subcontractors; (9) dealing with any internal or external conflict in an effective way with the aim of not stalling progress and limiting the impact of risk, e.g. financial, reputational, work relations, and so on; (10) ensuring that all activities undertaken are compliant with the relevant laws and regulations; and (11) deciding what needs to be studied and measured, and devising the best ways to gather, store, and communicate information.

Depending on circumstances, the direction of strategic thinking may differ widely. The strategy employed by a road safety authority to reduce road deaths is going to be completely different from, for example, that of a fledgling manufacturer of virtual reality equipment looking to provide a satisfactory rate of return to its venture capital investors. Similarly, those whose job it is to run a public hospital will operate with a different strategic mindset to those who run mature businesses operating in a particular market or, indeed, multinational conglomerates who have fingers in many pies. In all cases, though, the basic strategic elements we have explored apply – just in different ways and with different prioritisation.

Timing, location, and *positioning* are important aspects of strategy that have been proven to be key elements in success, particularly in the case of newer enterprises. Being willing and ready to act at the right time in the right place has been a persistent feature of those businesses that have managed to cross the *valley of death* between promising candidate to successful operator.

Earlier we introduced you to the work of Michael Porter along with some of his key messages and models, e.g. *five forces.* These include (a) truly thinking long-term when devising corporate strategy, i.e. 10 years ahead or more; (b) emphasising the importance of *strategic fit,* or how the existence of a good overall strategy can lead to many cost-saving synergies through resources and capabilities being effectively employed; (c) making decisions not to do certain things (accepting trade-offs), thereby focusing resources on what is important; and (d) the importance of differentiating oneself from the competition in a way that is difficult to replicate. Porter warns about the danger of incremental shifts away from a focused position, each insignificant on its own but collectively disastrous, as well as the risk of confusing management tools based around operational efficiency with the need for an effective replacement for strategy.

There are three main categories recognised by Porter in his *Generic Strategies* model, within which there are different types of strategic thinking aimed at achieving *competitive advantage.* Depending on the market environment with which you are dealing (e.g. oligopoly, etc.), various additional considerations will apply in terms of overall strategy. These categories are:

Cost leadership: this can be achieved in a number of ways. Firstly, by focusing on the cost of key items and ensuring that customers perceive the price of your products or services as lower than those of your competitors. We say "perception" because, although the prices of key items may be lower, the prices of other items of which customers are less price-aware may be higher. Asda, as well as its discount competitors Lidl and Aldi, have followed this strategy for some time, using low prices on common *selected* shopping basket items to encourage an overall sense of value for money amongst consumers. Secondly, by operational effectiveness, exploiting economies of scale and strategic fit, to secure a lower cost price for goods and enable competitive prices for customers with margins maintained at their current levels. Finally, innovation in product/service offerings, which can produce cost advantages relative to the competition in a variety of ways; for example by switching from germanium to silicon in the early days of microprocessors manufacturing.

Differentiation: the variety of products, services, or features offered exclusively by an enterprise, particularly if they are able to sustain that exclusivity. This strategic approach is ubiquitous across all sectors and can be realised in a number of different ways, e.g. through disruptive innovation where new products or services leapfrog the competition, dedicated investment along a particular theme over a long period, or first mover advantage in a given area.

Focus: segmentation of the market and personalisation, allowing you to meet the needs of the customer faster or in some way better than competitors. Again, there are many ways this can be achieved, and Amazon and other successful online sellers pursue this strategy to good effect. Features such as *"Look Inside"* in the Amazon bookstore, as well as integrated reviews and referrals (e.g. *"Customers Also Bought"* or *"Frequently Bought Together"*) are all good examples.

Alongside competitive advantage, Porter has written extensively about the related area of *competitive positioning* and recognises three main types, briefly described as follows: (a) variety-based – do what you do best, e.g. Ryman Stationery; (b) needs-based – do lots of things, but just in a well-tailored fashion for a segment of the market, e.g. IKEA; and (c) access-based – go to where the customers are, e.g. vending machines.

In Chapter 2, we described how Clayton Christensen explains a number of key aspects of business strategy. A point he frequently makes is how following the metric (marginal costs) can lead to completely unintended strategies and is an important cause of why incumbents gradually get overtaken by disruptive innovators. This is a conundrum in the modern world where many investors in publicly listed companies are looking for short-term performance and closely review quarterly results, at the expense of the longer term. Balancing the needs of such investors with the more sustainable long-term investment that an enterprise typically requires to stay ahead in their area of operations is not straightforward and has been termed the "Capitalist's Dilemma" by Christensen (Christensen & Van Bever, 2014). RONA (return on net assets), ROIC (return on invested capital), and IRR (internal rate of return) are three metrics widely analysed that simply relate to capital in the short term. Since real innovations often take five years or more to pay off, investing in such areas may not have much appeal on paper, as analysts only see less cash without a corresponding increase in the all-important ratios. In response, some large enterprises opt for the strategy of remaining privately owned, as it allows them better flexibility to think and act with the longer term in mind. This is of particular benefit in times of recession when they can position themselves well to take advantage of the next phase of growth which is sure to come.

Another influential thinker in the area of corporate strategy is William Edwards Deming (1900–1993), a prolific engineer, statistician, author, lecturer, and management consultant who played a major role in the advancement of Japanese industry beginning from 1950 onwards. He presented many of his prominent thoughts on industry in his 1986 book *Out of the Crisis*, which is credited with launching the Total Quality Management movement. His strategic thinking is very much based around instilling a strong quality and innovation culture that becomes second nature and provides employees with a safe environment in which to excel in their work and use their initiative. He does not advocate rigid management by the measurement of performance metrics and focus on short-term profits. Instead, he advocates for continual, focused, long-range planning; leading rather than following; breaking down barriers between departments; having a strong apprenticeship system; and an overall shared desire to learn and improve. In dealings with suppliers and others, he emphasises relationships, trust, and loyalty and underplays contracts and litigation. To him, the importance of the "system" outweighs that of individual employees, and improving the system should be a continuous goal, with top-level management leading the way. His System of Profound Knowledge (SoPK) has four elements – "Appreciation for a System, Knowledge of Variation, Theory of Knowledge and Psychology" – and ties together his seminal theories into a coherent whole.

As markets evolve, different concepts on how to do business emerge. One of the more interesting overall approaches in recent times is presented by Alexander Osterwalder and Yves Pigneur in their book *Business Model Generation* (2010). Using a novel visual style to convey concepts, the book focuses on a generic strategy diagram that can be widely adopted for the formulation of business plans. There are nine *business model building blocks* that comprise the *Business Model Canvas* and these are: (1) customer segments; (2) value propositions; (3) channels; (4) customer relationships; (5) revenue streams; (6) key resources; (7) key activities; (8) key partnerships; and (9) cost structure. By using the canvas as a template, the nature of the different building blocks and the connections between them can be explored to arrive at an agreeable business strategy.

Customer-facing enterprises need to think carefully about their strategy for selecting, training, motivating and rewarding their employees as they have a vital role in ensuring operational success. Poor human resources strategy was identified by industry observers such as Robin Lewis (The Robin Report, n.d.) as one of several serious flaws that plagued the troubled US retail conglomerate RadioShack. To overcome the *principal-agent problem*, where the interests of the employee and employer diverge, you can employ a number of different strategies. Probably the most robust and sustainable strategy involves using techniques to generate loyalty in the form of a strong emotional connection between employees and enterprise and encourage closely shared values. Do it well and your employees will be motivated to do the job well and share a sense that *we are all in this together.*

There are plenty of examples of strategy in the world beyond business that can provide inspiration and analogy. In the book and television documentary *The Private Life of Plants*, for example, David Attenborough (1995) describes a broad range of strategies employed by the plant kingdom to promote survival and reproductive success. These include the many different ways in which plants advertise themselves to the mammals, insects, and birds that spread their pollen or seeds, use mimicry, or employ specific structures, skins, and lifecycles to survive in the harsh conditions of the desert or frozen tundra.

The wider natural world is filled with examples of behavioural strategies: patience and ambush by crocodiles, altruism in vampire bats, communal upbringing amongst elephants, and division of labour between ants. In human terms, we talk about strategy in terms of military combat, politics, business, entertainment, design, engineering, administration, environmental hazards, medical care, psychology, law, taxation, scientific research, individual and team sports and games, and even folk wisdom. We've included a selection of different concepts, adages, or observations for the purpose of stimulating thinking on strategy in whatever guise or setting you feel is relevant. These are not arranged in any particular order. You may feel that many of these are very obvious and/or overused clichés, but they still require careful consideration and should not be dismissed too lightly.

Concepts relating to offensive or defensive strategic positioning: *Fight or flight? – Laying siege to – Isolation – Immobilising threats – Grinding down and weakening of opponents – Strength in numbers – Intelligence gathering – Information security – Use of decoys/smokescreens – Divide and conquer – Making a sacrifice to gain position – Mutually assured destruction – Amassing stocks – Holding extra in reserve – Counter-attacking from a strong defensive position – First-mover advantage – Second-mover advantage – Waiting in the long grass – Shock and awe/blitzkrieg – Show of unity – An eye for an eye – Use of deterrents – Territorial control – Circling the wagons – Controlling the message*

More generalised strategic concepts: *Having a Plan A, a Plan B (....C, D, E, etc.) – Consensus building – Accurate diagnostics – Only worrying about what you have control over – Buying low, selling high – Outsourcing – Contrarian positioning – Message repetition – Brand promotion and recognition – Learning by doing – Reading the small print – Margin of safety – Carrot or stick? – Follow the money – Economies of scale – Evidence-based approach – Delegation of work – Allocation of responsibility – Accountability – Waiting for things to blow over – Getting out front and staying out front – Kick for touch – Mimicry – Creative destruction – Keeping tabs – Picking the low-hanging fruit first – Win/win – Playing the percentage game – Calling someone's bluff – Broadcast or bury news? – Keeping a high/low profile – Appealing to fear – Low energy (fuel) requirements – Little or no waste (reuse/recycle) – Passive versus active control systems (e.g. emergency shutdown, negative feedback loop) – Cooperation in areas of mutual benefit*

Negative or controversial strategies most often considered to be neither: (a) sustainable; (b) ethical; nor (c) likely to be acceptable in the court of public opinion: *Benefiting from moral hazard (i.e. taking more risks in the hope of gain because someone else bears the brunt of it when things do not work out) – Burying one's head in the sand – Appealing to the lowest common denominator – Free-riding (benefiting from the work of others without reciprocation) – Race to the bottom – Obfuscation (e.g. employing the use of jargon to justify greater rewards) – Turning a blind eye – Fake it till you make it – Playing one off against* the other – Veneer of authenticity (focusing on image rather than substance) – Disinformation (e.g. propaganda, appealing to false authority – Mudslinging (using insults and accusations, often unjustly, to attack the reputation of opponents) – FUD (fear, uncertainty, doubt) – Bait and switch/trap (enticing customers in on false premises) – Planned obsolescence

Famous quotes on the theme of strategy:

"When in Rome, do as the Romans do" – St. Ambrose

"Perception is strong and sight weak. In strategy it is important to see distant things as if they were close and to take a distanced view of close things" – Miyamoto Musashi

"Never interrupt your enemy when they are making a mistake" – Napoleon Bonaparte

"There is nothing so useless as doing efficiently that which should not be done at all" – Peter Drucker

"Simplicity is the ultimate sophistication" – Leonardo Da Vinci

"The art of taxation consists in so plucking the goose as to obtain the largest amount of feathers with the least possible amount of hissing" – Jean-Baptiste Colbert

Common folk sayings on the theme of strategy:

- Neither a borrower nor a lender be.
- Prevention is better than cure.
- Measure twice cut once.
- A stitch in time saves nine.
- Once bitten twice shy.
- Practice makes perfect.
- Two heads are better than one.
- Old habits die hard.
- A chain is as strong as its weakest link.
- A small leak will sink a great ship.
- No time like the present.

Complexity and strategic thinking

Think carefully about the pros and cons of introducing the concept of complexity as part of any strategy. On the positive side, the complex may well reflect what differentiates your organisation from the competition and is a key reason for better functioning; for example in areas such as intellectual property and technology. It also may be the only way certain difficult issues can be resolved. For example, legislation: laws and regulations are often made to address a small number of extreme situations. This can impose what seems like overly bureaucratic and complex procedures, but those involved in their drafting argue that a small inconvenience protects us from a far greater ill. On the negative side, consider the following statements: (a) complexity breeds complexity; (b) over-complexity introduces structural weakness; (c) managing complexity often involves more energy to make things work and to monitor and control them; (d) problems in complex systems are tricky to diagnose; and (e) complexity reduces flexibility. There has been an increasing trend over several decades now to have computers "do the thinking for us." Computers are excellent tools for solving complicated problems, but human judgement is required to deal with true complexity, which is most often involved in strategic thinking. Schank et al. (2010) provide an interesting summary of recent developments and future trends in this field that gives a greater insight into what can be achieved and where the boundaries lie.

Complex organisations, processes or governance are commonly used strategies within which to hide the true nature of things. Sometimes this may be done for entirely legitimate reasons, e.g. the use of complex offshore trust ownership structures to provide asset protection against various threats such as opportunistic litigation or totalitarian governments. On the flip side, however, complexity may be employed to conceal illegal, unethical, or simply questionable activity. Tax planning and management is a very active area of strategy among larger multinational companies today. At a typical headline rate of 39% (effective rates tend to be much lower), and applied to all global profits earned, corporate tax is high in the US in comparison to other jurisdictions and this has driven some organisations to change tax residency, resulting in some significant short-term gains. In some cases, the original company becomes a subsidiary of a new company in the low-tax jurisdiction and profits are shifted there using various mechanisms. The gains here though are marginal in the greater scheme of things and are no replacement for a proper growth strategy based on solid business fundamentals.

Subjectivity and strategic thinking

The personality, knowledge, and characteristic behaviour of an individual can significantly influence how they approach strategic thinking. Some people may be naturally optimistic, while others are pessimistic; some might be sceptical, while others tend to follow unquestioningly. For strategic decision making, broad representation is important so that any subjective biases can be analysed and debated within a group before consensus agreements are reached.

Evolution and strategic thinking

As a final word, never forget that strategic decisions can have knock-on and sometimes irreversible effects or trigger a chain of unintended consequences. Over time, decisions can take on a life of their own and have natural consequences that were never conceived of at the time the decision was made. For instance, the imposition of economic sanctions on a country to punish them for an infraction of international law can lead to *middle class flight*, making the country in question more unstable and prone to extreme politics. Alternatively, if you assemble and train a workforce up to a high level in a particular field, you need to then provide them with the environment and the work to exercise their skills, and, since knowledge acquisition is a process and not a destination, they will naturally want to then go from project to project in that field to gain from their unique knowledge and experience. Momentum, thus generated, is difficult to stop, but there can also be natural limits to this specialisation of work and new ways of thinking or methods of performing the same function may supersede the old. Take another example: where the decision to provide generous social welfare may help individuals and families to escape from extreme poverty, it may also create welfare traps, disincentivise people, and generate resentment among those who pay but get no benefits, e.g. those working in low-paid jobs and those who pay high taxes. As a final example, consider a government that decides to generously recompense public sector workers during prosperous economic times in order to spread the benefits. The same government can then be faced with a major problem when the next inevitable recession occurs. In all of these examples, there are no right or wrong answers. A successful strategy, as we have seen, involves choices, trade-offs and compromises.

Reflection points

- How would you describe your approach to strategic thinking? How does your personality influence this approach?
- Describe a strategy undertaken by an enterprise with which you are familiar with reference to the different strategic concepts we have listed. Are there some concepts we have overlooked and, if so, what are they?
- What is the strategic thinking behind prison privatisation in the UK and elsewhere? What is the reality of this strategy in practice?

Future vision

The purpose of the vision is to describe the future that is desired for an enterprise so that owners, managers, and employees alike can share and to which they can commit themselves. It can also have a positive influence on customers, users, future employees, and the wider community in general.

The vision reflects what an enterprise really aspires to become by evolving from, and improving upon, the status quo. It is meant to provide a realistic description of the status of an enterprise at a certain time in the future and may be deliberately either unambiguous or leave room for a certain amount of interpretation while still providing an overall sense of purpose and value. You should present your vision in such a way that the direction in which to proceed towards it is clear in the here and now, and you may even advocate a specific pathway to follow. Add a number of intermediate milestones along this pathway so that you can measure ongoing progress in relation to the overall journey. The vision is influenced in part by strategic thinking and must be based on the values and the mission of an enterprise as well as on the core competencies.

The vision statement itself should include short and concise descriptions of the future status of the enterprise and you may choose to set your horizon a short or long way ahead, although the vision itself should involve some clear and conclusive result. For instance, a key part of the strategic vision of a UK manufacturer might be that at least 50% of their EBITDA is from foreign markets by 2020. This will have been judged as being appropriate to insulate them from the effects of a domestic recession and will represent a conclusive achievement (provided, of course, that all the various assumptions made in the plans prove valid).

It is good to decide early in the process how far ahead to look. Should the vision be for three months, one year, three years, five years, or even longer? Credibility is very important as it is very difficult to convince people to set off on a journey that they consider impossible. The greater the distance between the present and the envisioned future, the greater the need for good leadership to bridge the gap and drive and maintain progress. As the Chinese philosopher Laozi (or Lao Tzu) said: "A journey of a thousand miles begins with a single step."

You'll need strong and charismatic leadership to sustain a belief in the value and feasibility of collaborative endeavours that may not produce tangible results for a considerable length of time. You'll also need to develop separate strategies to express the discrete elements within the vision and motivate all those involved in its realisation. Part of this involves presenting the vision to employees in such a way that they can imagine their own contribution towards the final result and can reconcile the vision of the enterprise with their own personal vision. The working atmosphere should be kept interesting and exciting so that employees are inspired to get positively involved and do not need to be cajoled into action.

Alongside employees, you'll need to convince a range of other important stakeholders. These may be enterprise executives, board members, co-investors, partner organisations, creditors, public funding bodies, local authorities, supporters, customers (including potential ones), or users. The emphasis here is on feasibility and whether there is a realistic chance that a successful outcome can be delivered. Patience and judgement may differ, and key stakeholders will often have very different views on what should be done – think of frugal professional football club owners faced with excitable fans demanding that they splash out on expensive "star" players. This can require careful management to keep all pulling in the same direction.

A good example of an unrealistic vision is the slogan *"drug free country by the year 2010"* put forward by the government of Iceland and the city of Reykjavik in 1997.

While everyone recognised the good intentions, everybody sensed from the outset that this was unrealistic and would never come true. Hence, the wider public never took this vision seriously. A good vision should contain the following key attributes in order for it to be viewed as feasible and inspirational:

- It should be daring but realistic, tailored to the particular characteristics of an enterprise, and well defined with regard to scope and time.
- It should be made relevant for all concerned (the actual scope will depend on the scope of the strategic planning, e.g. corporate, business unit, project, and so on), to generate interest and provide motivation.
- It should be comprehensible and clear to all who are impacted. Simple versus complex, and emotional as well as rational, since we are well able to understand the visionary if there is enough detail for us to complete the picture for ourselves.
- Regardless of what deadlines are decided, it should provide a call to immediate action.
- It should include expectations, hopes, and objectives, and account for relevant external forces.
- It should be put forward in such a way that it can be used as the basis of goal setting.
- It should be under regular revision by top management.

It is a useful exercise to look at examples of how other enterprises present their future vision on their webpages, looking at key aspects like presentation and content. For example, the following is the long-term vision of the Port of Rotterdam (portofrottermam.com, 2011):

> "In 2030, Rotterdam is Europe's most important port and industrial complex. It is a strong combination of the Global Hub and Europe's Industrial Cluster, both leaders in efficiency and sustainability. Rotterdam is closely linked to other North West European industrial and logistics areas. Leading businesses make long-term investments in the most modern facilities. Close cooperation between businesses, government and knowledge institutions results in a high-quality labour market, living environment and accessibility. Our adaptive powers are unique. This makes the complex an important cornerstone for the welfare of the region, the Netherlands and Europe in 2030."

As we have explained in some detail, inputs into the process of strategic planning such as determining a strong future vision can employ a top-down, bottom-up, or a combined approach. In this book, we encourage a combined approach whenever possible and particularly so, in this case, as the future vision is a key anchor point in strategic planning to help align everyone on the same page.

Reflection points

- Assess the "Drug free country by the year 2010" vision based on the attributes of a good vision, what is good and what is not so good?
- Describe the current vision of an enterprise with which you are familiar. Does it have the attributes of a good vision? Explain.

Determining strategy and formulating the strategic action plan

All of the different aspects that have been discussed so far come together to determine our final strategy. Marrying the future vision and ways of strategic thinking with the realities of the internal and external environments of an organisation have all required careful reflection. Circumstances will differ each time you make a decision on a significant element of strategy, but the following offers you a useful criteria checklist to go through before committing to any one course of action:

- Do-nothing scenario – How does this impact upon the future vision?
- Value – Will the chosen strategy assist in achieving your agreed goals?
- Feasibility – Is the chosen strategy practical, given resource constraints and capacity?
- Appropriateness – Is the chosen strategy consistent with the values, mission, and operating principles of an enterprise?
- Acceptability – Is the chosen strategy acceptable to the Board, key employees, and other stakeholders?
- Cost-benefit – Is the chosen strategy likely to lead to sufficient benefits to justify the costs in time and other resources?
- Timing – Can and should the organisation implement the chosen strategy at this time, given external factors and competing demands?
- Opportunity costs – What else can be done instead and why should it not be done?

Determining strategy and developing detailed plans is likely to be an iterative and interactive process involving plenty of analysis. The overall process will typically open with a general agreement between those involved about the decision-making process, and subsequently, after various rounds of informed debate, the broad strategic direction to be undertaken. The latter might be in the form of a high-level statement with further work then focused on refining the strategic plan to the level of detail needed for the final specification. Various tools such as mind maps, concept diagrams, and flowcharts can be used to good effect throughout the brainstorming stage, and there is now a range of hardware such as interactive whiteboards to assist in this process in a professional setting. Steering groups are often set up to guide the broad direction of the work with offshoot groups then tasked with fleshing out the details. You may like to follow a process for breaking down the work similar to that described at the end of Chapter 1. According to this, the latest strategic approach that comes out of each stage of the decision-making process is written up in the form of a draft strategic plan to be used as the basis for the next level of consultation.

There are more formal approaches to decision-making, particularly relevant in high-stakes complex areas. One prominent example is the Delphi method, originally developed in the US military in the 1950s and 1960s. This is a method of soliciting and refining group judgements in which a facilitator collects and then feeds back the responses so that with each round, individual contributors can learn and modify their thinking on the basis of the response of their peers. There are three main features of Delphi: (1) anonymised response; (2) iteration and controlled feedback; and (3) statistical group response. These features are employed to minimise the biasing effects of dominant individuals, of irrelevant communications, and of group pressure towards conformity. Dalkey and Helmer (1963) outline the foundations of the method and it has remained in use ever since, with various small modifications and advancements made over the years (see Figure 8.5).

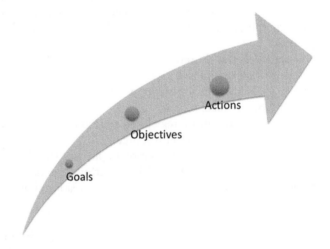

Figure 8.5

A strategic action plan.

Once you have chosen a cohesive strategy your focus becomes more specific. Action must follow words, but you must ensure that things are done in the right order. A strategic action plan is a holistic plan defining the goals of the organisation, which are then broken down into objectives, which are further broken down into actions or projects that always need to be seen and managed in light of their alignment with the strategy and vision of the organisation. We can describe the strategic plan as a bridge from the current status to the desired status, or future vision. In order to reach the objectives you've decided upon, and consequently goals, you need to execute a set of actions. The strategic plan can, therefore, take the form of a rather detailed and accurate work plan. This work plan is not a static document but regularly updated, and it should also include the business or organisational benefits that are to be realised. The goals are defined, the objectives are defined and prioritised and, finally, the actions are also defined and prioritised. More detailed project plans for particular sub-elements can be made on the basis of the strategic plan and do not have to be part of the main document. The plan itself is the core of the strategic planning work – this is where everything comes together and should describe accurately what goals must be reached and how to reach them. This does not diminish the importance of defining the values, mission, current status, and vision of an enterprise as we have talked about. One leads into the other.

By executing the plan, the organisation hopefully fulfils the strategic goals and the tactical and operational objectives. The ambition of your vision can only become tangible if the objectives are measurable and if the specifics of the actions are made clear. This part of the strategic planning, transforming the general ideas of the vision to well-structured plans, can be difficult for some of the participants. Now it becomes clearer how realistic the ambition is and whether it is reasonable that the enterprise commits itself to reach certain goals and whether it is likely that the defined vision will become reality. In some cases, the level of ambition is modest, and it is likely that all of the actions in the strategic plan will be executed ahead of time. In other cases, the level of ambition is unrealistically high and will need to be adjusted so it is in line with the resources available and other boundary conditions.

Goals

Goals are short sentences that answer the following question: what should be done to realise the future vision? Goals are plural because a future vision is most often comprised of a number of different distinct aspects. For example, stating that a hospital will be a world-class centre of excellence in the future will mean that: (a) its standards of hygiene must be very high; (b) it needs to have the latest/best facilities to allow for optimum treatment; (c) the medical staff need to be highly trained and of good international standing; and so on.

When defining goals, you need to refer to key points or themes that are put forward in the vision and use well-phrased sentences that reflect the right level of ambition. The goals themselves do not need to be measurable because they are further broken down into measurable objectives at a later stage. The purpose of the goals is to focus the attention and the ambition of the enterprise in certain directions and to create unity. The goals, therefore, become guides that are used by every employee in their daily routine. For goals to be of the greatest use, they should be independent, short, transparent, understandable and mutually compatible. For example, it may be problematic to have the goal of "outsourcing operations" alongside that of "increasing employee loyalty" as these goals may be conflicting. Your aim should be to try to avoid overlap between goals, but this may be unavoidable. Using goals that are short and memorable is effective in enabling employees to understand and adopt them into their everyday thinking. For example:

- *Ground breaking innovation.*
- *High profit margins.*
- *Products renowned for quality.*
- *Fast delivery.*
- *Fun working environment.*

For comparison, the following sentence is somewhat more confusing and considerably less memorable:

> *"Our goals are to realign our focus more with the needs of the user in collaboration with other relevant institutions in an environment where we are less dependent on our domestic operations due to greater emphasis on consulting, information gathering and other services."*

The advantage of clear goals is that all relevant parties understand completely what is expected when they turn up for work. They are the kinds of goals that come into your mind when you wake up in the morning. The goal statements themselves are rarely detailed and consequently allow for imagination and flexibility in their realisation.

Objectives

Once your goals have been defined it is time to break them down into objectives. Objectives are crafted in such a way that they can be used for monitoring and follow-up. Sometimes they are called sub-goals. The difference between a goal and an objective is that an objective is measurable, and the chosen metric should be included in its definition. For an objective to be useful it must be SMART (specific, measurable, agreed, relevant, and time-bound). Offering a clear scale for success, as opposed to a binary "succeeded or failed," increases the likelihood that an objective is reached as the effort required is much better understood. Each objective must have a timescale and you should allocate responsibility for its achievement to a named individual. Defining your success criteria allows you to measure the success of the strategic planning but also to detect any deviations that occur in the implementation of the plan itself. Success criteria often include a mixture of objective financial figures and more subjective elements such as the viewpoints of interested parties. An example of a financial objective could be:

"Grow revenue, stepwise, by 200% between 2018 and 2020."

In this example, the scale is well defined, as well as the criteria. All further description of how to reach this objective must be presented in an action plan, which might include a more detailed description of, for example, the steps that are mentioned in the statement. Another simple example of an objective is:

"90% of our clients are either "happy" or "very happy" with the service of the organisation in the service survey for 2019."

In this example, the objective is linked to the views of clients. The scale is known and based on a standardised survey that the organisation is doing on a regular basis. The reference is well defined and descriptions of the actions that need to be taken in order to reach this objective are to be found in the action plan. Compare these with the objective: "revenue is to increase in the coming years." The scale is not defined and there is no definite period of time involved, which makes a very blunt tool for planning, communication, or measurement.

Actions

Once you have defined the objectives, it is time to break them down to clearly defined actions that state what is to be done, those who are responsible, when the action is to be started and finished, and how it is to be carried out. In addition, you'll find it useful to provide an estimate of how much the action will cost, what revenue it will deliver, or how much it is supposed to save, if this is the case.

A set of well-defined actions means that the person in charge of implementing the strategic plan can delegate the actions to the different people, capable of carrying them out. Those people can then define the actions further, if needed, to help execute them. If everything goes as planned, all actions are carried out as they are defined in the strategic plan. You've reached your objectives, achieved your goals and realised your desired vision

Once you have formed your strategic action plan, you need to bring it to life by presenting it widely and explaining it clearly. The key word here is communication and every effort should be made to avoid misunderstandings. Whilst the plan itself can be presented in the form of a structured text, defining every goal and its subsequent objectives, and listing the actions for each objective, remember to do this in the context of the bigger picture: the value and benefits of the plan and what the organisation or its work will look like when you have finished. The following is a simple example, showing two goals and their objectives and actions. Also shown are clear key performance indicators (KPI) for each objective. In general, such measures can either be leading; preceding an event or a milestone, communicating change in the environment and can be used for control purposes – or lagging; following an event or a milestone and presenting what has already happened.

Goal 1. A financially stable family business

Objective i:	Increase operating margin to at least 10%
Action a:	Increase the service fee to 30% on average Responsibility: John Finished: By January 1st 2020
Action b:	Reduce inventory costs to less than 10% of inventory value Responsibility: Shirley Finished: By June 1st 2020
Action c:	Reduce variable costs by 10%. Responsibility: Shirley Finished: By January 1st 2020
Action d:	Process mapping of procedures for selling Responsibility: Beverly Finished: By April 1st 2020
Objective ii:	To increase market share to 15% by the end of the year 2020
Action a:	Undertake a detailed client analysis including each organisation's importance in terms of their business with us. Responsibility: John Finished: By February 1st 2020
Action b:	Implement a procedure for assessing client satisfaction Responsibility: Beverly Finished: The surveys will be done in June each year from 2018 onwards
Action c:	Increase business with present clients by 20% through closer communication with them Responsibility: John Finished: By April 1st 2020
Action d:	Work out a market plan, expand the number of clients by 15% by participating in exhibitions and by direct communication Responsibility: Beverly Finished: By October 1st 2020

Goal 2. Improved employee engagement

Objective i:	To increase the competencies of employees
Action a:	Define the need for continuous education and map how this will be achieved. Responsibility: Melissa Finished: By February 1st 2021

Action b:	Each employee attends two relevant courses or presentations annually. Responsibility: Melissa Finished: In operation starting with year 2018
Action c:	Implement a human resource policy Responsibility: John Finished: By January 15th 2021
Action d:	Implement annual employee interviews Responsibility: Melissa Finished: In operation starting with year 2018
Objective ii:	To assess and improve employee satisfaction
Action a:	Implement a formal organogram and job descriptions Responsibility: John Finished: By February 1st 2021
Action b:	Design, test and implement a survey for assessing employee satisfaction annually Responsibility: Beverly Finished: Surveys in June, in operation starting with year 2019
Action c:	Start an employee community of practice Responsibility: Beverly Finished: By May 1st 2021
Action d:	Map a descriptive process for daily information flow to employees Responsibility: John Finished: By March 1st 2021

You may prefer to use a table (see Table 8.1) to represent the goals. Using a shared spreadsheet can make calculations easier and allows for various extra information columns to be included. One drawback is that there is less space for descriptive text.

Depending on preferences, other more visual formats such as mind maps can also be used to convey the same information as above. A mind map can give a good overview of extensive information, is easy to understand for those involved in the process, and can be a good way to motivate and engage people in creative teamwork.

Detailed plans

Sub-elements of a strategic action plan may go into quite some detail on how exactly actions will be performed. A procurement strategy, for example, will typically contain an options analysis and a range of recommendations relating to the final selection. These would include items such as length and type of contract, the nature of the suppliers required, and supplier contract management. These additional items may be presented in the Appendix or as separate supporting documents so as not to interrupt the flow of the main strategic planning report with unnecessary detail.

Table 8.1 Example of strategic action plan

Action	Responsibility	Due date	Cost (GBP)	Progress
Goal 1: A financially stable family business				
Objective i: Increase operating margin to at least 10%				
a Increase the service fee to 30% on average	John	01/01/2020		
b Reduce inventory cost to 10% of inventory value	Shirley	01/06/2020		
c Reduce variable costs by 10%	Shirley	01/01/2020		
d Process mapping of procedures for selling	Beverly	01/04/2020	1,000	
Objective ii: To increase market share to 15% by the end of 2018				
a Undertake a detailed client analysis	John	01/02/2020	1,000	
b Implement procedure for assessing client satisfaction	Beverly	(annual) June 2017	2,000	
c Increase business with clients by 20%	John	01/04/2020		
d Prepare a market plan, expand number of clients by 15%	Beverly	01/10/2020	5,000	
Goal 2: Good work morale				
Objective i: To increase the competencies of employees				
a Define the need for continuous education	Melissa	01/02/2020	1,000	
b Each employee attends two courses annually	Melissa	Begin 2017	1,000	
c Implement a human resources policy	John	15/01/2020		
d Implement annual employee interviews	Melissa	Begin 2017	2,000	
Objective ii: To assess and improve employee satisfaction				
a Implement a formal organogram and job descriptions	John	01/02/2021	1,000	
b Implement a survey for assessing employee satisfaction	Beverly	(annual) June 2017		
c Establish a formal employee society	Beverly	01/05/2021	500	
d Map a descriptive process for daily information flow	John	01/03/2021	2,000	

Product presentation – the strategic planning report and delivery

A well-written strategic planning report is the key deliverable in determining the course of action to be taken and there are a number of important considerations when it comes to finalising strategy and committing things to paper. A good strategy document should be simple and accessible, short and concise, and free of jargon. It should be written with the key target audience in mind and the tone tailored accordingly. The format and layout of a strategy document, as well as its standard of writing, can have considerable impact when it comes to the reader assessing its contents. Spelling and grammar are important in the sense that errors can convey the wrong impression of the material contained therein. There is always the danger that the reader overlooks the quality of the contents because the poor layout and writing of a report make a bad impression.

A combination of catchy and informative titles/subtitles can be useful, enabling you to engage and inform at the same time. For example, "Horizon 2020," which is used to encompass a whole series of interconnected growth strategies currently being pursued by the EU as a lead body together with a broad range of national bodies within member states; the title is forward and outward looking but would have benefitted from a subtitle to explain the nature of the programme.

In order to give your strategy document's main messages impact, include a concise summary (preferably no more than three pages) at the start. After this, you can introduce the topic in the main body of text more fully and add a more detailed discussion on the strategic planning process, such as clarifications, analyses, and results. For many people graphics such as photographs, tables, and charts are a useful shortcut to understanding and an aid to memory as they convey concepts and information visually and spatially. Sources of information should be cited in the report, where applicable, with a list of references at the end. It is appropriate to list and thank all who have contributed to it in such a way that they can easily identify themselves. For instance, employees, members, chairpersons, board members, committees and directors may be referred to, with the work of those who contributed most highlighted (individuals should be named in this case).

Overall, there is no one ideal fixed layout for a strategic planning report and there are various ways in which you may structure and write it. It is basically a foundation for discussion; a document that needs to be assimilated by management and workers alike. For this reason, you may want to save time by formatting the report in such a way as to make it suitable for presentations, e.g. with a computer screen projector, and for reading in print. This can be done using presentation software such as Keynote or PowerPoint instead of customary word processors. Another option is to present the report as a web page, for instance on an organisation's intranet. This approach may open up new possibilities for presentation and distribution and enable users to access the report when it suits them.

We encourage you to use the process diagram outlined in Chapter 2 as a template to help you write your report. Different contexts will mean that you need to vary how you emphasise the different elements, but we believe all of them should always be referred to, however briefly. We stress again that each enterprise needs to be fully aware of its own internal and external environment and all the different factors there that can influence events and impact the achievement of objectives. The following, then, could act as a basic strategic planning report template that you can modify to suit differing circumstances:

i   Title page
Include the name of the enterprise, the report's title, the authors' names, and the place and the date

ii   Acknowledgements/List of Contributors (can also be placed at the end as an afterword)

iii   Table of Contents (including a list of figures and tables if appropriate)

iv   (Executive) Summary
Outline of strategy and principal reasons for change
Implementation plans

v   Introduction
Need for strategic planning
How the plan was developed
Structure of report

vi   Current Status: Environmental Scan and SWOT Analysis
External environment – PESTLE analysis, market analysis, principal opportunities, and threats
Internal environment – Organisational structure, history, culture, operations/projects, finances, principal strengths and weaknesses
SWOT analysis summary

vii   Values, Mission, and Future Vision

viii   Goals, Objectives, and Action Plan
Should outline clear objectives and deadlines, as well as responsible individuals and budgets where appropriate

ix   Performance Indicators, Monitoring, and Review

x   References

xi   Appendices/Attachments
Further reading including more detailed supporting data and analysis where relevant

Reflection points

- What is the relationship between goals and the future vision? Explain by using an example.
- What is the difference between objectives and goals? Explain by using an example.

- Give an example of an ideal SMART objective in the strategic plan of your organisation.
- Give an example of an action that relates to the objective above.

Delivery – project management as a tool for realising future vision

Strategic planning and its implementation phase can be considered as a project or programme (a related series of projects) as they involve a special undertaking that is limited by time and resources, and that aims to realise a series of defined goals as part of the future vision. While the production of a strategic planning report typically represents an important undertaking, the real value is delivered through the actual implementation of the strategies that have been selected. It is only through action that you can achieve goals and realise a future vision. This implementation phase can be derailed in a variety of ways and it takes good strategic planning and, subsequently, dedicated management to ensure that this does not happen.

Even quite straightforward projects can involve many different facets and, if you approach them casually without critical reflection, you risk unnecessary mistakes or omissions. As a simple example, imagine an enterprise is looking to expand their business into a new area, but only realises subsequently that they require a licence to do so. Crucial time and resources are spent on abortive planning or rework; any commercial advantage may be lost, quite apart from any regulatory penalties the business may incur. If, on the other hand, a proper project management methodology is followed, requirements can be anticipated and scheduled as part of the project's *critical path* to success. The critical path refers to the logical sequencing of tasks such that a successful outcome is achieved in the shortest time. This concept, along with other aspects of project management delivery and methodology, are explained in much greater detail in the *Execution* book in this series (see Figure 8.6).

Project management is formally defined as a methodology to prepare, manage, and conclude unique time-bound undertakings that are defined as projects, while programme management refers to the equivalent in terms of a series of related projects. Additional considerations in programme management relate to the interfaces and dependencies between individual projects and the development of an organisation's capability to undertake something new. The term "critical success factors" is used to describe the various conditions that must be fulfilled in order for success to be achieved. They represent the objectives of a project and are directly linked to the goals of an enterprise as outlined earlier.

Project management involves technical methods, for instance, the creation and follow through of project plans and the management of physical resources. It also depends on a number of people management skills and an

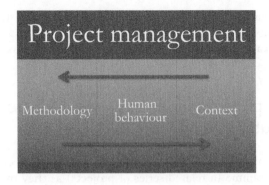

Figure 8.6

The fundamentals of project management.

understanding of human behaviour, e.g. the motivation of individuals and groups; how to respond to difficult situations such as conflict and exercise judgement in the face of moral dilemmas. In broader terms, it involves making sure that projects are justified on the basis of strategic positioning, the ethos of an enterprise and environmental and business realities. Project management in the context of strategy is therefore typically complex, requiring you to balance different competing demands and reach compromise. Whatever specific methodology you use, you will be breaking down this complexity into its associated parts, while still keeping an eye on the overall picture at the same time.

The method that we have followed in this book assumes that the output of the strategic planning process is a strategic action plan that contains the required goals, objectives, and actions. These actions can be defined in a planning table, designated with a descriptive title or taxonomy, allocated a responsible person, a due date, and perhaps a brief description. Uncomplicated actions (those that involve little risk and few resources and have a determined outcome from the start) can, of course, be implemented without any further planning. For more complicated actions, more thorough preparation is required, and this is the area of in-depth project management. For each of your projects, make sure you are appropriately prepared, and you have a credible project plan for its execution. This plan will define specifically how to execute the project and who will be involved in the different phases. The project is subsequently broken down into smaller parts, perhaps represented visually with something like a Gantt chart. Alongside this you'll need a plan for managing cost, resource requirements, communication, and dissemination of information. In the course of the implementation phase, your plans will need frequent reviews to check actual progress compared to what was planned and make adjustments as required. As we highlighted in the opening analysis diagram in Chapter 3, these reviews might lead back to the strategy itself to where iterative changes are needed. In any event you'll need to remain flexible in the face of uncertainty.

Reflection points

- What is likely to happen if the final report ends with a future vision, but no strategic plan? Explain.
- What is the connection between project management and strategic planning?

References

Attenborough, D. (1995). *The private life of plants: a natural history of plant behaviour.* London, UK: BBC.

Bbc.co.uk. (n.d.). BBC – Values – Inside the BBC. [online] bbc.co.uk. Available at: http://www.bbc.co.uk/aboutthebbc/insidethebbc/whoweare/mission_and_values/ [Accessed 24 May 2018].

Christensen, C. M., & Van Bever, D. (2014). The capitalist's dilemma. *Harvard Business Review*, 92(6): 60–68.

Dalkey, N. and Helmer, O. (1963). An experimental application of the Delphi Method to the use of experts. *Management Science* 9(3): 458–467.

Deming, W. E. (1986). *Out of the crisis.* Massachusetts Institute of Technology, Center for Advanced Engineering Study. Cambridge, MA: MIT Press.

Moz.com. (n.d.). Our Culture. [online] moz.com. Available at: https://moz.com/about/culture [Accessed 24 May 2018].

NHS England. (n.d.). NHS England: About NHS England. Retrieved from https://www.england.nhs.uk/about/about-nhs-england/

Osterwalder, A., & Pigneur, Y. (2010). *Business model generation: a handbook for visionaries, game changers, and challengers.* Hoboken, NJ: John Wiley & Sons.

Portofrotterdam.com. (2011). Port Vision 2030. [online] portofrotterdam.com. Available at: https://www.portofrotterdam.com/sites/default/files/upload/Port-Vision/Port-Vision-2030.pdf [Accessed 24 May 2018].

Schank, R., Lyas, D., Soloway, E. (2010). *The future of decision making: How revolutionary software can improve the ability to decide.* New York, NY: Palgrave & Macmillan.

Smith R (2005). Medical journals are an extension of the marketing arm of pharmaceutical companies. *PLoS Med*, 2(5): e138.

Squires, S. E. (2003). *Inside Arthur Andersen: Shifting values, unexpected consequences.* Upper Saddle River, NJ: FT Prentice Hall.

The Robin Report. (n.d.). Home Page – The Robin Report. [online] Available at: http://www.therobinreport.com [Accessed 24 May 2018].

Transport for London. (n.d.). What we do. [online] tfl.gov.uk. Available at: https://tfl.gov.uk/corporate/about-tfl/what-we-do [Accessed 24 May 2018].

Appendix: Working as an external strategy consultant

• •

There are a number of "musts" of which a good external strategy consultant needs to be aware of when working with an enterprise.

- Start by getting properly acquainted with the client in order to build up the trust necessary for collaboration. You need to become well aware of the client's needs and of the expectations people have for you as a consultant.
- You should propose a realistic process for the strategic planning work, but at the same time explain the inherent uncertainty involved.
- The financial costs in relation to strategic planning may be high for any enterprise, and you need to be able to demonstrate that the money is well spent, for instance by carefully managing the time that is put into the project and by keeping managers well-informed.
- They will need to oversee meetings with all relevant employees as well as with the executive management, board of directors, and individual departments. These may be a mixture of group meetings or one-on-one. Open the meetings by explaining the fundamentals of the strategic planning process as a whole and the role and contribution of each participant in relation to it.
- You may also need to hold meetings with interested parties in the external environment, e.g. suppliers and clients. At these meetings, you can gather the views and feelings of those involved with an enterprise in terms of the current situation and the future in a professional manner.

Be aware of boundaries and stay within your consulting role. Make it clear, at all times, that the real power resides in the hands of the enterprise's top executives. This means you must be able to step aside at appropriate moments, but at the same time guarantee that there is a continuum in the work and that all participants feel that it is advancing (or take a pause to reframe what you are doing if this is not the case). One of the things the consultant has to do is to work closely with the top executives of an enterprise and study their managerial approach, defining both positive and negative aspects. You also need to find out what their vision is. Perhaps an outcome of this could be to suggest that managers and even other employees might benefit from training in communication and leadership or in specific aspects of the strategic planning process.

As well as arranging all these meetings, you need to prepare the structure for them and lead them as a facilitator. The proceedings should be recorded faithfully, whether through written minutes, use of mind-mapping, or video, or some combination of these. You will need to edit this material to enable you to then present it back accurately in a clear and understandable way to all participating in the work. If the results of a previous meeting have a bearing on an upcoming meeting, make sure that you allow sufficient time for the attendees to assimilate and reflect on what you have presented. By ensuring that the participants feel that they have influenced and own the results of the strategic planning, you can encourage a sense of duty to work in the spirit of the outcome. This means, for instance, that you should facilitate the process, rather than direct too rigidly; the process should naturally develop in the workgroups, both among employees and managers. It is very important that each meeting takes place concurrently with the strategic planning process, the process, and schedule for which you shared with the employees at the beginning. Doing this, you guarantee that the participants are clued up about the purpose of the meetings and that they experience them as a part of the strategic planning process as a whole. This is an important part of creating a feeling of fairness and due process.

Even though meetings are a very common way to gather information, they are not the only solution. In very large organisations where working across different sites or even different countries is common, it may prove impossible to call each and every employee to attend a meeting. In which case, try alternative methods to engage the employees and gather their feedback, for instance: telephone interviews, surveys, emails, websites, and other communication methods that are appropriate for the culture of the organisation.

To illustrate the overall process in action, the following example relates to recent strategic planning work carried out by one of the authors acting as an external strategy consultant to the subsidiary of a large European civil engineering contractor running large and complex civil engineering projects.

Strategic planning within an engineering contractor

The strategic planning process was initiated by the CEO who wanted to produce an action plan to be used as a practical guideline for company management for the next two years or so. The participants in the planning process were to be a group of 15 senior executives, including department managers, key executives, and specialists. The purpose was to build up a common understanding in this group and construct an action plan involving wide employee

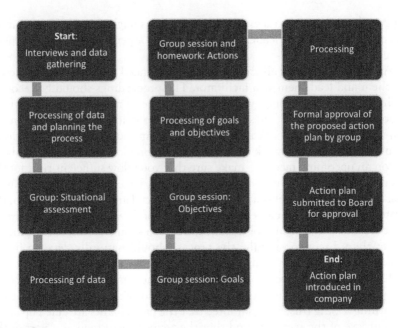

Figure A.1

Process for developing a strategic action plan for a civil engineering contractor.

participation that would then be applied to the whole organisation. Early inquiries showed that some of the basic elements of the strategic planning process had recently been carried out with participation from all employees such as agreement on the values and mission of the company.

Figure A.1 shows the planning process that was proposed along with the interaction between the strategy consultant and the group. The process took place mainly via well-planned and focused group sessions in which all 15 participants were present and actively participated. Between the group sessions, the strategy consultant processed the data that had been developed and the strategic action plan was gradually developed. The total period from start to finish was two months.

Index

Carr Square Village 7
cartel(s) 105, 141
Chandler, Alfred 10, 12
change management 8, 11
Christensen, Clayton 96, 107, 129, 187
clients 4, 33, 36, 82, 83, 95, 103, 109, 128,
    129, 133, 134, 136, 140, 175, 177, 179,
    181, 199, 200, 202, 208
climate change 91, 101, 152
clinical commissioning groups 183
closing out xix
cloud computing 96
Cognitive School, the 14
Colbert, Jean-Baptiste 190
commercial environment 103, 104
commodity(ies) 115, 116, 120, 125;
    prices 91
competence xix, 11, 64, 68, 123, 126, 127,
    139, 159, 181
competition 3, 11, 13, 21, 33, 54, 82, 97,
    99, 100, 104, 105, 108, 109, 112, 121,
    126, 127, 133, 135, 141, 147, 151, 160,
    161, 162, 164, 186, 190; authorities 106;
    perfect 104
competitive 4, 8, 11, 12, 13, 27, 30, 69,
    79, 81, 101, 104, 107, 108, 109, 111,
    112, 113, 114, 126, 127, 131, 139, 141,
    177, 186, 187; dialogue procedures
    125; edge 120; market strategies 108;
    tendering 125
competitiveness 4, 51, 82, 111, 112
competitors 4, 27, 38, 44, 81, 82, 83,
    103, 105, 107, 109, 111, 112, 113, 117,
    127, 132, 139, 140, 141, 161, 162, 164,
    177, 186
complex xv, 5, 7, 9, 10, 14, 22, 37, 55,
    61, 62, 64, 65, 70, 74, 101, 103, 112,
    116, 122, 125, 135, 137, 145, 153, 156,
    165, 167, 172, 174, 177, 179, 184, 185,
    190, 191, 194, 206, 209; adaptive
    systems 153
compliance 97, 125, 160, 161
Configuration School, the 15, 16
conflict 25, 56, 58, 64, 66, 90, 156, 169,
    174, 175, 185, 206
connectivity 4, 86, 114
consumer sentiment 115
continuing professional development 8
contract negotiations 85

corporate social responsibility (CSR)
    52, 84
cost 3, 4, 44, 47, 64, 70, 74, 75, 77, 91,
    92, 93, 94, 95, 96, 98, 101, 103, 104,
    105, 106, 107, 109, 110, 111, 118, 125,
    126, 133, 139, 140, 147, 149, 154, 157,
    158, 166, 176, 183, 187, 188, 195, 199,
    200, 202, 206, 208; leadership 208;
    reduction 4, 96
cover pricing 127
creative thinking i, 13
critical thinking xx, 5, 156
CRM see customer relationship
    management (CRM)
Cultural School, the 15
culture 7, 9, 14, 15, 18, 25, 31, 32, 33, 35,
    37, 41, 46, 49, 50, 52, 53, 54, 55, 56, 57,
    58, 61, 62, 85, 92, 93, 95, 99, 124, 159,
    169, 172, 173, 177, 178, 179, 182, 187,
    204, 207, 209
currency exchange rates 91, 115, 151
customer(s) 2, 4, 8, 18, 21, 32, 33, 34, 41,
    50, 51, 52, 57, 62, 64, 65, 68, 69, 70,
    71, 82, 83, 84, 85, 95, 96, 193, 104,
    105, 106, 107, 108, 109, 110, 111, 112,
    113, 114, 116, 120, 122, 123, 125, 128,
    129, 130, 131, 132, 133, 135, 136, 137,
    138, 140, 147, 160, 163, 164, 172, 173,
    176, 179, 181, 184, 188, 190, 192, 193;
    archetypes 129, 130; capital 48, 51, 94;
    customer relationship management
    (CRM) 8, 131, 137, 138; experience
    4, 52, 131, 137; needs analysis 35;
    retention 131, 132, 133, 141
customs and traditions 47, 93, 179

Da Vinci, Leonardo 190
DBO see Design, build, operate (DBO)
decision(s) i, xx, 2, 3, 4, 6, 18, 19, 30, 32,
    53, 55, 56, 58, 62, 65, 70, 74, 76, 79, 90,
    91, 92, 103, 107, 119, 122, 125, 131, 135,
    145, 147, 149, 151, 155, 156, 161, 164,
    165, 169, 176, 178, 179, 183, 186, 192,
    195; making 50, 51, 52, 61, 64, 66, 68,
    78, 103, 107, 125, 138, 147, 153, 171,
    172, 173, 178, 180, 180, 181, 182, 183,
    185, 192, 196, 207
Deepwater Horizon 157, 158, 167
delivery models 109

non-governmental institutions 84
non-profit 2, 3, 10, 33, 35, 71, 77, 79, 81, 82, 97, 103, 180, 183
Norman, Jane 116
Northwestern University 174
NYSE *see* New York Stock Exchange (NYSE)

OCR *see* Optical character recognition (OCR)
OECD 83
Office of Fair Trading 127
Office of National Statistics 118
Official Journal of the European Union 123
oil and gas 95, 120, 158
O'Leary, Michael 111
oligopoly 105, 107, 186
oligopsony 106, 107
online 4, 5, 93, 94, 109, 116, 117, 118, 120, 122, 129, 135, 136, 137, 138, 147, 161, 187
open discussion 21, 58
opportunities 2, 3, 4, 12, 14, 19, 20, 25, 26, 31, 44, 77, 78, 81, 85, 92, 97, 98, 99, 100, 103, 121, 124, 145, 147, 148, 149, 150, 155, 158, 159, 160, 161, 162, 163, 164, 165, 175
optical character recognition 119
Organic Consumers Association 136
organisational 1, 6, 7, 11, 15, 18, 25, 29, 31, 46, 49, 50, 52, 53, 54, 55, 56, 57, 58, 61, 62, 63, 64, 65, 66, 67, 68, 85, 115, 133, 139, 159, 164, 169, 173, 182, 197; change 6, 62, 133; culture 7, 15, 18, 49, 50, 52, 53, 54, 55, 56, 57, 58, 61, 85, 159, 169, 173; Types 10, 16, 20, 62, 66
Osterweiler, Alexander 188
outcome 2, 26, 29, 75, 84, 122, 127, 146, 149, 165, 171, 184, 193, 205, 206, 208, 209
outsourcing 74, 92, 96, 127, 157, 198

Pareto 133, 134; analysis 133; principle 133; Vilfredo 133
patents 50, 76, 95, 106
peer influence 131
Pension Protection Fund 86
pension scheme 86, 87
Perrow, Charles 156

PESTLE 89, 90, 101, 124, 155, 161, 163, 204
PFI *see* Private Finance Initiative (PFI)
Pfizer 149
pharmaceuticals 69, 85, 175
Pigneur, Yves 188
Piper, Charles 127
planning and implementation 71, 169
Planning School, the 12–13
plan of action 36
policies 4, 50, 90, 92, 97, 100, 153, 154, 160
political 10, 11, 33, 76, 77, 82, 83, 84, 86, 90, 91, 94, 111, 124, 155, 183; factors 90; parties 84
Porter, Michael E. 10, 11, 13, 69, 108, 111, 161, 163, 186, 187
portfolio 1, 29, 31, 61, 66, 115, 136, 145, 148, 149
Port of Rotterdam 194
Positioning School, the 13
power, legitimacy and urgency 88–9
power and influence 15, 87
Power School, the 14, 15
power versus interest grid 86, 87, 88
preparation 6, 19, 50, 73, 178, 206
prescription 13, 16
principle agent problem 176, 188
Private Finance Initiative (PFI) 183
process structure 62, 64
procurement 65, 69, 70, 123, 125, 126, 127, 201 *see also* tendering
product development 26, 84, 147
products or services 5, 51, 82, 91, 92, 105, 108, 111, 122, 125, 129, 148, 149, 160, 186
product structure 62, 63, 64
professional 1, 8, 23, 27, 37, 42, 50, 53, 58, 83, 85, 109, 121, 123, 128, 129, 130, 136, 139, 173, 194, 196, 208; association 83, 85; certification 109
programme 1, 2, 29, 30, 43, 48, 53, 65, 78, 107, 109, 110, 136, 145, 146, 148, 171, 184, 203, 205
project management maturity 64
project management training 109
project-oriented organisation 64, 66
project plan 146, 197, 205, 206
projections 7, 94
project sponsor 45, 165

property market 91, 154
prototyping 86
Pruitt-Igoe 7, 154, 166
psychological needs 130
psychology 10, 14, 188, 189
public 1, 2, 14, 31, 34, 51, 58, 67, 71, 73, 74, 78, 79, 83, 84, 85, 86, 90, 91, 93, 94, 96, 98, 100, 104, 107, 114, 122, 123, 124, 125, 126, 129, 136, 139, 166, 176, 180, 182, 183, 184, 185, 187, 189, 192, 193, 194; infrastructure 85, 94; liability 98; reaction 86
purpose and direction 3, 7
put or take options 34

quantitative metrics xxii

radio frequency identification device (RFID) 119
RBS 113
regulation 3, 8, 20, 21, 53, 66, 97, 98, 99, 115, 118, 122, 124, 125, 126, 136, 138, 161, 172, 177, 180, 185, 191
religion 33, 53, 92
reputation 51, 52, 53, 85, 90, 93, 101, 104, 108, 109, 110, 122, 129, 135, 136, 147, 157, 174, 176, 185, 190
request 26, 41, 125; for information (RFI) 125; for quotation (RFQ) 125; for tender 125
resilience 50, 85
resistance 6, 15, 27, 54, 98
restructuring 6, 78, 86, 169
retail 86, 90, 112, 16, 117, 131, 134, 136, 137, 188
return on invested capital 187 (ROIC)
return on net assets 187 (RONA)
reward and recognition 47
Reydarfjördur 173
RFI see request for information (RFI); request for tender
RFID see radio frequency identification device (RFID)
RFQ see request for quotation (RFQ)
risk 2, 3, 4, 13, 20, 31, 38, 44, 45, 74, 75, 76, 78, 81, 85, 86, 87, 91, 92, 93, 94, 95, 96, 98, 99, 100, 101, 104, 110, 115, 148, 124, 128, 131, 145, 151, 155, 156, 157, 158, 165, 166, 169, 171, 172, 173,

177, 182, 185, 186, 189, 205, 206; brand 94; hedging 115; and impact 87; of litigation 104; reputational 104
Rogers, Everett 131
Roger's Bell Curve 131, 132
ROIC see return on invested capital (ROIC)
RONA see return on net assets (RONA)
Ryanair 4, 111

SaaS see Software as a service (SaaS)
Salesforce 129, 137
Salience Model 88, 89
Samek, Steve 175
scenario analysis 75, 88, 91, 98, 155–8, 166, 185
scenarios 1, 2, 22, 150, 153–8, 171
scheduling 4, 7
Schumpeter, Joseph 14
search engine optimisation 122
Selznik, Philip 12
Senge, Peter 10, 11
sense of belonging 8
service 1, 4, 5, 6, 35, 37, 44, 50–2, 57, 64–8, 69, 70, 71, 74, 82, 84, 91, 92, 95, 97, 103, 104–5, 108–9, 111, 112, 114, 115, 116, 118, 121–4, 125–8, 129–34, 135–8, 139–40, 148–9, 151, 158, 160, 161, 172, 180, 182–4, 186, 198, 199, 200, 202
session replay 119
Seydisfjordur 150
Sildenafil 149 see also Viagra
situational needs 130
Skanska 84
skills 8, 22, 23, 25, 26, 27, 48, 82, 109, 110, 159, 192, 205
Skype 138
smart cards 119
Smith, Richard 175
social 7, 15, 33, 47, 48, 49, 50, 51, 52, 53, 54, 57, 81, 93, 96, 98, 135, 153, 176, 183, 192; cohesion 7; and economic factors 7; factors 93; housing 7, 176; justice 87; media 93, 121, 122, 137, 138, 151, 157; needs 81, 130
socialisation of content 96
software 5, 50, 77, 95
software as a service (SaaS) 95, 129

trade unions 84
Transatlantic Trade and Investment
    Partnership (TTIP) 156
Transport for London (TfL) 182, 184
Travelers Insurance 86
TripAdvisor 96
Truven Health Analytics 140
TTIP *see* Transatlantic Trade and
    Investment Partnership (TTIP)
Twitter 121, 161
Tzu, Lao 193

Uber 117, 118, 138
uncertainty 1, 6, 9, 22, 63, 74, 123,
    149, 151, 155, 157, 158, 190,
    206, 208
urban decay 7, 154
user demand 94
user-generated content 95, 96

value chain model 11, 71
Vanderbilt University 10

Viagra 149 *see also* Sildenafil
voice recognition 119
Volkswagen 53, 176
VRBO 118
Vroom and Dreesmann (V&D) 117

Walmart 112
warning signs 7
weaknesses 2, 3, 8, 12, 25, 61, 70, 158–65, 204
wealth distribution 92
wellbeing 2, 73
Weltbild 116
Westwood, Douglas 120
white elephant projects 94
Whole Foods Market 112
Wimdu 118
Windows 106
WorldCom 175

Xing, Chen 171

YouTube 110, 121

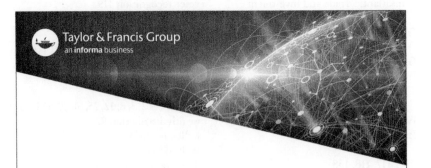